Marketing Democracy

Marketing Democracy

Power and Social Movements in Post-Dictatorship Chile

Julia Paley

UNIVERSITY OF CALIFORNIA PRESS

Berkeley   Los Angeles   London

University of California Press
Berkeley and Los Angeles, California

University of California Press, Ltd.
London, England

© 2001 by The Regents of the University of California

Library of Congress Cataloging-in-Publication Data

Paley, Julia, 1964–.
Marketing democracy: power and social movements in post-dictatorship
Chile / Julia Paley.
   p.   cm.
Includes bibliographical references and index.
ISBN 978-0-520-22768-2 (pbk. : alk paper)
1. Social movements—Chile.   2. Power (Social sciences)—Chile.
3. Chile—Politics and government—1988–.   4. Democracy—Chile.
I. Title.
HN293.5 .P34   2001
303.48′4′0983—dc21   00-037405
                                CIP

Manufactured in the United States of America
10   09   08

10 9 8 7 6 5

CONTENTS

ILLUSTRATIONS

ACKNOWLEDGMENTS

Books have one author but are, in reality, collective projects. Members of the health group Llareta were in many respects coauthors of this book, as they included me in their process of political analysis, gave feedback on mine, and made direct contributions to the text, most notably the ethnographic study presented at the end of the book. It is for the education they have given me and the enduring relationships we share that I thank Angélica, Digna, Flor, Isabel, Iván, Keka, Mari, Mariela, Marta, Mónica Janet, Quena, Sonia, Valeria, others who have participated over the years, and all their families. I also extend my warmest appreciation to *pobladores* in La Bandera and in neighboring *poblaciones* who challenged me with their insights and included me in their activities as I involved them in my research. Thanks go especially to Adelina, Angelina, Betty, Carola, Chana, Enriqueta, Janette, Juana, Juancho, Jorge, Leo, Mónica, Nidia, Rodrigo, Rosa, their families, and the many others who welcomed, inspired, and educated my husband and me over nearly a decade of fieldwork visits.

The conversations and activities that health promoters were engaged in linked them to a set of nongovernmental organizations (NGOs) that were themselves developing an analysis of the transition and new ways of acting within it. I am deeply indebted to Educación Popular en Salud (EPES), whose creativity and exceptional work will inspire me always. EPES staff members generously opened their office, activities, and ideas to my husband and myself, and I thank them all for their warmth and trust. Karen Anderson, Eladio Recabarren, and María Eugenia Calvin in particular made profound contributions to this book, many times offering their analyses and suggestions, and always providing new analytical approaches to understanding the political transition. I also learned an enormous amount from staff members at Promoción e Intercambio de Recursos Educacionales y Tecnológicos (PIRET), in particular Rosa Quintanilla, who spent long hours discussing politics, economics, and social analysis with me and whose book has been an inspiration; and Fernando Leiva, who generously read this entire manuscript and has educated me both through numerous discussions and through his own very astute publications. Jenny Mason, pastor of the Lutheran chapel in La Bandera, was always welcoming, inviting us to participate in the Lutheran youth group, AIDS education work, and church activities, as well as providing a space for the public forum at which I presented material from this book. I would also like to thank the staff at the NGOs Educación y Comunicación (ECO) and FOLICO for making available resources, information, and ideas that proved invaluable to our local history workshop.

I benefited greatly from work and conversations with Chilean scholars. Gabriel Salazar, whose historical writings have had a profound effect on my thinking, offered insight into themes of social movements, government, and participation. Tomás Moulian, whose own book on the Chilean political situation has gained much well-deserved attention, provided valuable suggestions for this manuscript. Vicente Espinoza, a friend and interlocutor for nearly a decade, has provided detailed commentary on many versions of my work. Although we do not always agree, our differences have often been as enlightening as the places where our analyses converge. Juan Carrera has been an important intellectual influence. From the first days in 1991, when he provided us with Spanish lessons that immediately became lessons in Chilean politics and history, to his trip to the United States in 1995, when he and I jointly spoke at university colloquia and coauthored an article, to his repeated readings and critiques of drafts of my book, he has challenged my thinking in innumerable ways. I also thank Isabel Toledo for sharing materials from her extensive research on La Bandera's history, Ana María Pinto for providing statistical data from her study, and Mario Garcés, who invited me to participate in a very interesting seminar on local histories and whose own writings (with colleagues) on that subject have been of ongoing usefulness.

My entrée into Santiago's intellectual community was facilitated by letters of introduction from Genaro Arriagada and Hugo Frühling, who were visiting professors at Harvard during my graduate school years. Their backing led to an affiliation with Facultad Latinamericana de Ciencias Sociales (FLACSO-Chile). There I benefited from office space, use of the library, faculty seminars, and conversations with José Joaquín Brunner, Alicia Frohmann, Manuel Antonio Garretón, Sergio Gómez, Teresa Valdés, Marisa Weinstein, and other faculty and staff. I especially thank Sergio Rojas for fascinating descriptions of eradications and public policy, Cristián Cox for taking the time from his work at the Ministry of Education to guide my research, and Enrique Hermosilla, whose friendship and insights into Chilean society will be appreciated always. At FLACSO I was fortunate to meet North American graduate students conducting research, particularly Patrick Barrett, Robert Barros, and Thomas Klubock.

I gained much from visits to other research organizations and universities in Santiago as well. These included Centro de Investigación y Desarrollo de la Educación (CIDE), where José Weinstein discussed with me ways to study identity construction among youth, and Programa Interdisciplinario de Investigación en Educación (PIIE), where Verónica Edwards helped me design an early proposal for ethnographic fieldwork in a municipal school. Programa de Economia del Trabajo (PET) was a source of crucial information on economics and popular organizations. SUR Profesionales became a second home; I thank Alfredo Rodriguez for opening space for me to work, and Rosita Barria for her help in locating books and other documents. Nelly Richard directed a fascinating three-year seminar, Postdictatorship and Democratic Transition, at the Universidad de las Artes y las Ciencias Sociales (ARCIS), in which I was honored to participate in late 1999. Thanks go to all the participants in that seminar, and especially to Margot Olavarría, who proved a constant source of intellectual engagement.

Staff at a number of government and university departments were exceedingly helpful. Architects at SERVIU remembered back to their early days planning the *población* La Bandera and dug out of their archives blueprints of their initial plans. The Municipality of San Ramón provided statistical data, aerial photographs, and information about service provision in the *comuna*, and the director and teachers at San Ramón's technical-vocational high school graciously facilitated months of ethnographic fieldwork. Workers at the Instituto Nacional de Estadísticas (INE) offered census data and explained the computer software necessary to use it, and employees at the University of Chile's Department of Economics helped select survey data that would illuminate La Bandera's changing demographic and employment structure. To all these workers at Santiago's various organizations and ministries, I offer my heartfelt thanks.

If the bulk of this research took place in Chile, preparation for it began much earlier, in my own formal education. In particular, my mentors at Harvard have had a permanent impact on my work. Byron Good's approach to meaning-centered anthropology and the education he offered in medical anthropology's theory and methods have been crucial bases for all my work. Sally Falk Moore's brilliant formulation of process theory and her challenging seminars have shaped a generation of scholars of which I am pleased to be a part. Robert LeVine's specialization in human development guided my early interest in education, and Frances Hagopian introduced me to political science analyses of regime transitions in Latin America and later helped me select Chile as a research site. Dorinne Kondo provided an introduction to experimental ethnographic writing, which became a fruitful source of ideas for writing this book.

During my graduate education, I was fortunate to spend three semesters as an exchange scholar in the anthropology department at Princeton University. There, Kay Warren's dynamic graduate seminars became a place to theorize themes of politics and identity encountered during fieldwork. Michael Jiménez's riveting lectures on Latin American history provided a framework within which to situate contemporary Chilean politics; I am forever grateful to him for sharing the perceptive analysis of Latin American democracy that he was developing in those years. Vincanne Adams's graduate seminar opened me to theory on media, knowledge, and power that has become productive for thinking through the Chilean material. At Princeton, Latin American studies bibliographer Peter Johnson guided me through the remarkable collection of Chile ephemera that the library had wisely commissioned a Chilean *poblador* to collect during the 1980s. My inquiries into Chilean history and politics were further advanced by participation in the colloquium series sponsored by Princeton's Program in Latin American Studies.

As important to my intellectual development as meetings with faculty and attendance at university seminars were interactions with graduate school peers. Kelly Askew, Tara Av-Ruskin, Bart Dean, Maya Dumeruth, Hudita Mustafa, and Isabel Zambrano provided many fascinating discussions, and I was delighted to find my relationship with Julie Goldman renewed as she initiated her own fieldwork in Chile. Lawrence Cohen, Kaila Compton, Lindsay French, Kate Hoshour, and Ana Ortiz have been crucial intellectual companions with whom I have had ongoing conversations on social theory, ethnographic method, and anthropological ethics, and who continue to be stimulating interlocutors and close friends. I have also enjoyed interaction over the years with Paul Farmer and Jim Kim, who, along with Anne Hyson and the entire staff at Partners in Health, have developed important models for combining academia with real-world action around health.

My own education reaches back to undergraduate work at the University of Pennsylvania, where Michelle Fine's course on feminist psychology and her ethnographic fieldwork on schooling provided important reference points for my later work. Bambi Schieffelin's creative instruction in ethnographic methods and the opportunity to conduct my first ethnographic study were formative for both my fieldwork in Chile and the course I now teach on urban ethnography. I also thank faculty in the urban studies program, including Ira Harkavy, for a stimulating curriculum that took me into Philadelphia's neighborhoods and community organizations and provided a context for thinking about urban public policy.

My return to the University of Pennsylvania as a faculty member in 1994 brought a new opportunity for intellectual development and involvement in Penn's scholarly community. The anthropology department has been a warm home for completing this book, and I deeply appreciate the support and interest of departmental colleagues. Thanks in particular go to Sandra Barnes, Paula Sabloff, Peggy Sanday, and Greg Urban, whose wise comments on my writing have significantly advanced this work. Michael Katz and Kathleen Hall have been unfailingly supportive colleagues, and I thank Dana Barron, Christine Kray, Demie Kurz, Ann Matter, Elaine Simon, Barbara von Schlegell, and Tom Sugrue for their feedback and encouragement. It has been an absolute pleasure to have writing groups with Ann Farnsworth-Alvear, Laura Grindstaff, Ayako Kano, and Barbara Savage, and to write in the company of María Rodríguez and Dina Siddiqi. I thank students in my seminars Urban Social Theory, Theory and Ethnography of Latin America, and Urban Neighborhoods for their feedback on various drafts of this book, and I am most grateful to Marcela Aliaga and Elisa Muñoz-Franco for their assistance with the final revisions of this text. Above all, two graduate students deserve special mention for their impact on this book. Clare Ignatowski, who read many early drafts, challenged me to develop humanist approaches to ethnographic writing, and Fernando Armstrong, with whom I established an ongoing dialogue in the later stages of book editing, pushed my thinking on social theory in productive new directions.

Perhaps the greatest delight of these last few years has been receiving the feedback of a wide range of anthropological and Latin Americanist scholars. Gene Burnes, Micaela di Leonardo, Charles Hale, Cathy Schneider, and Orin Starn's extensive commentaries on my dissertation have benefited this project ever since. Charles Briggs, John Burdick, Fernando Coronil, Karin Rosemblatt, Verónica Schild, and Peter Winn all provided indispensable suggestions on my manuscript that shaped the final product in profound ways. I have also benefited deeply from conversations with Andrew Apter, Teresa Caldeira, John Comaroff, Miguel Díaz-Barriga, James Ferguson, Carlos Fontes, Lisa Fontes, Carol Greenhouse, Katherine Hite, James Holston, Susan Hyatt, John Kelly, Maxwell Owusu, Michael Silverstein, and Michel-Rolph Truillot.

The opportunity for some of this feedback came from seminars at which I presented my work, including colloquia at the University of Chicago Department of Anthropology, Princeton University Library, University of California at San Diego Department of Ethnic Studies, and Temple University Department of Anthropology and conferences at Villanova University, the New School for Social Research, and the Institute of Latin American and Iberian Studies at Columbia University. I have also benefited from commentary on presentations I gave at the University of Pennsylvania, including the Department of Anthropology colloquium series, the Ethnohistory Workshop, the Urban Studies Faculty–Graduate Student Research Seminar, and the Latin American Cultures Program speakers' series. In addition, I presented work at meetings of the Latin American Studies Association, the American Anthropological Association, the American Historical Association, the Social Science History Association, and the Nineteenth Latin American Congress of Sociology in Caracas, Venezuela, where commentary by discussants and audience members contributed to the ideas being formulated for this book. For her fruitful suggestions for revision, particularly the idea of developing characters, and for bringing this book at last to publication, I thank Naomi Schneider, executive editor at the University of California Press, and express my appreciation to other staff who have worked on the many tasks involved in the publishing process.

Research and writing of this manuscript were facilitated by funding from a variety of sources. I gratefully acknowledge financial support from a Jacob Javits Fellowship, a Mellon Foundation Dissertation Completion Fellowship, and a Rockefeller Foundation Humanities Grant. Funding from Harvard University, the University of Pennsylvania Research Foundation, and the Trustees' Council of Penn Women made various stages of the project possible.

If all writing is collective, nothing could be more indispensable to a research project than the support and contributions of friends and family. For years, Rosemary

Barbera and Eduardo Villegas have shared with me their analyses of Chilean politics and their commitments to human rights, with both passion and a sense of humor. They and Mary Catherine Arbour have given very perceptive commentary on my work. Vivian Schatz ran the Chile Committee for Human Rights in Philadelphia for over twenty years and with others provided a local cultural context and community in which to write. Abigail Gillman, Lisa Maisels, Eva Moskowitz and Eric Grannis, and Debby Freedman and David Wycoff have been great sources of encouragement, joy, and support; I am blessed to have them as friends. I also thank Patrice Brodeur, Peter Cicchino, Craig Levine, Stuart Rudoler, and Jonathan Springer for provocative discussions and moral support. I am most indebted to my family, a group that has believed in me always and supported this work for many years. Annette, Norton, Ellen, Hubert, Bessie, and Susan Paley and Danny Farkas have always been ready with encouraging words and sound advice; their love has made this long journey possible. I recall with sweet memories my grandparents Florence and Walter Rosenfeld and Elias Paley, whose love nurtured my early personal growth, and express my appreciation to Walter Rosenfeld Jr. for interesting conversations over the years. Sylvia and Lewis Whitman provided warmth and beautiful atmospheres in which to write, and I thank Brad Whitman, Jim Whitman, and Anna El-Eini for their companionship and faith. Above all, my love and respect go to Gordon Whitman, the person with whom I most closely share my life. He has participated in every aspect of developing this book—from photography to statistical analysis, from field notes to editing—and his creativity and perceptiveness are woven throughout. It is with great joy that we now welcome our children and future fieldwork companions, Natalia Rose and Isaiah, into the world.

Prologue

We are gathered around Valeria's dining room table just before lunch. The winter air has left the house cold and damp, and we wrap our hands around mugs of tea to warm us. Two weeks ago, when I arrived in Chile for the fourth time, I didn't notice the cold. The summer heat seemed to accompany me from Philadelphia, clinging to the T-shirt I still wore. But when I got off the bus and entered their house, I found Valeria and her husband, Jorge, sitting close to the space heater, shivering. They were telling stories, hoping to keep distracted if not warm. During my year and a half of fieldwork in La Bandera—a *población* (shantytown) in the southern part of Santiago—shared conditions like the weather had connected us. This time, when I returned, my inability to perceive the cold seemed to underscore the fact that I was entering the scene after a long absence, during which I had lived in very different conditions. The coldness they felt had not built up in a moment; it had gathered over weeks, or maybe years. It's the *falta de caldo* (the lack of broth), Valeria told me. You can't get warm when you have nothing to eat.

Two weeks have passed since my arrival. Now I, too, feel permeated by the cold, wet weather and can feel the hunger gnawing at my stomach as the hour gets late. Early in the day I went shopping at the outdoor market, filling my bag with fresh fish and vegetables and remembering to pick up liter bottles of soda and two kilos of bread. Now in the kitchen we hear batter sizzling as it hits hot oil and smell the pleasing aroma of frying fish wafting into the dining room. Valeria's sister Sonia is cooking the food and has delegated the preparation of salads to adults and children alike.

I shift my attention from the goings-on in the kitchen back to the dining and living room area where we are seated. Valeria's house is artfully decorated. Batiks brought home from Africa and necklaces from Easter Island grace her walls. The floor is of polished wood, and new cushions sewn by Sonia brighten the couch. She has the stereo playing dance music and popular songs. Thinking back, I can recall the stages through which Valeria and her husband built this house. Over the course of years, they replaced cardboard walls with wood, filled in the open walls of the kitchen where the wind had blown in, and installed plumbing and electrical wiring. They bought materials using Jorge's income from driving a bus, a job he held periodically between long bouts of unemployment. For them, it was a constant balancing act between the long-term need to fortify the house and the daily urgency of buying food.

The women gathered in Valeria's house today are members of the health group Llareta,[1] a grassroots organization, with whom I spent many months during my fieldwork in 1991 and 1992. Created in 1984, the health group has been working for a decade, educating neighbors about preventive health care, responding to emergencies, and attempting to hold government officials accountable for meeting the community's needs. Today, Llareta's members arrive at the luncheon at different moments, leaving their housework, their jobs, and their organizational activities completed or arranged for. Each of these people has a different life story, and piecing together their personal histories offers a window into the processes converging in the history of this *población*.

Valeria has a bright smile, intense eyes, and flowing brown hair. Lively and outgoing, she is one of the most outspoken members of the group and has been a community leader for more than fifteen years. She comes from a family that has long been involved in political activity and can remember her grandfather telling stories about political party organizing in Chile's northern copper mines early in the century. She, too, participated in political activities during the dictatorship. But with the end of the military government, political parties have become distant from popular sectors: both relatively inactive and undervaluing poor people's work. So Valeria now searches for other ways to organize her neighbors. As the health group's coordinator, she takes an active role in many public activities such as health campaigns in the open-air markets, public assemblies, and district seminars. And in 1990 she traveled to Tanzania to represent Santiago's health groups at an international conference.

The opportunity to travel was new to her, for Valeria's history, like that of the other health promoters, was one of poverty, hunger, and the humiliation of never having owned what she needed. As a teenager, Valeria dropped out of school because she could afford neither pencils nor shoes. At last, in her thirties, with the economic assistance of a nongovernmental organization, she finished a high school degree with honors. Despite the severe economic obstacles that now confront her, she dreams of studying psychology at a university in Santiago. Today, as we gather for our meeting, her two youngest children and her husband join the luncheon and later weave their way in and out of the dining room and the discussion.

Glancing up, I see Sonia, making a grand entrance with the first two plates of food. She is short and energetic, with her long brown hair pulled back in a braid, playful eyes, and a great sense of humor. She is wearing a blouse she made herself, and her skirt seems to move to the rhythm of the music as she enters. Raising four children on her own, Sonia has worked as a hairstylist, a salesperson, and now a seamstress. She makes furniture covers for customers in wealthier parts of the city, sews clothing in a small nearby factory, and does piecework at home. The closing of textile factories in Santiago and the imports of used American clothing have often left her out of work. Although she never completed the final requirements for a high school degree, like Valeria she has studied in many educational programs, both popular education and formal institutes, on themes ranging from fashion to family counseling to political analysis.

It was years ago that Sonia learned of the availability of land in La Bandera through her sister Cristina, who had led one of the committees of the homeless to gain land here in 1969. Sonia obtained a spot on a broad avenue on the edge of the *población*. With her oldest daughter's help, she built her house by hand, laying the bricks for the front rooms and adding a makeshift skylight in the kitchen. She decorated the living room with Pablo Neruda's poetry and his pictures, and in her teenage daughter's bedroom, the ceiling is still covered with posters of rallies and popular organizations from the 1980s. Looking at Sonia now, I recall many a party in her house, with the *cumbia, merengue,* and *lambada* music playing loudly, the cakes of a "thousand layers" filled with *manjar* (caramelized milk) waiting for us on the table, and friends and relatives dancing long into the night. Yet I also remember the days when a pot of salty rice or potatoes or noodles left over from the day before was the only food besides tea; the days when she would leave the children unattended to make money sewing clothes; or other days when she stayed home from a health group meeting, reasoning that if her children were to go hungry, at least she should be with them. Today her youngest daughter accompanies her. She announces in a proud voice and with the right number of fingers raised, "I am six." From the tiny four-year-old she was when I last saw her, she has grown into a still small but beautiful girl.

Angélica has brought along her knitting, and as she chats with others around the table, she works on a sweater for her niece. She wears her gray hair short and uses glasses, which she hangs around her neck on a string. Older and quieter than the other health promoters, Angélica grew up in a rural area north of the capital. She came to Santiago in the 1950s to work as a maid and through many meetings and conversations strove to generate class consciousness among the domestic servants she knew. She and her husband later squatted by the banks of a river in Las Condes, an otherwise wealthy section of Santiago. In 1982, the military forcibly relocated the settlers to the poorer southern zone of the city, purportedly to provide them with solid, permanent houses. But in reality, the plan was intended mainly to remove poor people from wealthy sections of the city. Angélica's relatives and neighbors still dream of their old community, with its larger houses and green areas, as well as work for them as golf caddies, maids, and gardeners. They have found their new location difficult to adjust to—dangerous, without good public services, far from work, in cramped quarters, and across the street from people they neither know nor trust. But Angélica says she feels at home here. In the *población* she no longer experiences the daily tension of living a life of poverty amid wealth. Here she relates better to people who, in terms of life experience, are much more like herself. She has been active in the church in her sector, and the health promoters with whom she sits at the table today have become a central part of her life.

Mónica Janet enters Valeria's house with fanfare, greeting all the others with kisses and hugs. She leaves her son and daughter to play with the other children, then returns quickly to her mother's house to bring another chair as the crowd steadily grows. Mónica Janet is young but stout: her body has swollen from the side effects of a kidney illness she has had for years. Raising two small children, she participates in myriad organizations, including housing committees, human rights organizations, and the health group. During the years of national protests, she took her young daughter with her to marches and land seizures, always teaching her not to be afraid. These days she routinely walks long blocks on dusty or muddy roads to pick up her children at school or to coordinate events, all while struggling with her illness. In 1992, the health group launched a campaign to finance medicine for her, and later it held a large cultural event at which twenty-two dance, musical, and theater groups performed in order to raise more funds.

Nearly all her life, Mónica Janet has lived in the house that her parents built in 1970. They acquired their site through the 26 de enero land seizure that both helped initiate La Bandera and made it famous. But after many years of waiting, Mónica Janet has at last obtained her own apartment in a new housing development about twenty minutes by bus to the south. There she is beginning to organize her neighbors, while remaining deeply tied to the health group and La Bandera.

Mónica Janet's sister Digna has not arrived—she sends a message with one of her children that she will come as soon as her husband returns from purchasing goods in the center of Santiago, but until then she must stay home to watch her sons. Her husband, Guillermo, who is dying of disease brought on by alcoholism, is too sick to hold a job. A gentle man, he spends most days taking care of their three children. It is an unusual task for Chilean men, who typically insist that wives take on all domestic responsibilities. But Guillermo is different. In the mornings he cooks the main meal and cleans the house while his wife goes out to work.

Digna earns money in various ways. She washes clothes at her sister's for a small amount of cash, cleans houses one day a week, and sells linens in the outdoor market. On market days, she transports a bundle of curtains and bedclothes in a wheelbarrow and spreads them out on a ground cloth near the far end of the market. Around her other workers bring their wares: inexpensive clothing; old, worn-out shoes; assorted faucets and pipes—and farther up the road people with stands sell meat or fruits and vegetables. But recently business has been particularly slow, and Digna has been talking about finding a new source of income, perhaps selling cosmetics to her neighbors. She would no doubt be good at that, for her sense of fashion is adventurous, and she always puts together surprisingly stylish outfits from the used American clothing sold at the market. She has never participated in a social organization before, but, inspired by her sister Mónica Janet, has begun to attend meetings of the health group this year. After delivering the message that his mother will come when she can, her oldest son says good-bye and returns to his home.

We are already enjoying our meal by the time he leaves. Mariela passes the bread and pours everyone drinks before beginning her own lunch. Having grown up in the village of Lo Espejo near Santiago, Mariela moved to La Bandera with her parents and later married a young man here. The couple and their small son now rent a room in a hand-built house in the back of another family's yard. Petite and lively, with her straight brown hair cut short, Mariela plays soccer on Sundays and enjoys hanging out with her friends. But in large groups she is shy, and this is the first organization in which she has been involved. She chats enthusiastically with the others during lunch but tends to say little at health group meetings. For now, just a few months since she has joined, she prefers to listen to what others have to say.

Not so for Iván, who is sitting next to me at the table. The only man in Llareta, he is also one of the group's most active, and most vocal, members. He first arrived in La Bandera during the same land seizure as Mónica Janet and Digna did, when they were small children and he was twelve years old. He remembers vividly the cultural activities for youth in those early years of the *población*—especially dance and theater—and the school that neighbors jointly built. The number of community organizations he has participated in and led since that time are numerous: a union of the unemployed, a cooking cooperative, a human rights committee, and, in 1992, a commemoration protesting official celebrations of the Columbus Quincentenary. An office clerk at an international church organization during the week, he sells homemade fried food—like *sopaipilla*s and meat- or cheese-filled *empanadas*—in the market on weekends and helps organize a union of vendors. Now he, his wife, and two little children live in another working-class neighborhood in Santiago. But like Mónica Janet, he returns to La Bandera regularly to participate in its organizations, especially the Christian Base Community and the health group. In recent years he has traveled to Argentina and Ecuador as part of international seminars, and he participates in an international ecumenical organization, Proceso Sao Paulo.

When most of us are mopping the last bits of sauce off our plates with our bread, María Eugenia arrives. She is a staff member of Educación Popular en Salud (EPES), the health education cooperative that helped train Llareta ten years earlier and has worked with the group ever since. She brings greetings from other members of EPES who would have liked to join us but are occupied with many other aspects of their jobs—training *población* health teams like this one; producing educational games on themes such as adolescence, AIDS, and respiratory illnesses; coordinating citywide health events; preparing for international conferences; and writing a book based on interviews with health promoters throughout

Santiago and the southern city of Concepción. After greeting the health promoters, María Eugenia pulls up a chair and joins the conversation.

Being back with these people with whom I spent over a year is a powerful experience. A flood of memories is triggered by the sensory impact of this place: the taste of dark, sweetened tea and the firm texture of Chilean bread, the pungent aroma of eucalyptus leaves escaping from the water-filled cans perched on space heaters, the lingering headache caused by Santiago's winter smog, the stilted Spanish of dubbed Brazilian *telenovelas* playing in the background, the spirited voices and laughter of children in another room. Back in the United States, as I went through my field notes and listened to recorded interviews, the months I had spent in Chile swirled together in my mind. The health promoters' animated voices repeated the same opinions endlessly as I played and replayed my tapes. Now the world has fast-forwarded to 1994, and the people I sit with are alive with energy and initiative. Their comments are new and in immediate dialogue with my own. The two years I missed have given me heightened awareness of how things have changed and how they have persisted. Now I am ready to bring the health group members along with me into that juxtaposition of time. Together, we will debate and discuss one slice of the past, one aspect of recent history.

The meal has ended, and as the plates are cleared away, I pull out the materials I have spent the week preparing. On the wall, I tape large sheets of brown paper covered with ideas, just as I have seen these community leaders do at so many workshops and presentations. The sheets lay out the goals for my presentation and outline the methodologies I used in my research two years ago. One has a glossary defining words such as *ethnography* and another displays a large time line showing periods in recent Chilean history. I pass out nine-page stapled handouts, onto which I have translated into Spanish my ideas about political change, power, and community organizations' changing strategies. And just before we start, I circulate my dissertation, a thick manuscript written in English. With the last of the dishes cleared off the table, we get down to work.

"Here are the objectives for this presentation, and for this visit to Chile," I say, pointing to a sheet of brown paper on the wall. "First, to share the analysis in my dissertation so that people here have access to things usually presented in English, in the United States. Hopefully it will contribute to work going on here. Second, to generate debate—it would be good to have a long-term discussion of these themes.... And finally to hear everyone's commentary, in order to improve the analysis in the upcoming book." Two women adjust their positions in their seats, a child gets hushed and sent out of the room, a dog barks in the background, and the presentation begins.

Introduction

On October 16, 1998, General Augusto Pinochet was arrested in London on an extradition request from Spain. The charge was crimes against humanity, including the killing and disappearance of more than three thousand persons. Human rights groups lauded the arrest, citing it as an advance in international human rights law. By contrast, the Chilean government pressed for the general's release, "arguing that a prolonged detention of the former dictator will jeopardize Chile's stability and transition to democracy" (Krauss 1998). The disjuncture between the symbolic construction of Pinochet in Chile, where the general had been sworn into Congress as senator-for-life, and the international human rights discourse branding Pinochet a tyrant puts into stark relief the contradictions in Chile's transition to democracy. The spectacle of an elected president defending the ex-dictator in the name of democracy compels us to inquire into the nature of Chilean democracy itself.

This book is just such an inquiry. It explores the social constructions and institutional practices of Chilean democracy, from the perspectives of community groups in an urban neighborhood *(población)* and the writings and activities of intellectuals and government officials. It seeks to offer an ethnographic and processual account of changing conditions and strategies.

In examining Chile's transition to democracy ethnographically, my work joins that of a small number of anthropologists who have begun to explore the variety of meanings and experiences of contemporary democracy. Until recently, democracy has been examined mainly by political scientists, whose concern with formal regime shifts (the reopening of legislatures, the revival of political parties, and the onset of elections) and the consolidation of political democracy has established the framework and set the boundaries for debate (see, for example, O'Donnell and Schmitter 1986; Diamond et al. 1999). Anthropologists, at times working in interdisciplinary contexts (Alvarez, Dagnino, and Escobar 1998), have only recently begun to provide alternatives to this framework. Seeing through and beyond formal regime transitions, these approaches to studying democracy can be described as falling into five major groups. These categories are not bounded and separate but instead blend into each other in revealing ways.

Generated by anthropologists who have played a role in constitution writing or other aspects of governance (e.g., Owusu 1997), a first set of essays offers programmatic suggestions for how governmental systems can become more democratic, for example, through ideals of grassroots participatory democracy (Owusu 1995). Optimistic in tone, this approach draws heavily from the public sphere and civil society ideas, which gained popularity in the 1980s amid political transitions in Eastern Europe. Anthropological literature of this sort is strongly represented in studies of Africa (see, e.g., Chikwendu 1996), perhaps because of the historical strength of political anthropology in that continent, while in Latin America it is more commonly sociologists who both write about and participate in governance.

Another set of anthropologists, who share the aspiration for making systems more democratic, has focused on the qualities and characteristics of citizenship. Drawing on ethnographic material from Brazil, Holston and Caldeira (1998) call democracy "disjunctive," indicating that while formal political institutions have been reformed, civil rights remain unenforced. In the context of transnational flows, in which emerging democracies (and other contemporary political systems) are situated, citizenships may be multiple and overlapping as well (Holston and Appadurai 1996).

Applying to contemporary political situations anthropology's classic task of identifying local meanings, a third set of studies is less directly interested in reforming governmental institutions or emphasizing their internal inconsistencies than in showing the ways in which formal regime transitions contrast with or are reappropriated by culturally different native traditions (Comaroff and Comaroff 1997; Schaffer 1997). Such studies attempt to shed light on local responses to political change by exploring indigenous understandings of power and politics (Apter 1987). These studies often provide a critical view of Western democratic systems by way of revealing their situational inappropriateness or political contradictions in non-Western settings (e.g., Go 1997).

Unlike those who demonstrate entrenched cultural difference, a fourth set of studies traces the circulation of multiple meanings and strategic uses of the term *democracy* itself. Coronil (1997), for example, shows how in Venezuela democracy took on a widely divergent set of meanings ranging from universal suffrage (132), to the population's sharing in national oil wealth (88–89) while being excluded from political rights (176), to the premise that military regimes safeguard democracy (147). Apter (1999) traces the "condition of verisimilitude and dissimulation" through which the "electoral charade of 'pro forma democracy'" operated in Nigeria—a situation in which the head of state choreographed elections as performance without really being elected through them. While such studies have been insightful in showing the multiple uses of democracy as discourse, they have largely focused on elite political actors, a situation that begs examination of effects through on-the-ground ethnography.

Finally, a fifth set of writings builds on Michel Foucault's (1991) concept of governmentality—as elaborated by such scholars as Colin Gordon (1991), Nikolas Rose (1996), and Timothy Mitchell (1991)—to examine how power operates in new ways in political democracies. Here democracy is viewed not as utopian dream following authoritarian or totalitarian regimes but rather as an exercise of power in its own right, at times more effective in enacting control over the population (by acting through it), or achieving quiescence of social movements, than military repression had been. While this theoretical inclination holds great promise for understanding democracy within "advanced liberalism" or amid neoliberal economics, we are only now seeing the beginning of detailed ethnographic accounts along these lines (see, e.g., Nelson 1999, 102, and work by the political scientist Schild [1998], who writes with an ethnographic sensibility).

This book shares elements of these various approaches in analyzing Chile's particular experience of democracy. Focusing on historically specific constructions about politics, it contrasts views of democracy promulgated by politicians during the transition with conceptions voiced by the health group Llareta. As such, it examines a variety of discourses of democracy circulating in Santiago in the early 1990s. Although my intention is not to offer programmatic suggestions for reform of government, recommendations in this direction are voiced by the book's central characters, as health group members articulate their aspirations for democracy in speeches and activities that emphasize their quest to hold government accountable. Finally, and most significantly, the book seeks to examine how power is exercised in political democracy, particularly through the use of public opinion polls, pressure for grassroots organizations to "participate" by providing social services, and technocratic decision making that excludes the poor. These practices enact a kind of governmentality that requires the health group to devise innovative forms of action attuned to the conditions specific to the post-dictatorship period.

An entry point for anthropological inquiry into democracy in Latin America is the variety of discourses circulating about the elected governments that now predominate in the region. Some have described contemporary political systems not as democracy plain and simple but as *democracia con apellidos*—democracy with last names ("last names" refers to the adjective, which in Spanish follows the noun). In Chile it is not uncommon to hear the current system described as *democracia restringida* (restricted democracy), *democracia cupular* (elite democracy), *democracia lite* (low-fat democracy), and *democracia entre comillas* (democracy in quotation marks).

By speaking of *democracia con apellidos*, Chileans were in part calling into question the democratic character of the new political institutions. After Chile's regime transition there were nonelected senators, an ongoing influence of the military, a constitution written by the former dictator, and electoral rules skewed to favor Pinochet's followers. Through these mechanisms, the prior military government was deeply embedded in post-dictatorship political life. Under these conditions, just how democratic could the resulting system be?

But the critique went beyond the nature of formal political institutions. Those who used these phrases were also questioning the impact citizens could have on political processes. The term *democracia cupular*, for example, describes a situation in which only a small circle of elite politicians has access to negotiating the structure of the political system and the particular policy decisions it makes.

Members of the *población* health group Llareta were some of those most preoccupied with the influence they could have on policy during democracy. When, in a workshop in 1992, I asked what democracy meant to them, Mónica Janet, Digna, and Mariela offered definitions that converged. They said that democracy meant "being listened to," "having one's opinions taken into account," and "being taken seriously." The valuing of participants' viewpoints was characteristic of grassroots organizations in which members expressed their ideas and had an impact on resulting decisions. With the coming of political democracy in the country, the health group wanted agendas and priorities generated in poor communities to influence public policy. The health promoters' definition of democracy focused not on elections and political regimes but on the influence ordinary people and organized community groups could bring to bear on the decisions that affected their lives.

The nature of democracy and the influence citizens could have on policy in the late twentieth century were shaped not only by national politics but also by international economic processes. In public discourse, U.S. foreign policy makers and Latin American politicians have linked free market economic policy to democracy, seeing them as twin pillars of freedom around the world. Yet as citizens in places as diverse as Africa, Latin America, and countries of the former Soviet Union acquired the right to vote in national elections in the 1980s and 1990s, they often had little ability to influence public policy. By the 1980s and 1990s, these countries' economic frameworks were largely determined not by citizens but by employees of multinational corporations, experts within financial institutions, or staff of transnational lending bodies such as the International Monetary Fund. Staff persons were hired for their expertise, having gained credentials and technical competence at world-class universities. As nonelected technocrats expanded their areas of responsibility, basic decisions about national economies shifted out of public control and societal debate. At the very moment when countries regained democratic political institutions, key decisions about public life and the economy had moved outside the ambit of elections, beyond the reach of the electorate—indeed, beyond the reach of the nation-state. Elections may have been heralded as the sign of democracy, but in the context of neoliberal economics, they had largely been emptied of democratic force.

POWER AND SOCIAL MOVEMENT STRATEGY
IN POST-DICTATORSHIP CHILE

As an ethnography of democracy, this book interweaves two central preoccupations: the changing nature of political power in Chile, and the changing strategies of urban social movements under new political conditions. With regard to the first theme I ask: How have forms of power transformed with the onset of a political democracy? That is, what new mechanisms of power come into effect when military repression is no longer the key political force?

This inquiry is inspired by an apparent paradox in the Chilean transition to democracy. Social movements, which had been strong amid the land seizures and housing mobilizations of the late 1960s, the factory takeovers during Salvador Allende's Popular Unity government in the early 1970s, and the protests against the military regime in the mid-1980s, largely diminished with the onset of post-dictatorship democracy in the early 1990s. This quieting of social movement activity at what appeared to be a moment of openness for political activity is striking. It calls for investigation into the ways in which contemporary democracy might convince people not to mobilize.

In setting the groundwork for an examination of how power functioned, I note that the basic economic model installed by General Pinochet was maintained during the political transition. Through new cultural forms and practices, political democracy played a key role in generating consent and providing legitimacy for neoliberal economics. The cultural and political work sustaining neoliberalism were part of a new approach called *neostructuralism*, a term coined by the United Nations' Economic Commission on Latin America and the Caribbean (ECLAC) in the late 1980s (Green 1995, 188–89). In this framework, creating "growth with equity" or giving capitalism a "human face" required the state to take on a new role in developing political consensus, achieving some degree of economic redistribution, and investing citizens in a common national project of economic growth (Petras and Leiva 1994, 65).[1]

Discussion of the kinds of power that replace repression have often drawn on the concept of hegemony. Following Antonio Gramsci, theorists have noted that when power does not operate primarily through repression it may generate subtle forms of consent. Such an effort may initially operate "consciously and programmatically" but "increasingly [becomes] the 'natural' and unreflected administration or reproduction of a given way of doing things." At least in the beginning, it requires "a continuous labor of creative ideological intervention" that has "to be systematically worked at" (Eley 1994, 323–24).

A mixture of the programmatic and the seemingly natural, the change in political culture in the post-dictatorship period in Chile, which included demobilization, was produced through the mechanisms of contemporary democracy. These included election campaigns, opinion polls, mass media publicity, and exhortations to the population to "participate" in democracy. Theorists of hegemony have observed that dominant paradigms can be resisted, and James Scott (1985, 304–50) has rightly noted that just because reigning forms are not overtly protested does not mean that the population finds them convincing. Yet whether or not they are accepted or resisted, these practices are powerful to the degree that they produce particular types of subjects, in this case citizen-consumers constituted as individuals through the mutually reinforcing mechanisms of the market and contemporary politics.

I use the concept "marketing democracy" to refer to this intersection of politics and economics, and I attribute to the concept two intertwined meanings: the infusion and shaping of democracy by free market economics, and the production of political images that promote democracy as a positive value. In Chile, the idea of democracy was strategically deployed and imbued with a series of meanings by a variety of actors, including health group members and government officials. Accompanying these shifting discourses and strategic uses of the term were the techniques of political marketing that solicit citizens' opinions so that policy decisions appear to be the product of their own choice.

A related way in which power functioned in post-dictatorship Chile was by attempting to stimulate citizen participation. In Chile, community groups were asked to "participate" by giving of their labor, often to activities previously performed by the welfare state. While framed as a way of bolstering democracy by strengthening civil society, this kind of participation subsidized and fortified neoliberal economic reforms. It constituted a kind of "governmentality" (Foucault 1991) in which citizens became agents in their own governance (see also Cruikshank 1999; Rose 1996).

Finally, power operated in the post-dictatorship period through the insistence that only those with formal educational credentials participate in policy-making processes. The professionalization of knowledge and the migration of former nongovernmental organization staff members into government jobs or work funded through government contracts left few sources from which to establish a critical perspective on the transition.

Questions about power lead to a second set of questions having to do with social movement strategy. In the face of changing forms of political power, I ask, how have social movements analyzed the political conditions in which they are situated? Once open protest had been abandoned in the post-dictatorship period, what kinds of strategies did grassroots groups develop to respond to forms of power that operate less through repression than through a discourse of participation? How might the poor manage to gain some influence over public decision making when that privilege has been reserved for those with formal credentials and expertise? In short, what forms of social movement activity have community groups found to be suitable to address the new political circumstances?

My research in the *población* La Bandera reveals a series of emergent approaches used by community organizations. Among them are the critique and appropriation of professionalized forms of knowledge, and resistance by community groups to providing public services by demanding "real participation" in decision making and searching for ways of holding government accountable. Together, these approaches constitute an emphasis on intellectual work and political analysis that contrast with more limited forms of participation and an expertise-driven legitimation of knowledge in the post-dictatorship period.

CHILE: MODEL OF AND MODEL FOR DEMOCRACY

Chile is a particularly enlightening case to study because the relationships between economic and political processes have been so clearly drawn. In the late 1960s and early 1970s an upswell of social movement activity in Chile culminated in the presidency of Socialist Salvador Allende, the first Marxist president in the hemisphere to gain power through elections. Antagonizing the United States government, multinational corporations, and Chilean elites, Allende nationalized industries and redistributed income—thereby combining political democracy with a socialist economic experiment and a period of cultural vitality for the political Left. This period ended abruptly in 1973—the same year oil shocks catapulted the world economy into an era of unprecedented capital mobility—with a military coup that introduced one of the most comprehensive free market restructurings ever attempted worldwide. General Pinochet's government privatized industry and public services, opened the economy to imported products, and promoted exports based on primary goods. This economic transformation was facilitated by brutal repression against labor and social movements. In 1990, after economic restructuring was virtually complete, a political transition to an elected civilian government made Chile an internationally touted model for combining free markets and democracy. As this book details, the new government largely perpetuated the structures, both political and economic, instituted by its military predecessor, while instituting new forms of power and reaping the legitimacy gained from democracy.

The links among free markets, democracy, and the changing role of the state in Chile provide a useful lens for looking at other contemporary political transitions. In both South Africa and Haiti, for example, leaders of resistance movements took power through elections, only to find their economic policies constrained by structural adjustment policies of international financial institutions. The case of Chile also provides a new way of looking at Eastern Europe, which has been constructed in the West's public imagination as gaining freedom through the joint arrival of democracy and free market capitalism. The parallels with these other countries are not merely coincidental, for Chile has become an international model in recent years. Eastern European nations have turned to Chilean financial experts for advice on privatizing their economies, and in South Africa, Chile's National Commission of Truth and Reconciliation became one of the precedents (though with fundamental differences) for its own process of confronting past human rights abuses. As these historical borrowings and political parallels demonstrate, the Chilean story is a particularly important entry point into an analysis of the relationship between democracy and free market economics throughout the world.

This study of the Chilean political transition also has implications for understanding the challenges facing democracy in the United States. Declining voter turnout, the blurring of ideological boundaries between political parties, and the rapid increase in campaign spending have raised questions about the nature of democracy in the United States. As in Chile, these questions take place in the context of efforts to limit and restructure the role of government, for example, through welfare reform, and increased globalization of the economy. There are also important parallels between the discourse on volunteerism in the United States, as seen during the 1997 Summit on America's Future held in Philadelphia and efforts at national unity, such as the Clinton administration's conversations on race, and the emphasis on citizen participation and civil society during the Chilean transition.

If Chile and the United States are undergoing related processes, they have also directly influenced each other's policies. The United States' involvement in the Chilean coup is well documented. More recently, the United States' two-party system and political marketing campaigns have been models and resources for the transformation of Chile's political system. This borrowing is reciprocal, for Chile has also been a testing ground for public policy ideas generated in the United States. The "Chicago Boys"—Chilean economists who implemented General Pinochet's economic strategy—received their initial training in the economics department at the University of Chicago, funded in part by the United States Agency for International Development (USAID). Free market ideas, which met resistance from organized interest groups, such as senior citizens and legislators in the United States, found their full expression under a military dictatorship in Chile, where the Congress had been shut down and social movements repressed. By the 1990s, proponents of privatizing the U.S. Social Security system would use the Chilean experience as the model for the United States despite the fact that it had been implemented under an authoritarian government.

LA BANDERA: HISTORY AND ORGANIZATIONS

If Chile is a prime location for examining international political processes connecting democracy to free markets, the Santiago *población* La Bandera is an excellent site for seeing how these processes unfold for social movements and within daily life.[2] The *población*'s history exemplifies the political and economic processes occurring during the last three decades in Chile. Created in the late 1960s, La Bandera came into existence at a time of significant state involvement in urban neighborhoods, political democracy, and robust social movements. Following the military coup, which occurred just a few years after its birth, La Bandera residents (particularly those involved in political and community organizations) endured severe repression. Moreover, the neoliberal economic model created high unemployment rates and widespread hunger in La Bandera. In the immediate post-dictatorship period, economic deprivation persisted, while avenues for political change became unclear.

It is this last point—shifting strategies for political change—that makes La Bandera a pertinent site for the questions about democracy raised in this book. La Bandera is a place in which the changing strategies and fluctuating strength of social movements have been particularly notable. Committees for housing involving thousands of people led the impetus to populate the southern zone of Santiago in the late 1960s, and in 1970 a land seizure gave La Bandera a reputation as one of the most highly politicized places in Chile. In the mid-1980s, protests against the military regime confirmed La Bandera's image as a combative urban neighborhood. Yet after being one of the most highly mobilized *poblaciones* in the 1960s through the 1980s, La Bandera became strikingly demobilized in the 1990s. Many community organizations that were on their last legs when I did my fieldwork in 1991 had completely collapsed when I returned in 1997. Into their place had stepped an increased role of the municipality, televised symbols of national identity and participation, and periodic elections. Local leaders faced co-optation, while others struggled to find new avenues for organization. Because of its history of social mobilization, the decline of social organizations, and the dilemmas community leaders faced in the 1990s, La Bandera is a window into the local impact of a particular kind of political democracy situated within neoliberal economics.

THE HEALTH GROUP LLARETA

This book looks at the impact of changing political conditions on the social organizations functioning within La Bandera. Based on research with various community groups, the book follows one organization—the health group Llareta—particularly closely. Over time the specific participants in the group have changed and the exact number of members fluctuated, but in the early 1990s the group consisted of seven women and one man, mainly in their twenties and thirties.[3] The leaders who constituted Llareta traced their own entrance into political activity to different historical moments—some as early as the 1950s, when they campaigned for candidates or organized workers, some as late as the 1990s, when they first joined the health group. Llareta itself originated in 1984, during the military regime. While many of La Bandera's organizations dissolved after the transition to democracy, some organizations, including Llareta, continued to be active, although their ongoing existence was often precarious. Llareta's longevity and durability distinguish it from groups that did not survive the political transition, as well as from those created in the post-dictatorship period. The group's long history is useful for analysis, however, because it reflects the changes in Chile and La Bandera in a way that the history of an organization that disappears at the end of one political context or arises in a new one does not. The specific ways Chile's political processes have played out in the organization are unique to Llareta, in part reflecting the very distinct training and nongovernmental organization support the group has received. But the group's characteristics—whom it attracts, its methods of organization, its enduring principles and shifting tactics—express the pressures community groups were under and the options they faced in different historical times.

A look at the health group's priorities and tactics helps illuminate changing political scenes in La Bandera's and Chile's histories. Llareta was born in 1984 as a result of a training seminar held by a nongovernmental organization known as EPES (Educación Popular en Salud, or Popular Education in Health). EPES had been created in 1982 by a U.S.-born Lutheran missionary and three other women—a Canadian doctor, a Chilean social worker, and a Chilean health educator. Initiated in Santiago, it expanded to the city of Concepción in 1983. Its purpose was to train health teams in various *poblaciones*. Drawing on the work of Paulo Freire, EPES sought to build on people's own knowledge. The staff of EPES invited leaders from La Bandera's existing organizations to participate in the seminar, anticipating that they would later have an impact on the common kitchens, women's groups, and other organizations to which they belonged.

From the outset, EPES's work went beyond teaching the technicalities of first aid and how to administer injections, though these skills were included in its programs. The organization's focus was on training health promoters to engage in critical analysis of the political-economic processes that affected their health broadly conceived. The staff had developed an analysis of the health system that involved examining the impact of the dismantling of the national health service, the privatization of insurance, and the impacts of environment and poverty on health. EPES staff members sought to increase the overall health in poor neighborhoods by involving residents in identifying problems, making decisions, and taking actions to improve conditions in their communities. Residents would do this not only or even primarily by providing their own health services but by developing agendas, formulating demands, educating, and taking part in societal debates. EPES emphasized the importance of building networks and strengthening existing social organizations in the *poblaciones* in which they worked. To the degree that they sought to organize the poor in the 1980s, members of EPES inserted themselves into a broad-based popular movement trying to restore democracy to Chile.

In the mid-1980s, during the years of national protest against the military regime, community leaders faced dire health emergencies in the *población*, not the least of which were bullet wounds when military police fired into crowds and sicknesses that an underfunded local health clinic was not equipped to address. Confronted with these exigencies, twenty-three people signed up for EPES's training course. After the seminar, a smaller group remained and became the health group Llareta.

Valeria, who at the time I did my fieldwork was Llareta's coordinator, remembers the initial encounters with EPES as a time of conceptual transformation. Initially she and other community leaders were interested in how to treat injuries and cure disease. This seemed logical, she said, because at the time, "the concept that we used as *pobladores* was that 'health' was *not being sick.*" Valeria later wrote, "As [EPES] delivered the contents [of their training workshop], our concept of health changed. Through [this] process...we came to see a concept of health that is much broader.... We began to glimpse that health was housing, education, work, environment, etcetera. A series of situations that we lived."

Over time, the group's members moved away from providing direct services— what they called *asistencialismo*—and turned their efforts to *educación* and *denuncia:*

Figure 1. Health promoters play "Getting to Know Your Community," a game developed by EPES, during training for a new health team. Photo: Gordon Whitman.

educating their neighbors and voicing a critique of the dictatorship through the theme of health. To this day, the tension between these different roles persists. Health promoters gain some of their credibility by giving neighbors injections and healing wounds. But they do not see providing these services as their main role. Although health promoters in some of Santiago's groups kept a first aid box in the house, others refused to keep supplies on hand. Valeria, who would scramble for bandages and medicines when emergencies arose, told me she did not store supplies at home because she did not want her neighbors to get a false sense of security from the idea that health promoters could provide for their needs. She wanted fellow residents of La Bandera to see the existing shortages and search for more enduring solutions. Members of Llareta defined health care as a right, and they expected services to be provided by the state. They saw their primary function as educating their neighbors by making available to them preventive information ordinarily known only by professionals, and holding the government accountable for meeting the community's needs.

By the 1990s, Llareta was experiencing many of the dilemmas confronting other social organizations during the transition to democracy. Asked to provide services formerly offered by the state, discredited because its members lacked professional degrees, determined to resist co-optation, and frustrated by overall demobilization, the group had to develop its own analysis of the political situation and create new strategies suitable for the post-dictatorship period. These struggles to understand contemporary political conditions and to develop ways to deal with them are presented in part two of this book. There, I detail Llareta's dilemmas and the group's efforts to resolve them through a series of ethnographic stories about struggles over the meaning of democracy. In a meningitis campaign described in chapter 4, for example, a representative at the Ministry of Health aims to convince health promoters not to hold a demonstration because doing so would undermine democracy. Health promoters contest his discourse during the meeting but find the citywide leadership of health groups divided and their ability to protest health policy weakened by the attractiveness to some health promoters of the concept of democracy promulgated by government officials. "Participation" similarly acts as a powerful discourse to limit the oppositional activity of social movements. During Llareta's campaign to prevent the spread of cholera (described in chapter 5), a congressional representative suggests that community groups "participate" by cleaning garbage from littered fields. This construction of the problem sparks debate among community groups over the meaning of participation and exposes different understandings of the meaning of health. If, as Lila Abu-Lughod (1990a) suggests, by looking at resistance we can better understand power, an examination of Llareta's experiences gives us a view into both changing mechanisms of power and shifting forms of strategic resistance in a succession of political contexts in Chile. Llareta is an especially rewarding case study, moreover, because the group has reflected on its own shifting tactics and analyzed the country's political reality as part of its work.

EXTRACTING KNOWLEDGE FROM THE *POBLACIÓN*

For both Llareta and EPES, knowledge was deeply tied to power. When members of Llareta asserted that in a democracy their ideas should have an impact on decision making, they were advancing the idea that politics is inextricably tied to the use and legitimation of knowledge. Similarly, when they engaged in their own political analysis, they were using knowledge and intellectual work as a strategic resistance appropriate to the kinds of power operating in the post-dictatorship period.[4]

In La Bandera, community leaders critiqued the power relations embedded in the production and distribution of knowledge. The following anecdote illustrates how direct this critique was. The story relates an experience I had upon introducing myself to members of the neighborhood council *(junta de vecinos)* soon after arriving in La Bandera. The *junta de vecinos*, also known as the *unidad vecinal*, is an official institution meant to represent the needs of residents in a subsection of the *población*. Each cluster of houses sends a delegate to periodic meetings. During the dictatorship the military government had appointed representatives, but by the time I did my research in 1991, a new board had been popularly elected.

For the purposes of my research, meeting with members of the *unidad vecinal* was not absolutely necessary, since they were not official gatekeepers of the community, nor did they monitor relationships in the *población*. Nonetheless, it seemed respectful to announce my presence to community leaders and useful to meet members of the local council. And so I went one evening to introduce myself. Once initial presentations had been made, the group sat down around a long wooden table. The council members asked me to describe my work, which I did.

After hearing about the proposed research, members of the neighborhood council confronted me immediately with their own views of power relations and knowledge. The president told me that for centuries, Europeans, North Americans, and now the Japanese had come to take the natural resources and products of Chilean labor out of Chile. Similarly, he said, researchers come to take knowledge out of our community. They do surveys, the results of which we never see. They publish photos of our children looking dirty and miserable. All of this is justified as a mechanism to diminish poverty, but it never does. We continue to live with hunger and dirt, while researchers receive salaries for their work. He addressed me seriously. Why should we cooperate with you if your research is going to take more of our knowledge away from us? How will your work directly benefit the *población?*

As a researcher, I felt that the stakes in giving an acceptable answer that evening were high. As members of the council and I knew, social science research—particularly the ethnographic method I had proposed—depends on interviews, photographs, the gathering of documentation, introductions to acquaintances, invitations to events, and agreements to attend discussion groups. It depends, in short, on the goodwill of people to extend access to local knowledge. The council president was challenging me to reformulate my study to compensate for inequalities of power. He conditioned his own cooperation on those criteria.

That evening I argued that writing books that exposed the difficulty of life in La Bandera and revealed instances of injustice could contribute to changes that would ameliorate poverty. It was an argument that presented the anthropologist as a channel for the "voices" of the poor,[5] and one that saw usefulness in writing books that could be read by policy-making elites. I argued that this could be an effective mechanism for creating proposed changes or altering relations of power.

After hearing my response, the president of the council paused. The members of the *unidad vecinal* had been reading between the lines, listening to my discourse for the political affiliation, ideology, and social networks it implied.[6] During some moments of silence, the president seemed to mull over the available evidence. Finally he indicated that if there was anything he and the other council members could do to help with my work, I should just let them know. My answer seemed to have been accepted. I now believe that that acceptance was due more to assumptions about the politics revealed in my discourse than to confidence that my work would have any useful effect.

While I seemed to have survived the initial litmus test for research in the *población*, I was aware that access functioned along a sliding scale, and that in the following months my actions would be judged more strictly than my words. It was fast becoming clear to me that because of its recent experience of dictatorship, its traditions of clandestine organizing, and the fractured nature of its political networks, La Bandera was a place where a researcher needed to build trust, and where it was impossible to forge relationships without choosing sides. The initial experience with the *junta de vecinos* illustrated that a critical recurring issue in the community would be efforts of community leaders to limit outsiders' appropriation of their knowledge and to resist being situated as objects of study. This raised a key question for me as an ethnographer: What sort of research methodology could one create in a place where social science itself had been problematized?

TOWARD AN ETHNOGRAPHY OF POLITICAL PROCESS

In the 1980s, the trend in anthropology for dealing with power-knowledge inequalities was reflexivity: greater scrutiny of the categories and practices of inquiry and writing (Rabinow and Sullivan 1987, 27; Marcus and Fischer 1986; Clifford and Marcus 1986). Scholars committed to this outlook rightfully questioned the way textual representation enacted power. But while such self-examination advanced an awareness of knowledge inequalities and the construction of ethnographic authority, its overemphasis on the written text created limitations in addressing issues of power more broadly.

A response more suitable to addressing power-knowledge inequalities in the political context in which people struggle and live situates the traditional objects of ethnographic inquiry as producers of knowledge. Recently, a number of anthropological studies have rendered informants' critiques of knowledge explicit and have begun to look at intellectual production by indigenous peoples themselves.[7] These "indigenous intellectuals" are often in direct dialogue with, appropriating from, or launching a critique of standard social science (Warren 1998; Campbell 1996). The studies recognize that while power operates through knowledge as a form of domination, production, and control, it also provides strategies of resistance for social movements. When grassroots leaders and organizations question knowledge-power relations, they compel researchers from groups traditionally identified as knowledge producers to create new kinds of methodology (see also Hale 1994, 16; Burdick 1993, viii–x).

From the start, the theoretical and methodological challenges presented by *pobladores'* refusal to be positioned as objects of study reconfigured my work. They forced me to reconsider how I would contribute to the local community. Sometime after my conversation with the neighborhood council, I reflected back on that meeting and considered a different resolution to the power-knowledge problem. In my talk that evening, I had proposed writing particular kinds of books for policy-making elites as a way to benefit residents of La Bandera. However, my approach underestimated the degree to which inequality of access to information—and differentials in who got to be authors of knowledge—was precisely the form of power that members of the *unidad vecinal* had critiqued. I realized that my research would have to contribute to intellectual work already under way in the *población*.

The decision to engage in intellectual work with people in La Bandera grew out of the practices and methods of the place and time. In the year and a half I was there, a number of adult leaders had gone back to finish high school degrees. Some had given talks at national and international conferences, in Cuba, Tanzania, Ecuador, Argentina, and Spain. Three people I knew were writing books: one woman from a different Santiago *población* had recently published a compendium of life histories of *pobladora* women (Quintanilla n.d.), another was drafting an autobiography, and a young man was in the middle of composing a novel. *Talleres,* or educational workshops, operated frequently in *poblaciones*. They included analyses of the causes of hunger, seminars on health, and educational sessions on the legal rights of workers. In *poblaciones* all over Santiago, libraries and documentation centers were opening up. Intellectual activities were not the only or even the primary concern in people's lives, which were dedicated to working, caring for children, cleaning and repairing houses, and other exigencies of daily life. Nor were they engaged in by all residents. However, for community leaders seeking new organizational tactics in the post-dictatorship years, critical thinking, political analysis, and historical investigation were priorities.

In this context, I saw myself as studying political processes *with* the urban poor rather than studying them, their actions, their beliefs, or their behavior. This relationship is perhaps best captured by George Marcus's (1998, 122) term "complicity," which he describes as "an affinity, marking equivalence, between fieldworker and informant. This affinity arises from their mutual curiosity and anxiety about their relationship to a 'third.'" In the context of my fieldwork, the "third" that both the health group and I focused on was the transition to democracy and the development of social movement strategy. Marcus states that the "acknowledged fascination between anthropologist and informant regarding the outside 'world'" creates "the bond that makes their fieldwork relationship effective." Since the central questions facing *poblador* community leaders in 1991 were how to analyze new power relations affecting community organizations' relations with the state, and how to assess which strategies might be useful in confronting them, I sought to understand, with them, the power dynamics and discourses that made particular options feasible for social movements at that historical juncture. My object of study became not residents of poor communities but rather the political processes they were experiencing, resisting, and helping to generate. In concrete terms, I was studying the transition to democracy from a location in the *población;* I was looking at the changing landscape of political options available to *poblador* social organizations and, in that context, understanding the ones they chose and why.

In seeking to understand local, national, and international politics, I worked in tandem with *poblador* leaders engaged in analysis. Far from initiating such reflection, I inserted myself into already existing organizations in which they were conducting an ongoing process of analysis: popular education workshops, Christian base communities, and in more informal locales such as around kitchen tables or in homes while people watched the television news. The fact that *poblador* leaders routinely theorized the political processes shaping their lives means that as much of the theory in this book takes place in their voices as my own. Rather than objects of study, *pobladores* became intellectual colleagues; rather than a researcher of them, I became someone with and through whom the traditional objects of anthropological study reflected on the political processes they shaped and faced. How each of us—anthropologist and community leaders—was situated varied significantly. We had different things at stake, and we have generated different products through our work. But our process of analyzing and the uses to which our work was put intertwined and overlapped.

In the places where I did initiate discussions or raise questions, *poblador* community leaders soon melded my techniques into their own genres and used them for their own purposes. What elsewhere would have been a focus group, participants transformed into a *taller* (popular education workshop). They taught me how to begin with an ice breaker *(dinámica)*, state my objectives, use markers to record points on large pieces of brown paper *(papelógrafo)*, conduct an activity or pose questions for discussion, give people the opportunity to speak in small groups and report on their findings to the larger assembly *(plenario)*, and take time for evaluation. Participants absorbed what they learned in these sessions into their own personal processes of education and growth.

Members of these workshops also insisted that reflection lead quickly to action and that analytic work be used systematically for social change. Their inclination toward taking action meant that my study was not limited to describing preexisting social organizations. I was also actively involved in seeing how people evaluated and implemented strategies to rework those organizations in an ongoing way. This kind of participation enriched my study. At a time when mass mobilization had subsided, it was not possible to find popular organizing in large-scale demonstrations or rallies in the streets. Instead, organizing relationships were built in "submerged networks" (Melucci 1989), and decisions were made as part of ongoing debates. Researching the question of collective action meant gaining detailed knowledge of the day-to-day functioning of social organizations and being present at informal daily conversations.

An example will help make these points clear. In one workshop session in which health group members and others participated, we analyzed 1970s blueprints of La Bandera that I had obtained from the housing authority. The blueprints showed that empty fields filled with garbage had been designated two decades earlier for public services: a popular laundromat, a swimming pool, parks, a nursery school, and a supermarket. I was interested in sharing the information and taperecording community leaders' comments for my study. However, after discussing the blueprints, workshop participants wanted to take immediate action. They set a date to exhibit the blueprints in the *población*. In the process of planning the event, they determined the best location (outdoors, rather than in a building, where guards might refuse to let certain people enter; on a street without traffic, where many pedestrians would pass by) and the best time (during the hours of the open air market, so people would see the exhibit on their way to shop; on the day the municipality had scheduled a celebration of the recent paving of that street, to make the point that the pavement had been promised and delayed for over twenty years). Prior to the day we would display the materials, we decorated the maps with commentary to contrast what had been planned with what existed there now; on the day of the activity, we hung photos of the garbage that now occupied the open areas and created signs explaining the group's analysis of the use of public space. The participants then incorporated the information collected for this exhibit into their campaign to get the municipality to convert empty and garbage-filled fields into parks. The process through which materials gathered during my research were used for local activities gave me knowledge of the dynamics and changing tactics of organization in the post-dictatorship period.

As another way of developing a methodology that would begin to address the power-knowledge conditions raised by community leaders, in April 1991 my husband, Gordon, and I began a history workshop.[8] I later learned that history workshops were one of the most prominent forms of intellectual activity then occurring in poor neighborhoods in Chile. At a 1991 seminar on histories of the *poblaciones*, thirty authors of local history books (professionals and *pobladores*) gathered to share ideas (Farias, Garcés, and Nicholls 1993). A bibliography distributed through that seminar included fourteen published books on the histories of *poblaciones*,[9] one of which was a collection of nine historical essays written by different *pobladores* (Avello et al. 1989). There were also efforts to write the history of *poblaciones* concurrent with their process of formation, as seen in a 1992 workshop at a land seizure in the northeastern section of Santiago.

Participants in our workshop were neighborhood teenagers. At the beginning of our working process, the group divided the history of La Bandera into periods, which we set out to research in turn. For the various periods we used documents and interviews to produce a comic-book bulletin that could be distributed to neighbors. The bulletins included editorials written by the teenagers, newspaper headlines, fictional dialogue that portrayed the debates of the time, and poetry. We set up a stand and gave out the booklets in the marketplace.

The history workshop advanced my work in a number of ways. It allowed me to contribute to the *población* by expanding space for intellectual inquiry by *pobladores*. It provided a mechanism for repatriating a collection of materials that had been researched in and written about La Bandera by others but had never before been accessible to the majority of its residents. These documents included theses by social work and architectural students,[10] book chapters,[11] urban planning blueprints from the Ministry of Housing,[12] statistical data,[13] newspaper articles,[14] and human rights information,[15] as well as videos (Shaffer 1989) and cassette recordings.[16] And the history workshop benefited my research directly by providing a forum from which to gather local residents' interpretations of history.

The decision not only to participate in daily and organizational life but also to initiate activities provided one possible resolution of the methodological dilemma inherent in studying strategies adopted by grassroots organizations during the transition to democracy. This idea is best contextualized by the writings of Pierre Bourdieu, who has attempted to construct a methodology for the study of practice. In his book *Outline of a Theory of Practice* (1977), he writes:

> The anthropologist's particular relation to the object of his study contains the makings of a theoretical distortion inasmuch as his situation as an observer, excluded from the real play of social activities by the fact that he has no place (except by choice or by way of a game) in the system observed and has no need to make a place for himself there, inclines him to a hermeneutic representation of practices, leading him to reduce all social relations to communicative relations, and, more precisely, to decoding operations.... *[There is a] tendency to* intellectualism *implied in observing language from the standpoint of the listening subject rather than that of the speaking subject* [emphasis added]. (1)

According to Bourdieu, an approach to fieldwork in which the anthropologist positions herself at a distance in order to understand objective models leads the researcher to see social action as spectacle rather than as decision. What to actors is irreversible action appears to the researcher as a reversible series of options. As an outsider approaching an unknown place, the researcher sees the landscape as a map and speech as a dictionary: a depiction of all possible routes or phrases, rather than as a set of distinct pathways one must choose to get from here to there, and on which, over time, there is no going back (see also de Certeau 1984, 35).

In problematizing objectivism, Bourdieu does not call for phenomenology—the study of subjective experience rather than objective structures—but rather for a theory (and methodology) of practice, which can capture the sense of time and sequence through which people act. Using a history workshop as one research tool allowed me to face some of the constraints that confronted neighborhood leaders and better understand the strategies adopted in response to those conditions. To create the workshop, I had to learn methods of popular education, face the difficulty of getting neighbors to come to activities, design meeting agendas and work plans, and receive critical comments about the work. By doing my own organizing, I had to deal with questions such as the following: Where would materials and financial support come from? Where could we meet? How should we divide responsibilities? How many people, and of what ages, should participate in the workshop? What kind of final product would be the best to create, and how would it be distributed? Why were people skipping meetings? The activities gave insight into the context of organizing in La Bandera in 1991 in a way that a methodology restricted to observing or participating in existing organizations could not.

STRUCTURE OF THE BOOK

Each of the chapters of this book weaves together the linked questions of how power functioned and what kinds of strategies social movements were developing within the political climate of the time. Part one sets the stage by dealing with these questions historically, from the mid-1960s to the late 1980s. Part two, the heart of the book, analyzes the kinds of power and resistances functioning in post-dictatorship Chile.

Chapters 1 and 2 describe La Bandera's history of collective action. Embedding La Bandera's past within the recent history of Chile, they show how the place was created through the organized activity of social movements, and how these movements' forms of collective action have changed over time as political conditions transformed. The chapters are thus a history of politics and strategy, tacking back and forth between national events and the memories and experiences of La Bandera's residents.

Chapter 3 focuses on the political process known as the "transition to democracy," which followed the protest period and continued into the 1990s. Beginning with a sketch of demobilization following the onset of democracy, the chapter flashes back to the political processes through which the demobilization of social movements was achieved. Because this necessitates a look less at local organizations than at national politics, the chapter traces the evolving strategy of the opposition to the dictatorship and follows the politicians and intellectuals as they negotiate with the military regime for a return to civilian rule. The chapter closes by reexamining grassroots demobilization of the 1990s, in light of the particular kind of transition that had taken place.

Part two analyzes the forms of power operating within political democracy. Focusing on the "marketing of democracy," chapter 4 suggests that the idea of democracy has been imbued with different meanings and used strategically by a range of actors. The chapter examines techniques such as opinion polls and political marketing, through which implicit consent for the model is sustained.

One of the ways in which the state can limit pressures from below is by investing citizens in the system. While chapter 4 examines that proposition through reference to opinion polls, chapter 5 delves into the "paradox of participation." Using the health group's campaign against cholera as an example, the chapter shows that within the discourse of participation, citizens are welcomed to join organizations of civil society where, through their own efforts, they can help improve living conditions in their community. The promotion of civil society is at once a political and an economic strategy, for cutbacks in government services prescribed by neo-liberalism are thereby delegated to citizen volunteers and grassroots organizations to fill the gap. In post-dictatorship Chile, the term *participation* itself became a centerpiece of debate, as community leaders competed with government officials to achieve hegemony over its meaning.

In chapter 5, the health group Llareta's view of what "real" participation means is that community leaders set agendas and take an active role in all aspects of a campaign (designing it, carrying out activities, and evaluating the outcomes)—rather than just implement programs designed by experts. Chapter 6, "Legitimation of Knowledge," describes how the professionalization that accompanied economic restructuring under the military regime has persisted within the elected government. In both political systems, professionals, technocrats, and "apolitical" experts manage the economy with little input from the citizenry. Whereas health group members regarded democracy as having their ideas taken seriously, professionalization that excluded those without formal credentials ensured that *pobladores* would have little political influence. The example of a health seminar in which Llareta played an important role illustrates how community leaders both critiqued professional forms of knowledge as a kind of power and appropriated them as a form of resistance strategically tailored to the post-dictatorship political landscape.

Weaving through the book, and positioned at the beginning of chapters, are a series of incidents that offer commentary on the text by showing temporal change, highlighting contradictions and tensions in the analysis, identifying local debates, and positioning *pobladores* as intellectuals engaged in their own political projects. In part one the chapter preludes show the teenage members of our local history workshop debating the content and process of doing history. The chapter preludes in part two relate events that took place mainly after the years of primary fieldwork, sometimes outside the boundaries of Chile. The book begins with the moment in 1994 when I returned to Chile to present my dissertation in La Bandera (prologue) and ends in December 1997, when I held a workshop to teach health promoters ethnographic methodology (epilogue). The book concludes with the health group members' own ethnographic study of the process through which a soccer field in their neighborhood became a garbage dump. This "ethnography within an ethnography" is, I think, a fitting response to a way of legitimating knowledge that systematically underestimates the ability of the urban poor, particularly women, to engage in their own research and create their own political analysis. It is also an attempt to envision how ethnographic method might operate in a more democratic way.

La Bandera in the Social Imaginary

Geographically speaking, one can reach the *población* La Bandera by taking a bus south from the center of Santiago and turning westward along one of several roads. But a visitor coming from outside the *población* rarely finds the neighborhood without first encountering the imaginary that has been created around it.

"The mystique," says a young man who moved there about a decade earlier. "Some people think 'La Bandeeeeeera.'" His meaning comes through in his intonation—the drawing out of the penultimate syllable of the word. He refers to what goes unspoken: the powerful images that the name "La Bandera" evokes. For almost everyone in Santiago, mention of the name calls up a strong reaction—images of danger, chaos, poverty, subversion, resistance, or struggle.

Living in the place called La Bandera—as researcher or as resident—means negotiating these images daily. I am told by a professor not to work there: it is far too dangerous. A librarian and her intern at a research institute try to convince me not to move to a *población:* "You don't understand the unsanitary conditions. There's no hot water. A woman has to wash every day." When I say that if fifty thousand women currently live there, surely I can too, she insists that it's different: "They are accustomed to that filth, to cold water, to living on tea and bread. You are not." In a gesture I have seen countless times before, a taxi driver slides his right forefinger across his throat: La Bandera means delinquency, muggings, violence, death. "I don't know if you've noticed or not," says the young man quoted earlier. "When the newspapers speak of La Bandera, they speak of assaults, muggings,...of epidemics of lice, scabies, meningitis, of the child from the school across the street who died just recently. All things that don't move us forward, that don't give a person much desire to live in this *población*."

The reputation extends not only to poverty, disease, and crime but also to political activity. Residents say that the *población* was designated to be bombed at the time of the military coup in 1973 because the regime assumed that everyone there was a communist. In 1991, a Chilean sociologist working with the Ministry of Education tells me that my work will be of little interest to Chilean social scientists because La Bandera is such a politically active, and therefore atypical, place. Interlocutors routinely confuse it with other *poblaciones* noted for their activism. "Ah yes, La Bandera," says one. "I saw the documentary about it on television last month." The documentary he refers to was not about La Bandera but about La Victoria, a *población* also known for its activism. His confusion reveals how incidental the place itself is to the image it calls forth.

The mystique is manifested not only in stigma but also in the creation of a legendary history and an identity. People told me that the *población* was called La Bandera because when squatters first occupied the land they stuck a *bandera* (flag) in the ground to symbolize their victory. For years, annual celebrations of the anniversary of the *población* have taken place on January 26, the date of a famous land seizure in 1970. The land seizure is highlighted because it symbolizes protagonism and unity of *pobladores*. But the *población*'s history began earlier, when participants in committees of the homeless pressured the government to expropriate farmland for housing sites. And the area got its name not from the heroic actions of squatters but from the name the land had had for decades as an agricultural zone: *Fundo* (farm) La Bandera.

Myths and memories of collective action are highlighted by residents' sense that people living in the *población* have created everything they own. A neighbor describes the empty piece of land she arrived at in 1970—just a plot of dirt marked off by a line of chalk. She recalls the stages through which she built her house—first a tent made out of spare materials, then a shack put together with cardboard and wood, later a one-room structure, and at last an enlarging and changing house. I am told about children bringing their own chairs to the school neighbors were helping to build in 1971; in 1991, I walk by a community garden operated by neighbors, a store recently opened in someone's house, a newly paved segment of sidewalk. People's houses seem to be in a constant state of flux, as they rearrange the furniture and switch the uses of the rooms. One evening, a neighbor walks over sweating and exhausted to borrow a tool. Now that his married siblings had finally found other places to live, his parents were rearranging the structure of their house. He and his father had just knocked down a wall and put it up in a different spot, only to have his mother say she wanted it relocated again.

The fact that residents built their own homes leaves the *población* with a variety of housing styles, in a panoply of colors, shapes, and sizes. Houses with two stories stand next to small wooden shacks; properties with tall painted fences abut sites with only a crooked wooden gate. This wide assortment of styles makes the usual translation for *población*, "shantytown," a misleading image, for it conjures up only the most decrepit of homes. The architectural heterogeneity also reflects people's reluctance to leave. "I had the opportunity to buy a house in another place," said Digna, who had lived all her life in the *población* and who would later become a member of the health group Llareta. "But I bought my house in La Bandera instead." Valeria's husband, Jorge, who had lived in La Bandera for ten years, insisted that if he were to suddenly become wealthy he would not move out of La

Figure 2. La Bandera as seen from Sonia's rooftop. Photo: Gordon Whitman.

Bandera. "I would stay, fix up the house, and rebuild it from solid materials. I'd keep the same friends, think the same way, not have to change." "In the *barrio alto* [upscale neighborhoods] it's different," he said. "As soon as they hear that all you have is a high school degree, it doesn't matter how much money you have, they won't accept you, won't talk with you, will throw your children out of school. So people who get money and have moved to Las Condes [a wealthy section of Santiago] come back to the *población*. Here they get respect." Those who have the means to do so invest in their houses, but they stay.

The strong feelings of place and the relationships between people are in part the product of long-standing ties among generations that had arrived together through collective action. They are also the results of organized efforts to infuse the space of the *población* with culture. Murals, in the styles characteristic of various political parties and community groups, adorn walls all over La Bandera. Walking down a dirt road one day, I see a group of teenagers painting a mural for the prevention of AIDS. After an aborted land seizure in 1992, a mural goes up by the side of the *unidad vecinal* where the families had been given a place to stay, as if to explain and symbolize the event. Another mural depicts laborers doing construction work. Some of the paintings reference artists themselves: large images of the poet Pablo Neruda and the musician Víctor Jara cover the side of one apartment complex; a painting with poetry and images of women reaches three stories up another. And some public art depicts the *población* as it is, turning the precarious houses themselves into symbols. When asked what she could envision in the *población*, Angélica's teenage daughter described an outside wall painted with "pictures alluding to the *población*": houses with rocks holding down the roofs and diapers hanging on the clothesline. "It's not that I like these things so much, it's that they're so much *of* the *población*. On [greeting] cards or on the *arpilleras* [tapestries], these things look really pretty because they are your own." One community leader, who aimed to reclaim creativity for the *población* by doing art, puppetry, radio programs, street theater, and music, chose to interpret art itself as a popular creation. "Art is ours, poetry is ours, *modismos*—the way people talk—they are ours. They're of the *pueblo*."

While houses and public art reflect the stylistic creativity of residents, public utilities and urban infrastructure were also constructed by La Bandera's inhabitants. Working in minimum wage subsistence programs during the dictatorship, they had paved the roads and seeded the parks. Given the changes they had witnessed and created, and the fact that the very existence of the *población* was a result of organized activity, collective action and agency are central to the history and imagery of La Bandera. In the 1990s, community organizations would draw on the stories and symbols of collective action to assert the important role of the poor amid the elite negotiations structuring the new democracy.

The images surrounding the name La Bandera seem to project a place easily characterized—a logical unity, dangerous because of crime, or rising up in rebellion. But among the streets and passageways of the space delimited by the name La Bandera, the contours and fragmentation are more remarkable than any unity. Many of the images fostered by outsiders are applied by residents to smaller areas carved out along divisions in the local landscape. Afraid of what they call *delincuencia* (crime), for example, residents make meticulous distinctions about space. A friend living a few blocks to the north walks me only halfway home. "I walk until this point and no farther," she says. When I ask her what she expects to find on the next block, she is taken aback—she has never walked beyond this spot, so she does not know. A person waiting for the bus stands on her own side of the main road and crosses the street to board only after the bus has arrived. A woman is nearly trembling as she drives me home. "If I had known you lived in this part of the *población*, I would never have agreed to give you a ride," she tells me. In large part the mistrust reflects the fault lines of the wide variety of migration histories and the violence and fear new arrivals faced. It is for these rejections and hesitations, for the euphemisms and evasions, for the segmentation and stigmatization of people across a street, that the young man who had lived in La Bandera since the mid-1980s says that "there isn't a general sense of identity" in the *población*.

The resonance of the name La Bandera in the social imaginary has additional significance given the intense symbolic work used to market Chile internationally. Glossy brochures urging foreign investment and magazine ads publicizing exports aim to sell not just the product but also the country.[1] Indeed, Chile has been marketed internationally as a model for combining free markets with democracy.

Figure 3. Mural of two cultural icons of the Left on the side of an apartment building in the *población*. Photo: Gordon Whitman.

Figure 4. Lutheran youth group from La Bandera paints HIV mural in the *población*. Photo: Gordon Whitman.

Given this globally circulating image, it is striking that La Bandera is said to be everything that Chile is not—radicalized, poor, and dangerous. The gap between the national imagery and the *población*'s reputation has been treated in various ways: with physical repression (soon after the coup and during the protest period), geographic segregation (intensified through forced relocation by class), and a sense of cognitive dissonance for residents, who experience the disjuncture between the images of consumer abundance in television advertisements and the reality of poverty in the *población*. In the 1990s, as politicians promoted the ideas of consensus and democracy, *poblador* community leaders used the images and history of the *población* to create heroic narratives that could contest official representations and motivate social movements' revival.

Where did these images come from? The creation of La Bandera's reputation and the material production of the *población* are rooted in processes begun decades ago. Understanding them requires examining the origins of the neighborhood and its subsequent history.

PART ONE

History of Collective Action

We are sitting around the dining room table in Marisol's house, a small wooden structure at the edge of one of the open dirt squares in La Bandera. Scattered on the table before us are notebooks, pens, a tape recorder, and an assortment of newspaper articles from the late 1960s and early 1970s. It is the second meeting of our history workshop. I have conceptualized this workshop as a way to return materials I have gathered to people in the *población*, contribute to local intellectual work, and strengthen community organizations, all while collecting historical material and local interpretations of it. The health group Llareta is supporting this effort. Its members want to see another generation of youth become community leaders, and they hope to foster the development of organizations in the *población*. They are also interested in creating space for cultural activities. And so, a few weeks ago, Valeria helped me develop a work plan for the history workshop—a written program that includes objectives, activities, and a time line for events.

So far, my husband, Gordon, and I have managed to recruit three teenagers for the history workshop. Diego and Laura, both nineteen-year-old high school graduates, are at the moment falling in love with each other. They spend their days looking for jobs in the city center, Diego as a waiter or clerk and Laura as a secretary. Serena, seventeen, is still in school. Having passed her childhood in a squatter's settlement elsewhere in Santiago, she was relocated with her family to housing adjacent to La Bandera about a decade ago and comes here daily to care for her niece.

These teenagers were born between 1972 and 1974, around the time of the military coup. They are part of the generation of urban youth that, until the election of Patricio Aylwin a year and a half ago, has never witnessed a presidential election—a generation whose entire life has been lived under military rule and whose most common response to political issues in the mostly demobilized early years of democracy is *"No estoy ni ahí"* (I couldn't care less) or *"No me meto en política"* (I don't involve myself in politics).

But they are also from a generation of youth who remember the protests. They recall the street theater, the recreational day camps for children, the slogans, and the fights with police. And in the post-dictatorship period, they are left with a longing, a sense of boredom and letdown as the transition gets under way. It is this disquiet, combined with the urgings of family members and supportive older friends, that convinces Diego, Laura, and Serena to join our history workshop. And while the idea of writing local history is new to them, participating in community activities is not.

Serena comes from the most politically involved family: in the mid-1980s her mother and brother helped lead the protest movements, and now they are active in workers' organizations, political parties, and elections. Serena participates in a government-funded cultural center where youth learn painting, music, printmaking, and radio. In the summers she joins volunteer brigades to build houses among the Mapuche in the south. Diego's and Laura's families, less politically active, are more focused on making a living than on achieving social change. But both Diego and Laura have been involved in their churches, and they have adult and teenage friends who participate in political parties and community groups. Initially reluctant, at the first session of our workshop they hear us out and decide to join the group.

We spent the first meeting, a week ago, settling on objectives. The five of us agreed that the goals for the workshop had to do with political organizing as much as historical content. All of us wanted to *concientizar* youth—that is, increase the political awareness and involvement of young people. Although there were only three teenage members at the beginning, we decided to create activities that could attract more young people—perhaps street theater about local history, or cultural events with music and art. Substantively, we aimed to write a history of La Bandera "because," in Diego's words, "it has not been written."

The other task at our first meeting was to determine the procedures we would follow. To gather historical material, we decided to interview persons who had participated in land seizures and organizations, find newspaper stories about La Bandera's history at the national library, and visit nongovernmental organizations that might have information on historical events. After doing the research, we would create a tangible product that could be distributed widely in the *población*. The five of us brainstormed to come up with possibilities: a colorful poster with illustrations of events in La Bandera's history that residents could hang on their walls, and thus provoke numerous informal conversations; an exhibition with historical photos, old documents, and tape-recorded interviews that could be set up for neighbors to view in the church or at a school; a binder filled with stories and illustrations that could be left at the neighborhood council building for people to peruse; or a series of brochures, detailing episodes of La Bandera's history, that we could hand out in the *feria* (outdoor market) one weekend. Still needing to figure out the logistics and determine how to pay for the materials, we decided to put off the question of the product and move on to the research itself.

Now we are at our second meeting. Our agenda for this session is to divide the history of the *población* into periods, each of which we will study in turn. The history for all of us is murky, and the criteria for distinguishing one historical era from another a matter for debate. By this time, Gordon and I have learned from members of Llareta basic aspects of popular education methodology. We know to begin the meeting with an icebreaker and to start from people's own experience. So Gordon and I ask Laura, Serena, and Diego to tap into their memories about the *población*. The teens point out that they are too young to recall La Bandera's early years, which occurred before they were born. So our conversation starts with the 1980s, then weaves backward into the late sixties and early seventies, times they have pieced together from comments they have heard and books they have read.

The fact that they had not yet been born is only one reason that the teenagers know little about the early 1970s. As we discuss those years, it becomes clear that they have not learned about that historical period in school. The dictatorship created an official history that censored key moments of the past. That may be one reason that popular and local histories have recently taken on importance in popular neighborhoods in Santiago, and why our history workshop makes sense to community leaders in the political climate currently existing in La Bandera.

When we ask the teenagers about the 1970s, the conversation goes like this:

Diego: ... In my case ... what am I going to know of [19]70? ... Okay, in seventy, we begin with the issue of the election of President Salvador Allende.... [It] is like a stage in history, that up to the present is [not] in the books. Because the history of Chile gets up to seventy and nothing else. From there on out there is still no written history.... the social, history, geography, ... all the books in elementary school ... and including in high school, they don't teach you anything from [nineteen] seventy forward. They start talking about independence, colonialism ... and they only get up to seventy. Nor do they give you the election of Allende. They bring you up to seventy.

Gordon: The end of history.

Serena: ... [Up to] the election of the president Salvador Allende and from there [on] no.

Diego: ... They don't tell you what happened in his government, what happened in the three years, what they did, what they didn't do....

Laura: ... Chile between '70 and '73 disappeared from the map. It doesn't exist. It died.... It's as if we don't exist between '70 and '73.

Julia: I heard that ... they ... ripped ... the pages out of the books....

Laura: No, no, they didn't [write] them!

Diego: ... But we speak of the official history, [of that] there is none.... But there is what we said earlier: clandestine [history].

Serena: Popular history.

Diego: That history. Popular history ... that there is from seventy forward.... But it's not officialized, understand? Like to work on it in the high schools or in the educational programs, there is none. For us [there is], if we want to investigate and find books.

Laura: Including, there is a video that I saw about seventy-three ... the coup, that's called *Battle of Chile.*

Diego: I have a book that is called *Dialogue....* That is the government of Allende, when he won. An old book. It's from the time of his government. It's like taking the newspaper and reading what happened yesterday. But from the time [of Allende]....

As the young people talk, it becomes clear that the significance of this workshop goes beyond my interest in giving research back to the *población.* People produce their own historical accounts because in official versions of history parts of the past do not even exist. Information circulates subterraneanly in videos seen, books borrowed and lent, education workshops sponsored by nongovernmental organizations. In every case the material is actively produced and purposefully used—to inspire, to inform, to incite. History is political because its erasure has been a political act.

But there is another history not tapped even in these clandestinely circulating documents, and that is the past lived and experienced by *pobladores.* Behind the election of Allende and the shock of the military coup lies what La Bandera's residents remember. These are varied histories—multiple experiences with multiple trajectories—and they provoke disagreement along the way. As we strive to divide the early years of La Bandera's history into periods for study, we quickly encounter disputes. One disagreement is mentioned in an oral history thesis written by a Chilean anthropology student. The controversy is over whether or not the famous land seizure 26 de enero, popularly credited with beginning the *población,* is its founding moment.

Gordon: We heard yesterday that there was a dispute about...the beginning of La Bandera.

Serena: The first land seizure was on January 26 [of 1970].

Julia: But they say that there were at least two land seizures before January 26. In La Bandera.

Diego: [Reading out loud from a newspaper article we had brought]...It says it in this document..., "five hundred families without housing...illegally occupied the lands that are next to the *población* La Bandera."...[So] we are reading here that there already was a *población* La Bandera....[The people from the land seizure] didn't create it....According to what it says here, it already existed.

Julia: ...Diego, I think that your family arrived in '69. Or '68. Your mom said so.

Diego: Yes...when my parents arrived here there wasn't anything...there was nothing but yards. Land. But...my parents arrived through Operación Sitio....they didn't arrive in a seizure illegal[ly]...They arrived to nothing but sites...marked with chalk....So they had to put up their tent and guard the site because...from the very same land seizure there were people who could come and see that the site was empty...and take it....I'm going to have to ask my parents...if they know of the land seizure..., what it was like here before, [and what] was here already.

We probe them to think about the multiple histories of the *población* and the various interpretations of them.

Gordon: This interests me. They say the anniversary is January 26, and on this date the *población* began. But it was a seizure outside of La Bandera, and it was after people had arrived....

Diego: ...What we are [saying here] is that the *población* was not born on January 26 of '70.

Gordon: But they say that it was! [laughs]

Diego: They say so. But...I ask my old lady and [she] says that the *población* was not born on that day.

Serena: That day was the land seizure.

Diego: ...What we want to know is the history of the *población*....Not [the history] of the land seizure.

Gordon: The histories of the *población*.

Diego: What we are seeing is that the *población* did not start on January 26.

Gordon: But it is possible that for many people it does begin on January 26.... What is the *población?* It's the physical terrain, but it's also the attitude. And if year after year they have the celebration on January 26— ...It's a question.

Diego: We have to look for people. We can try to make a questionnaire....

Julia: We can ask: "When did it begin?"

Diego: Right....Don't ask the people what...they think of the land seizure 26 de enero. Instead say to them, "When was the *población* born?" or "When did you arrive here?" Some [will say that they]...arrived in '69, others that they arrived in '68.

Julia: But one of them might say, "Um, it started on January 26 of 1970." And afterward we can say, "And when did you arrive?" And get the answer: "In 1968"! [laughing]

Diego: You know what's the best thing we can do?...Find the owner of the farm. We'll ask him, "When did they take the farm away from you?" And he's going to tell us in '67. And there we're going to discover the beginning of the history....It's going to be difficult to find [the guy, though].

Julia: For him the whole history ended in '68. [laughing]

Gordon: Yes, yes! [laughing] He'll tell us all about the cows.

By the end of our discussion the young people are devising questions to ask their older neighbors—ones that will elicit interpretations, not assume them. One of the first people they decide to interview is Iván, a member of Llareta. His experience as a child in the 26 de enero land seizure, and as a youth participating in cultural activities during the Popular Unity period, contrasts with and puts in perspective Diego, Laura, and Serena's experience of being teenagers during the protests against the dictatorship and now in the mostly depoliticized moment of the early 1990s.

In many ethnographies the history section is background, the information necessary to locate the ethnography in space and in time. In La Bandera, writing history was a collective project. Our history workshop operated for two years and produced two bulletins covering the 1967–70 and 1970–73 periods. After the first bulletin çame out in 1991, my husband and I left Chile, and the group continued to work on the second bulletin, which was printed in 1992 when we returned to Chile. As late as December 1999, when we last visited Santiago, a woman in the *población* who had originally helped recruit Diego and Laura to the workshop had, with others, constructed a small building that would serve as a popular library and house the historical materials the group had collected. The account that follows is in part the product of research done by the teenagers in that workshop. It is also the result of research that Gordon and I did, based on interviews, statistical data, architectural theses, and informal talks with residents in the *población*.

In asking the teenagers to divide the history into periods, we imposed an organization upon the past. Boundaries between the eras were a subject of debate and a product of our own collective constructions. Yet the assignment itself assumed that time congealed into political moments that could be arranged in sequential form. Such an organization runs counter to recent social theory that questions the linearity of history and problematizes the notion of epochs (Ferguson 1999), ethnohistorical research showing that conceptions of time vary cross-culturally (Rosaldo 1980; but see Gupta 1994), and processual anthropology that sees not ruptures between epochs but interrelated processes playing out over time (Moore 1987b).

Recent social theory has also emphasized that versions of the past are multiple, memory volatile, and metanarratives long gone. Members of the history workshop did discover disagreements over La Bandera's history: disputes between neighbors that implied that there was no single narrative, no final version of history upon which all would agree. But the creation of a narrative—even, or especially, a linear one—can be useful. The postmodern inclination toward fragmentation can undermine social movements' needs to create an identity that serves as the subject of collective action. When official histories exclude the urban poor from their tellings, or when a single dominant account erases alternative stories,

Figure 5. The history workshop of La Bandera produces its first bulletin: "Founding of the *Población* and the Land Seizure 26 de enero."

these silences provide people with a gap to fill, a foil against which to narrate their lives. When a community's past is replete with collective action, as La Bandera's is, history is particularly fertile ground on which to solidify identities. Under these circumstances, fashioning a historical account takes on strategic importance for action.

Our history bulletins represented multiple viewpoints yet also wove a coherent story that drew lessons from the past for contemporary collective action. A product of that process and a participant in that genre, the historical account that follows does the same. While reflecting multiple viewpoints, it offers a more or less linear story, with its tone emphasizing the protagonism and value of the urban poor. In so doing, it is a participant in a kind of history-making being practiced in *poblaciones* in Santiago in the early 1990s; a kind of history writing that searches for sources of inspiration, strategy, and identity in social movements that people remember from their own pasts. For some Chilean intellectuals, this mode of history writing is a remnant of the past—a focus on the highlights of conflictual struggle that misses the day-to-day dealings in poor communities. But I suggest in this book that this version of local history making is particularly attuned to political and epistemological conditions in the early 1990s, a time in which a discourse of reconciliation required a purposeful forgetting of the past, in which the nation (not class) was seen as the key appropriate identity, and in which the professionalization of knowledge dismissed the lived experience and political analysis of the poor. Although the account that follows is, of course, my own, and it often cites English-language sources, I adopt some of the tone of the popular history storytelling style to convey a spirit of the conventions in use at the time in Chile. I have also used this historical account as a forum in which to look not only at the history of La Bandera but also at the impact of that history on the personal development of community leaders who became members of Llareta.

In the account that follows, I tell La Bandera's history as a history of collective action. Without the housing committees that demanded land in the late 1960s, and the groups that pressured for public utilities in the early 1970s, I suggest, La Bandera as an urban neighborhood might not have come to exist. Because of this early history, collective action is deeply embedded in the personal and shared memories of the inhabitants. Indeed, the centrality of political organization to the history of the *población* makes La Bandera's demobilization in the early 1990s all the more notable.

But if collective action permeates the *población*'s history, the form that that action has taken has varied considerably. From the social mobilizations for housing during the Frei and Allende presidencies in the late 1960s and early 1970s, to the survival organizations immediately following the 1973 military coup, to the mid-1980s protests against General Pinochet, the modes of organization, political objectives, and strategic approaches of grassroots organizations have changed over time in relation to changing characteristics of national politics. Moreover, different kinds of collective action have existed at any given moment, reflecting in part the varying approaches of political parties. In the early years of the *población*'s history, for example, three quite different mechanisms—committees of the homeless, legalized site acquisition, and a radical land seizure—brought inhabitants to La Bandera. Examining the historical relation between local organizations' strategies and national political conditions from 1965 to 1990 enables us to ask similar questions about transforming modes of power and changing social movement strategies during the transition to democracy in the 1990s.

As important as the multiple types of collective action used in La Bandera are the variety of interpretations that have been generated around them. For this reason, the creation of historical narratives and the construction of identity are both contested and intertwined. Particularly in the 1990s, the historical accounts of collective action take on symbolic significance for creating images of popular protagonism and the possibility for renewed mobilization at a time when community organization had declined. Finding the sources for such symbol making requires us to look back to the early years of the *población* and its early interpretations.

CHAPTER ONE

The Founding of the *Población*

COMMITTEES OF THE HOMELESS

In the mid-1960s, the area called La Bandera was farmland. In the space that would later become the *población,* fields of wheat, corn, tomatoes, and onions filled a large expanse that blended into agricultural terrain to the south and abutted Santiago to the north. In the northeastern section of the land lay a densely forested area. There, flanked by palms, sat the landowner's spacious house.[1]

Just a short distance away, in the urban neighborhoods of Santiago, the landscape contrasted sharply. There, families lived doubled and tripled up in housing. The overcrowding stemmed from Santiago's dramatic population growth in the previous decades. As early as 1913, the Chilean state began facilitating the relocation of laborers from northern Chile to Santiago during periodic declines in nitrate production in the north (Bergquist 1986, 29). But it was after World War II, under an import-substitution national development model, that Santiago, like other Latin American cities, grew most rapidly. As the state promoted industrialization, and agriculture became more mechanized and commercial, subsistence farmers and contracted laborers were forced out of rural land and drawn to cities. The expansion of manufacturing in the capital, with its potential for industrial jobs and education, made Santiago a favored destination (Winn 1992, 209).

To get a sense of the scale of urban growth after World War II, it helps to look at one municipality, La Granja, which would later be a source of population for La Bandera. When La Granja was created in 1941, its inhabitants numbered four thousand. By 1967, the population of just one section of it, the *población* San Gregorio, had increased to forty thousand residents. Such rapid urban growth made that single *población* "larger than many cities in Chile."[2] Similar increases in population affected areas around Santiago.

The family whose daughters Valeria and Sonia would later become members of the health group Llareta was one of the households that relocated to San Gregorio in the middle to late 1950s. Cristina, born in 1944, was the second in the family of ten children. For much of Cristina's childhood, the family had lived on the property of wealthy families in Las Condes, where they served as caretakers, while the father also managed housing construction and the mother cooked meals for the workers. But when Cristina was twelve years old, her father died, leaving the family penniless and homeless. Raising ten children between the ages of one and fourteen on her own, Cristina's mother searched for housing, and through contacts eventually acquired a site in the newly created *población* San Gregorio. There, utilities such as water, electricity, and pavement were beginning to be put into place, and some housing was being built. While the younger children like Valeria and Sonia attended school, the older ones went to work to support the family. The eldest daughter cut hair; two brothers worked initially at a store and later learned to sew soccer balls, and Cristina sold produce in a market, bringing home leftovers for the family to eat.

While the family scraped by on the food they could bring home from the market and the little money they could earn, thousands like them experienced unemployment. The number of manufacturing jobs in Santiago did not nearly meet the quantity of people looking for jobs in the postwar period, and urban dwellers endured severe poverty. Nationally, the infant mortality rate reached 111 per thousand in 1967, and malnutrition affected 82 percent of families in the poorest sectors.[3] In poor areas, residents also suffered from inadequate schooling, lack of urban infrastructure, and epidemic disease.

In the midst of these problems, the second generation of urban dwellers—the grown offspring of urban industrial workers—confronted a housing crisis. Without land on which to build their homes, they lived overcrowded, with as many as ten people residing in rooms measuring about two by three meters. Growing up in a household with nine siblings, Cristina experienced overcrowding early. In 1960, at age sixteen, she had her first child, and by age nineteen, she was already a mother of three. She moved in with her in-laws, at a site they already shared with some of their other five offspring and their children. Constructing cramped, makeshift housing on their parents' and in-laws' sites, families like Cristina's were called *allegados*, meaning that they were living on others' property. They were also known as those *sin casa* (without housing), which, unlike the term *homeless* in the United States, did not mean sleeping on the street, but rather living in overcrowded homes with relatives.

Pressured by the overcrowded conditions, young couples with small children organized into *comités sin casa* (committees of the homeless). In La Granja, the first committees began in 1964, and by 1967 their number had reached thirty.[4] Many of the leaders of these groups were women like Cristina who were seeking housing for their families. When I asked Cristina why she became a community leader, she joked, "Because I loved to talk!" "I got involved in the leadership [*directiva*] because ... I fight all over the place, and I have always raised complaints about what seems wrong or illegal to me. ... Whatever was not right, I pointed it out." As a leader, she filled in for the president, the treasurer, and the secretary at meetings and helped to organize events.

The housing committee members engaged in marches, demonstrations, meetings, and letter writing, in coordination with *comités sin casa* throughout the region.

For two years, Cristina and other leaders went from one government office to another, sometimes waiting all day to meet with a public functionary, in an effort to convince officials to assign housing sites to members of their committees. The leaders brought with them piles of required papers from participants in their groups: identification cards, birth certificates, documents declaring the applicants had no criminal records, and, above all, bank statements demonstrating that the families had saved up sufficient funds. At other times, the committees held dances to raise money for families who could not afford their bank quotas and used some of the money they raised to pay leaders' transportation costs for meeting with public officials. On particularly memorable occasions, the committees organized massive marches to the presidential palace. Cristina emphasized the value she placed on people's own efforts to get their families homes: "Here, all the people were fighters [in the struggle] to get their housing sites."

One of the things that the *comités* were fighting for was participation in Operación Sitio, the Frei government's (1964–70) program to address the housing problem. Operación Sitio offered families a plot of land in exchange for money deposited in a savings account. Costs of participating in the program were high for people who were unemployed or living on low salaries, and Cristina explained that she often went without food in order to save the obligatory sixty-eight bank quotas. Although this was a public program, land was by no means being given away, for the cost to an individual family approximated the price of land on the private market. Yet with a shortage of land and severe overcrowding, this plan promised to relocate households more quickly than housing programs because families would build their own homes rather than await government construction.

But if Operación Sitio promised to find families housing solutions quickly, its size could not keep up with the demand. Whereas in 1952 the housing deficit at a national level had been 165,760 units, in 1965 it had reached 445,968 units.[5] According to a 1967 article, President "Frei promised to build 60,000 houses yearly,"[6] not nearly compensating for the housing deficit, which increased with each passing year. Even Operación Sitio, designed to provide solutions more quickly by promising only a piece of land without housing, could not accommodate the need. Within only fifteen days of when the program was opened to applications, sixty-five thousand families had applied. In two years, the program had reached little more than 10 percent of the registered families (Espinoza 1988, 278–79). In short, the proposed solutions did not nearly satisfy the mounting needs.

Thousands of homeless families of La Granja, many of whom had applied for housing and saved money in bank quotas, were among those who did not receive sites in the first phase of Operación Sitio in 1965. Local leaders attributed this not only to a paucity of sites, and the difficulty of saving money, but also to political party discrimination. Although official requirements were uniform—a quantity of money in savings, and a point system to identify families most in need—the limited sites went disproportionately to adherents of the governing political parties, particularly Christian Democrats. In La Granja, two major supporters of the housing struggles, Mayor Pascual Barraza and congressional representative Orlando Millas, were both members of the Communist Party. Cristina emphasized that neither the families *sin casa* nor the organizations to which they belonged were necessarily party members.[7] Yet because the *comités* were aided by the party and associated with it, the meetings often had to be held in secret, with people entering one by one to allay suspicion by authorities.

The Communist Party's support for the *comités* is a window into the role parties of the Left played in mobilizing the urban poor in the late 1960s. At that time, the Communist Party held a more moderate stance than the Socialist Party, in that it rejected armed struggle and favored an electoral road to socialism. Making organizing the urban masses central to its strategy, the party fostered popular sector networks and built local urban leadership. Political scientist Cathy Schneider (1995) has argued that by being involved in day-to-day styles of organization, creating a mass base, and developing a cultural ethos of collective action, the Communist Party generated organized *poblaciones* that were able to recuperate strength decades later during the protests of the 1980s.

Whether because of political discrimination, lack of funds, or a shortage of sites, the *comités sin casa* of La Granja continued to find themselves without solutions as the land designated for Operación Sitio filled up. Thus the *comités* shifted their efforts to a new strategy: convincing the government to appropriate a piece of farmland outside the southern boundary of the city. At first, government officials dismissed this demand to annex the place called La Bandera. They said they wanted to prevent the city from expanding into a designated *area verde* (agricultural area).[8] Administrators also objected to the costs. But at last, in October 1968, as a result of intense public pressure and social movements' mobilizations, housing officials purchased the land from the owners and designated it for residential use.

While pressure exerted by La Granja's housing committees had succeeded in getting La Bandera designated a residential area, it soon became clear that the committees had not succeeded in obtaining sites for their members. Shortly after purchasing the farmland La Bandera, the housing authority facilitated what have been called *auto-tomas* or *tomas legales*—small-scale land occupations sanctioned and protected by governing parties. In these instances, representatives of the Christian Democrat Party, and at times the National Party, would accompany committees of the homeless to the sites, ward off police, complete the paperwork, and legalize the transactions. As these families received sites in La Bandera, the committees of the homeless from La Granja again found themselves excluded from the land they had fought to secure.

Finally, in late 1969, residents of La Granja were assigned sites in La Bandera. Yet despite their accomplishment, their property ownership was still not assured. Other *pobladores,* coming from a land occupation nearby, seized the plots. I could see the indignation rising in Cristina's face as she explained the anger she had felt when sites assigned to members of her committee were taken by others:

After two years, [and] so many chores…it appeared that we were ready with the sites assigned to us—with the assignment card, with the…housing site number—and La Bandera was occupied. They seized the fourth sector that was [designated] for those of us who had fought and had gone around for two years saving [bank] quotas, tightening the belt to have a site.…They… put up a flag,…and there they added themselves to the site without having made any effort from one day to the next.

From Cristina's perspective, housing committee leaders like herself had worked tirelessly for years to obtain their housing sites. They had gone hungry in order to put their earnings into a savings account, attended meetings, held marches, and written letters to authorities. In contrast, the squatters intended to take land without making any effort, as far as Cristina could see—land, moreover, that had already been promised to committees from La Granja. Some of those who had been assigned the lots across from those granted to Cristina and other members of her committee did not hear about the seizure in time. They lost their assigned places to participants in the land occupation and eventually moved to other parts of Santiago. Cristina's committee, however, was able to take action. When Cristina and other leaders heard of the land takeover, they went immediately to meet with the government housing chief, Boris Tapia. According to Cristina:

[He]…said that we had to come because…other people were taking our sites. So the next day the trucks started to arrive with people, with people, with people. So right here in this place, he [gave us] the site. Put up your room. Put up your house [he said]. Whatever it is—even if it's a pair of sticks.…He filled out all the papers and in that moment gave us the sites. In a hurry…before they could take the sites.…We didn't have water, we didn't have electricity, we came just like this. To nothing but empty land.

While done with somewhat unusual haste, Cristina's experience of getting property typifies conditions under Operación Sitio. During the years it functioned, Operación Sitio became popularly known as Operación Tiza (Operation Chalk) because the majority of families received only a piece of land bounded by a chalk mark on the ground. The program provided neither building materials nor training in housing construction to new landowners. Despite promises that the areas would be "semiurbanized," the newly created *poblaciones* lacked infrastructure. Without water, electricity, sewage systems, pavement, or public lighting, most new residents made do in precariously erected tents until they could build first a one-room shack, then in stages expand their homes. The *poblaciones* created through Operación Sitio also lacked public services. Garbage collection, schooling, and health care were inadequate or absent. The situation was particularly dire given that the majority of applicants were young couples with small children.[9] Acquiring public services required more organizing and pressure on the state in the years to come.

This account of how La Bandera was created lets us examine the significance of collective action in the history of the *población*. For some of the initial inhabitants, collective action played a minor role. Those who arrived in "legal *tomas*" orchestrated by centrist political parties such as the Christian Democrats often had minimal prior involvement in political organizations. Obtaining housing through Operación Sitio involved bureaucratic actions such as filling out forms and individual acts such as saving money in bank accounts. Although the families belonged to committees, party representatives completed the paperwork, negotiated with the housing ministry, and handed over the sites. Far from mobilizing neighbors, establishing enduring community organizations, or learning to see housing as a right, these families mainly experienced their arrival in the *población* as meeting an immediate need for land and housing. Once they had gotten their sites, many of their committees disbanded (Toledo 1991, 68).

In contrast, for residents from La Granja and other parts of the city where committees fought for land, the process involved local and regional organization, relations with political parties of the Left, and a sense of cooperation, mobilization, and struggle. The *comités sin casa* like the one Cristina led forged networks, built relationships, developed leadership capacity among poor women and men, and created a political base that would outlast the early years of the *población*. They cultivated a culture of working together to solve common problems. How long this inclination to organize would last varied, however, and Cristina, unlike her sisters Valeria and Sonia, largely stopped participating in community organizations after the early years of the *población*.

The housing committees and mobilizations for the expansion of Santiago were a particular kind of collective action used by political parties and urban social movements in the late 1960s. At the time, the government was meeting some of the needs of *pobladores* by constructing housing and opening up land for settlement. In this context, community organizations put pressure on the state to accelerate that process. The concept of what it meant to join organizations and work collectively for needed services would influence the idea of participation advanced by community leaders in years to come.

To this day, the effects of collective action can be seen in the infrastructure of the *población*. The sidewalk in front of Cristina's house is continuous for the entire length of the block. Cristina's housing committee, which remained active after its arrival, pooled money to purchase cement. Across the street, in the sites assigned to members of the land seizure, the sidewalk skips houses—concrete appears in some places, dirt in others, and embedded stones in a few. On that side of the street, each family purchased sidewalk materials individually, to the extent that its income and inclination allowed.

As the story of La Bandera's origins demonstrates, the *población* was literally and physically created through collective action. Without housing committees pressuring the state, the *población* La Bandera might never have come to exist. But as the sidewalk patterns silently attest, the levels of organization, the forms of collective action, and the ideologies behind them varied. Who were the squatters who tried to take Cristina's assigned site, and how were they organized? The answer goes to the heart of La Bandera's legend.

LAND SEIZURE: "HOUSING OR DEATH"

In January 1970, before the La Granja families had moved to their designated sites, La Bandera became home to one of the most famous land seizures in Chilean history. On January 22, 240 families, totaling more than a thousand persons and organized into committees of the homeless, occupied land along the northwestern border of the new *población*. Lacking extensive organization, their first attempt at occupation came to an end three days later at the hands of police. But on January 26 the settlers, now numbering 575 families from many parts of Santiago, tried again. Police tore down the tents, smashed their belongings, set off tear gas bombs, and chased and beat the inhabitants, leaving a number of them injured.[10] This time, however, the settlers were bolstered both by experience gained during the previous day's events and by the support of university students, politicians, and dignitaries, as well as the radical movement MIR (Revolutionary Movement of the Left), which coordinated the land seizure. With a combination of physical resistance and political negotiation, they warded off police and established the settlement. They called their squatters' settlement 26 de enero after the date that the land occupation took hold.

Historically, land seizures in Chile had occurred as a last resort after years of negotiations with the government had produced no positive results. Unlike the scattered *callampas* that sprang up at the outskirts of the city, land seizures required planning and organization. Political parties of the Left interested in gaining adherents among the poor frequently supported these activities. During the Frei presidency, and later the Allende presidency (1970–73), land seizures became a widespread phenomenon. The number of land occupations occurring between 1967 and 1972 totaled 312 and involved participation by 54,710 families (Espinoza 1988, 275). Indeed, land seizures had become so common that they accounted for 40 percent of Santiago's growth between 1957 and 1973 (Schneider 1995, 45). Although illegal and repressed, squatting ultimately worked in tandem with official practices. Once police had been fought off and the land seizure taken hold, government offices would regulate and legalize the new residential areas.

Mónica Janet, who in her adult years would become a member of Llareta, was a child when her mother decided to participate in the land seizure. Like Cristina's family, Mónica Janet's parents had been living as caretakers on others' property. Seeking housing of their own, Mónica Janet's mother had joined a housing committee but found that "there wasn't a [housing] solution." Mónica Janet remembered,

She had the opportunity to go to this *campamento* [squatters' settlement], [so] we went. Without my father wanting to, because my father didn't want to go to a *campamento* at all. The men are ... more comfortable [where they are]. And my mother said no, that she was going because she wanted to have a house for all of us, since there were five of us. We were all little back then. And we lived [on land] that wasn't ours. And everyone needs to have their space, their house.... And from there my mom went to the *campamento* 26 de enero.

As in the cases of Mónica Janet's and Cristina's families, more often than not, the people who decided to take action to acquire land for their own housing were women. Women in La Bandera, both those who came through the land seizure and those who acquired land by joining *comités sin casa* and Operación Sitio, told me that their husbands had been more or less satisfied living in their parents' houses. They had the freedom to leave the house during the day and then return to a household in which both their wives and mothers cleaned, cared for children, and prepared meals. Young women, however, were confined to the home to take care of domestic and child care duties. Impatient at sharing a kitchen and living space with their mothers or mothers-in-law, they were desperate for their own homes. Women told stories of men hiding under the bed while their wives went out to battle police or negotiate with authorities at land seizures. While elite men dominated political party positions, and working-class men were active in labor unions, poor Chilean women were key players in social struggles for housing, as they would later be in survival organizations, human rights groups, and the health group Llareta.

Like those who participated in other land seizures, Mónica Janet and her family arrived on a bare plot of land. Sealed off with wire, the *campamento* occupied a treeless space of 50 by 150 meters, traversed by a broad dirt road. Squatters lived in tightly packed tents and shacks made of cardboard, cloth, and planks.[11] Mónica Janet remembered living in a tent sealed off with plastic. "In this room we had a bed, a little table, and a kerosene stove, [and that's] all we had." Water had to be fetched from a faucet two blocks away, the children washed in the dirty water of a canal, and six latrines served nearly three thousand people.[12] Living in these unhygienic conditions, residents suffered from outbreaks of diarrhea, typhus, and other diseases (Espinoza 1988, 302).

What distinguished the 26 de enero from prior land seizures—and what ultimately made it famous—was the ideology of its leaders. As members of the political movement MIR, which saw itself as revolutionary, the leaders of the *campamento* had objectives that went far beyond getting housing for participants. They sought to use the 26 de enero as the basis for revolutionary action. In the words of leader Victor Toro, "Experience has taught us that the definitive solution to our problems is through the taking of power by the workers, which can only happen after the violent destruction of our class enemies."[13] Given this agenda, the key question was not how to find housing sites quickly—such an outcome would disperse the population and dismantle the settlement—but rather how to use the settlement as a launching pad for revolutionary activity.

Using the *campamento* as a basis for taking power required constituting homeless families as social and political actors. To do this, the MIR sought to elevate the category *"poblador"* (which literally means those who populate [an area]) into a cultural identity whose meaning would be the struggle for the rights for one's class. They envisioned land seizures—illegal actions in conflict with the state—as the primary vehicle through which this actor could gain identity and seize power (Espinoza 1988, 313).

Creating *pobladores* as social actors necessitated cultural and organizational work within the *campamento*. The leaders of the settlement aimed to do that by making the 26 de enero into a model socialist community.[14] They hoped that the experience of "living socialism" would lead to the awakening of class consciousness in the participants.[15] To create this model community, leaders established a range of social organizations, including a collective kitchen, a system of getting food donations from the market, and a health clinic. With a system for accessing electricity and a set of rules banning wife beating, drinking, and gambling, 26 de enero became an exceedingly organized urban settlement.[16]

The goal of creating class consciousness that underlay the collective activities was advanced most directly through education. A cultural center in the *campamento* functioned as a "school of a new type" for both adults and children. University students and professors came to the 26 de enero in large numbers and helped "examine the history of Chile and its current reality from a revolutionary focus."[17] Children, many for the first time, attended a school in the *campamento*, where they were taught to read and write and received classes that were "adapted to socialist criteria," such as "a history of Chile speaking of the virtues and failures of the heroes, and of how the Independence didn't favor the *pueblo*, but rather the Creole bourgeoisie."[18]

In retrospect, the cultural center is significant not only because it reveals one current of thought and experience that shaped the initial development of La Bandera but also because it illuminates a role played by Chilean intellectuals in the late 1960s and early 1970s. Envisioning themselves as supporting a revolutionary movement, and seeing the urban poor as protagonists in that struggle, professors and students lent their active support at squatters' settlements. By the late 1980s and 1990s, in contrast, many leftist intellectuals would be involved in a very different project. Along with affirming the end of the grand Marxist narrative and questioning the political mistakes of the early 1970s, they would play a key role in dampening the popular movements they had once sought to activate.

At the 26 de enero, the education toward armed revolution was not only theoretical—it was embedded in the funding and organization of the settlement itself. In early March it became clear that the MIR had financed medicine for the *campamento*'s inhabitants through the proceeds of an armed bank assault in the city center. The MIR defended the action as "returning to the *pueblo* part of what the bosses have robbed from it."[19] Military preparation was also present in the internal organization of the 26 de enero. Volunteer groups called "popular militias" kept order within the settlement, enforced regulations, and protected the entrance to the *campamento* against incursions by police. The MIR leadership envisioned the militias as having a role that went beyond the internal regulation of the settlement; they saw them as the germ of armed forms of mass organization that could be replicated in other squatters' settlements and form the basis for large-scale actions.

As the formation of popular militias indicates, the MIR sought to use the 26 de enero as a base from which to coordinate other land seizures and develop a broader strategy. To this end, they hosted a three-day "Congress of *Pobladores* without Housing" in March 1970. Members of more than thirty housing committees and squatters' settlements around Santiago and Chile attended the event.[20] They sought to organize committees and coordinate land occupations throughout the province.

Expressing their divergence from the MIR's strategy of armed rebellion, leaders of the Central Unica de Trabajadores (CUT) workers union and the Communist Party objected to the congress. They accused the MIR of inciting division among *pobladores*. Their objections reflected an important split within the Left in the late 1960s and early 1970s between parties and movements that backed armed rebellion (the MIR and the left wing of the Socialist Party) and those that favored an electoral road to socialism (the Communist Party and the moderate branch of the Socialist Party).

While leaders planned revolution, and while the social organizations of the *campamento* tempered the stresses of daily life, residents in the squatters' settlement continued to endure squalid living conditions. As they struggled to survive the daily dramas of *campamento* living, their primary goal was to obtain housing.[21] One woman I interviewed, the oldest of six children and the daughter of an alcoholic father and an ill mother, went alone to the land seizure as a young girl. She recalled, "I arrived at twelve years [old] ... at a land seizure, where I passed almost from child to almost a mature adult, because I had to make the decision for my family [which had always lived] ... *allegada* [in other people's houses]. ... I had no idea of what a land occupation meant, but for me, it meant leaving my house to search for a solution for my family." Although she participated in the cultural events of the *campamento*, her overwhelming need was to find a site on which her family, still living overcrowded in another *población*, could live. More vivid in her mind than the political aspirations of the leaders were the traumas she was experiencing. Later in life she developed an outlook and set of practices that differed greatly from those of the MIR. During the dictatorship she became a member of the neighborhood council handpicked by the military, and in the 1990s she firmly told me, "I don't involve myself in politics."

Daily life in the *campamento* was difficult, but in May it became intolerable. The first major rainfall of the year destroyed the precarious housing and spread sickness among the children. The squatters demanded immediate resettlement. In an act that some news sources described as an occupation, members of the 26 de enero entered and refused to leave the government's housing office (CORHABIT) until members of the settlement were granted land.[22] It was at this crisis point that Cristina and her housing committee were warned that their sites would soon be taken. From the point of view of the squatters from the 26 de enero, however, the tactic proved effective. The following day, the government relocated settlers to permanent sites within La Bandera. MIR leaders went on to establish squatters' settlements elsewhere, most famously Nueva La Habana.

After moving to their new housing sites, the previous occupants of the *campamento* continued to engage in conflictual actions. Their actions and the mythic stories they generated would become an important part of the history later told of the *población*. Within a few days of the move, the newly arrived residents forcibly occupied the police station and refused to leave until authorities constructed a health clinic. Police responded with bullets, injuring eight *pobladores* and sustaining two police injuries as well. The incident was decried throughout Santiago for excessive use of police force. Nonetheless, the clinic was built, and to this day, La Bandera's health facility is located across the street from the police station. They also hijacked and sequestered a bus to establish a new transportation route to La Bandera. Furthermore, they occupied the Ministry of Housing, the National Congress, and other government offices to demand housing, drinking water, and electricity. Regardless of whether participants in the 26 de enero were convinced of the need for revolution, this kind of conflictual action created a clear connection in the experience of many residents between collective action and improvements in facilities and public services in the *población*.[23]

Years later, when participants talked about their life histories, autobiographies, and memories, they were rooted in collective action. The physical existence of the *población*, and each family's access to property, housing, and public services, could be attributed to organization and, for some, to conflict with the state. Such a history taught the indelible lesson that collective action was essential to one's own and one's community's very survival.

But initial collective action alone does not suffice for a sustained history of mobilization. Many *poblaciones* began as land seizures but later became depoliticized. The experience of collective action at the 26 de enero resonated years later in part because it had been narrated as it occurred. From the beginning, the story told of the 26 de enero was one of popular protagonism. It constructed an identity category of *pobladores* as social actors struggling for their rights. It interpreted the land occupation as a heroic action. Although Cristina claimed that those who went to *tomas* were just hoping for a free ride, those who participated in the 26 de enero told a differ-ent story. A woman who lived across the street from Cristina held that the families who acquired land through Operación Sitio had it easy. All they needed to do was complete paperwork, and they would be given their sites. In contrast, she argued, participants in the 26 de enero settlement like herself lived in squalor and uncertainty for months, enduring repression by police and the stigma of being from a squatters' settlement. Unlike the people who had simply followed the rules, those who took the risk of illegally seizing land were the real fighters of the *población*.

It was this tale of heroism, the fact that every step of the event was accompanied by an interpretation, that gave it its symbolic power and allowed it to be used for many years as a cultural and political resource. In reflecting on a study about popular memory of the Dirty War in the shantytowns of Córdoba, Argentina, William Rowe and Vivian Schelling (1991, 119–20) argue that if events are not narrated as they occur, there can be a massive erasure of memory. They describe

> an absence of memory of the period of military government (1976–85) as compared with the years preceding it. This silence is not the result of fear.... Nor does it indicate lack of knowledge.... What it showed was that during the time of military totalitarianism there was a *lack of any "discourse about the collective sphere,"* and that this related to "the lack of any space in which together with other people one could act upon reality." All of this amounts to the lack of place for the articulation of memory, its former location in everyday life having been suppressed [emphasis added].

Because people in these Argentine shantytowns were so isolated from each other during the military regime, no common discourse emerged through which events were articulated as they occurred. As a result of this lack of public discourse while events were in progress, decades later people found the occurrences impossible to recall.

Throughout the existence of the *campamento* 26 de enero, in contrast, leaders theorized the process as it occurred. Through cultural centers, schools, and slogans, they promoted a narrative of revolutionary struggle. They created *"poblador"* as a powerful identity category—one that would have meaning for decades to come. These messages transcended the local context and took on national and international importance. Indeed, the *campamento* gained publicity abroad through an article in a 1970 issue of *Time* magazine.[24] Through all of these efforts, the 26 de enero squatters' settlement, and by extension the *población* La Bandera, emerged as a national and international symbol.

Because the events were narrated as they occurred, the symbols generated by the land seizure could be recaptured years later, when they took on new strategic importance. During the transition to democracy in the late 1980s and early 1990s, popular groups around Chile began to create "local histories" that highlighted popular sector protagonism.[25] Faced with an elite political system, leaders of local history efforts sought to make struggles of the urban poor visible.[26] The local histories appeared in the form of workshops, theater, and books circulated through nongovernmental organizations and in the *poblaciones.* They used the local accounts to historicize discussions of society, at a time (after the dictatorship) when forgetting had become an intentional cultural practice and elite political strategy. By prioritizing events in poor urban sectors, they hoped not only to historicize but also to create popular alternatives to official history. Still usable years later at a key historical juncture, symbolism ended up being the 26 de enero's most lasting, and perhaps most politically important, legacy.

While its symbolism seems unequivocal, the 26 de enero leaves us with a paradox. Despite the practice of conflict with the state, and beyond the narrative of heroic struggle, the 26 de enero ended up much like other urban movements for housing. In the end, residents were resettled by the national housing authority to permanent sites in La Bandera. They then proceeded to pressure the state into providing public services. This fact requires extending this account of La Bandera's history beyond popular collective action, toward the state's role in creating urban neighborhoods.

THE ROLE OF THE STATE

Government Planning and Urban Design

Although land seizures and homeless committees grew out of collective action by popular sectors supported by parties of the Left, the *población* La Bandera is also the product of sophisticated state-led urban design. The Ministry of Housing's blueprints from the late 1960s reveal that far from merely zoning the area for urban expansion, architects and city planners designed La Bandera as a model community. Planners at the Ministry of Housing and Urbanization sectioned the large area into quadrants. They left open a broad swath of land so that a band of services—a "popular laundromat," a hospital, a supermarket, a gymnasium, schools, churches, and jungle gyms—could run down the center of the *población* from north to south.[27] Moreover, each quadrant would have its own smaller set of services—a church, child care, parking, a nursery school. The forest from the original rural landscape was left intact as a park, and the old farm mansion became a cultural center.

La Bandera's fourth sector received particularly innovative planning. Rather than have long streets bordered by housing, the planners clustered housing sites around open spaces so that residents could socialize with ease. While they intended for major roads to be paved, Frei's urban planners planned for the inner passageways to be filled with grass. Along the northern border of the *población*, city planners left space for a long park that would provide recreation for inhabitants. The park served a double purpose, for it would also present a pleasing view to motorists traveling along Manuel Rodríguez, the main road bordering the *población*. In an ironic and tacit acknowledgment of the living conditions in urban neighborhoods, city planners lined the park with apartment buildings. These solid four-story structures were intended to create a facade that could hide the precarious, self-constructed housing that predominated within the *población* from those traveling on Manuel Rodríguez.

The creative design that went into producing La Bandera remained a source of pride among city planners. During the 1970s and 1980s, architecture students writing theses at Santiago's universities studied and admired the *población*'s layout, while contrasting the plans with what it had actually become. And in 1991, city planners I interviewed at the housing ministry waxed eloquent as they described and praised its design. Not unlike the stories of the 26 de enero told by community leaders, the urban planning of La Bandera had taken on legendary proportions.

La Bandera's place in the city planners' imagination became most vivid for me on a visit to the municipal government in the early 1990s. An architect there shared with me multiple official representations of La Bandera: aerial photographs, planning sketches, and maps colored to indicate different qualities of housing stock. He drew my attention to a map illustrating land use in the *población*. I was momentarily seduced by the image: there, hanging on his wall, was a depiction of La Bandera with all the "green areas" *(areas verdes)*—totaling 40 percent of the land—shaded in the color green. It was as if that architectural depiction of grass could somehow redefine the grim reality of dust, mud, and garbage located just a few minutes' walk away.

As the contrast between the *areas verdes* on the map and the dirt in the fields suggests, few of the plans came to fruition. The old mansion did become a cultural center, and the forest remained a park, though both of these later burned down. And, indeed, some schools and churches were built on public property. But much of the area designated for public services and plazas remained barren spaces filled with mud in the winter and blowing dirt and dust in the summer. The contradictions between plans and reality provided evidence of the cracks in the Chilean development model in the 1960s. The state could not comply with its ambitiously announced plans, and the period of state provision of public services would be short-lived.

Export Model of Development

President Frei's decision to institute Operación Sitio and the pressures that led to the creation of *poblaciones* like La Bandera were embedded in an import-substitution economic model initiated in the 1930s.[28] Import substitution, which supplanted an economic policy focused on the export of raw materials, sought to industrialize the country by replacing imports with locally manufactured goods. The model required an active role for the state in promoting capitalist economic development. To advance this effort, in 1939 the Popular Front created the Chilean Development Corporation. CORFO, as it was called, invested in such industries as steel and textiles, while supporting the development of electricity, transport, and communications infrastructure. In addition, the government improved public services such as social security, health, housing, and education (Collins and Lear 1995, 14). The period came to be known as the "Compromise State" because it represented a rapprochement between government, capital, and labor. It was the state-led effort toward industrialization that contributed to the flow of rural migrants to Santiago in the postwar period.

By the late 1950s and early 1960s, the tensions in the import-substitution model were increasingly evident in Chile and throughout Latin America. As the housing situation in La Granja illustrated, industrialization and urbanization placed intense demands on the state—a situation common to governments throughout Latin America. In the wake of the 1959 Cuban Revolution, the Kennedy administration created the Alliance for Progress to address social inequities and forestall the spread of communism in Latin America. The Alliance for Progress sought to prevent social unrest by ameliorating poverty that led people to rebel. Chile, where the Left had been gaining increasing support, seemed a strategic location to implement the program.

As Chile's 1964 elections approached, the Christian Democratic Party appeared to be the political force in Chile most closely allied with the goals of the Alliance for Progress. In his campaign, presidential candidate Eduardo Frei had committed himself to a "Revolution in Liberty." He sought to create a "third option" that would provide an alternative to both full socialism and unrestrained capitalism. In their place, he advocated "communitarianism"—a concept that promised to promote "community responses to social and economic problems" within an overall capitalist economic framework (Oppenheim 1993, 25). The concept, like the Christian Democrat Party itself, had roots in the social doctrine of the Catholic Church, which sought to improve living conditions of the poor while warding off communism. Frei's policy framework suited the Alliance for Progress agenda well, particularly with the growing strength of Salvador Allende on his left, and his campaign received millions of dollars from the United States government and U.S.-based transnational corporations (Collins and Lear 1995, 16). In 1964, Frei took office, and the following year his party won a majority in the congressional elections.

Promoción Popular

To ameliorate urban poverty and temper popular dissatisfaction, President Frei recommended that the Chilean state promote the creation of social organizations in popular urban sectors. His approach drew philosophical coherence from work by the research institute DESAL, the Center for Latin American and Social Development (Centro para el Desarrollo Económico y Social de America Latina) (Perlman 1976, 118). Run by a Belgian Jesuit, Roger Vekemans, DESAL explained poverty as a product of "marginality." In this conceptual framework, the poor were unable to achieve social mobility because they "participated" in neither the material benefits of the economy (passive participation) nor the political decision-making process (active participation). Proponents of this theory warned that those living in the belts of misery surrounding the city were a potentially explosive force, and that the frustration they had accumulated during years of hunger and misery could easily lead to violence. In the spirit of anticommunism prevalent at the time, DESAL recommended that to avert mass rebellion, *pobladores* should be "integrated" into the society through local organizations. Because the poor were plagued by "internal disintegration"—characterized by unstable families and the lack of organizations—they could not overcome their poverty by themselves. Organizations would have to be initiated by an outside agent, specifically the state (Espinoza 1988, 332).

The theory of marginality gave Frei the conceptual underpinnings for a new program he called Promoción Popular. Through this effort, the state would generate, regulate, and legalize social organizations in poor communities (Fleet 1985, 87). The neighborhood organizations Frei promoted included territorial institutions like civic associations *(juntas de vecinos* or *unidades vecinales)* and thematic groups such as sports clubs and mothers' centers. The Law of Neighborhood Councils and Community Organizations passed in August 1968, and thousands of shantytown dwellers joined these groups. In La Bandera, those who arrived in the legal *tomas* orchestrated by the Christian Democratic Party may have seen their *comites sin casa* dilute soon after their arrival, but they were able to join other organizations in their neighborhood, including mothers' centers and the local *junta de vecinos.*

By involving thousands of people in community groups it had structured, the Christian Democratic Party was able to garner broad-based political support. Most important, the program acknowledged and channeled popular demands, while keeping organizations of the poor subordinate to the state and elite decision making. The goal of *Promoción Popular* was to satisfy some of the needs of popular sectors without changing either the dominant political regime or the prevailing economic system.[29]

By the end of the sixties it seemed clear that Frei's program of Promoción Popular was a victim of its own success. Encouraged to join community organizations, *pobladores* and workers mobilized in large numbers, as evidenced in the many seizures of land around Santiago. As the poor heeded government promises of solutions to their problems, their expectations of concrete benefits rose exponentially, as was the case for the *comités sin casa* from La Granja. Yet government programs could not keep up with escalating popular demands. The state could not satisfy the pressures for housing and land that the rural migrants and their urban offspring had generated. That promises made in the Frei era remained unfulfilled testifies to the fact that the economic-political system was breaking down exactly when La Bandera was being created. The next three years would see the acceleration of political party organizing, union militancy, and popular social movements. It would quickly be followed by the end of elected government, the opening of the Chilean economy to international markets, and the dismantling of the welfare state.

POPULAR UNITY

Democratic Road to Socialism

The mobilizations for housing and social services that transformed Santiago in the late 1960s found political expression in the campaign of Salvador Allende. Backed by a movement of left-wing political parties, the former health minister and senator had run for the highest elected office four times since 1952. Allende was almost elected in 1958 and received a large percentage of votes in 1964, but it was not until 1970, in a three-way election, that he had won with only slightly more than a third of the vote, just outpacing the Right's candidate, Jorge Alessandri. The close results required the Chilean Congress to decide whether or not to ratify Allende's presidency. It did, but only after demanding explicit guarantees that he would uphold the constitution and the law. Widespread expectations for improved living conditions, cultural movements of the Left, and extensive grassroots organizing in the countryside and shantytowns added intensity to his election and his call for a "democratic road to socialism."

Allende's narrow victory reflected deep divisions in Chilean society, and his policies once in office would intensify those divisions. As a Socialist, Allende sought a downward redistribution of power and wealth. For Allende, the state would take on a stronger role than that envisioned by former president Frei. Whereas Frei had sought the "Chileanization" of foreign enterprises, Allende sought their nationalization. To accomplish that, he created an area of "social property" under which enterprises of key importance—particularly copper, industry, and banks—could be expropriated by the state. Whereas Frei's agrarian reform had applied to workers of larger plots, Allende sought to create cooperatives through which even day laborers would benefit. And whereas Frei had increased government funding for public education, Allende proposed to reorganize the educational system in order to create a "new man" who would be prepared to live within socialism.

Economic policies of the Unidad Popular were designed to redistribute income toward the poor. Allende accomplished this early on by raising wages while holding prices stable. Allende's economic policies—which some have described as more Keynesian than Marxist (Schneider 1995, 67)—increased demand and consumption of industrial and agricultural goods. Allende's promises were manifested in the provision of milk to all children and were symbolized by the dream of wine and an *empanada* for every Chilean. In the first years of the Unidad Popular, lower food prices and higher wages meant that workers and the urban poor not only could afford food but also had access to it. By 1972, when food shortages became severe, thousands of food distribution groups called Juntas de Abastecimiento y Precio (JAPs) were created to distribute groceries through workplaces, *unidades vecinales,* and political party networks (Loveman 1988, 299).

Iván, who would become an active leader in Llareta and many other community organizations, was fourteen years old in 1972. His family had come to La Bandera through the 26 de enero land seizure. He remembered the Popular Unity period in La Bandera's history as one in which food was readily available through organizations: "Once a week we had chicken... and a package consisting of sugar, coffee, all the basic foods. Detergent. And bread. The people... organize[d] in such a way that all the *manzanas* [blocks] had a delegate... [who] bought bread directly from the bakery, and would bring it to the *población.*" Some of La Bandera's residents criticized the program. They complained of favoritism in the distribution of goods and held that there were inadequate supplies (Toledo 1991).

Others described this as one of the first periods in their lives when they could remember having a steady source of food.

In wealthier neighborhoods, the reaction was different. Price freezes plagued merchants, who experienced declines in their profits. Resisting price controls, some producers sold food at a markup on the black market. Meanwhile, customers waited on long lines at stores only to encounter shortages. A survey conducted in 1972 illustrated how differently the various social classes experienced Allende's economic program. While 75 percent of lower socioeconomic groups at the time found it easy to buy essential household items, 99 percent of upper-income households considered it difficult (Valenzuela 1978, 58). Of course this was a matter of perception, since the wealthy continued to have better nutrition than the poor (Winn 1992). But the relative availability of food in each set of neighborhoods had changed.

Popular Culture

The Popular Unity government had a symbolic impact that went far beyond economic policy. To some Chileans on the political Right, Allende represented the scourge and danger of Marxism. To others on the political Left, his administration symbolized the dignity of the working class and the cultural resurgence of popular sectors. Music, magazines, and other manifestations of popular culture that had emerged in the late 1960s flourished during his time in office. Pablo Neruda's poetry, colorful mural art on shantytown walls, puppet shows, and popular theater appeared in Santiago. Chile's New Song movement expressed the culture of popular sectors. The lyrics of folksinger Víctor Jara's songs, for example, evoked the suffering and hopes of *pobladores*. Songs on his album *La Población* incorporate the voices of women participating in land seizures and the words of men speaking in the vernacular of the shantytowns.[30] In these expressions of art, the urban poor, who had long been known by the derogatory expression *los rotos* (the broken ones), became recognized in the most idealized sense as protagonists in struggle, and at the most basic level as valued human beings.

The proliferation of art and popular culture in La Bandera's early years deeply affected Iván, who was a teenager in the early 1970s. Looking back with nostalgia on this formative moment in his development, he described a vivid social life in the streets and public use of the open spaces. Iván participated in a cultural center where youth engaged in theater and dance and produced a newspaper. For him, the popularization of art was a mechanism through which residents' opinions and efforts were valued. He said, "There was a different sense of participation that we lived [then]. It was what we thought, what the neighbors thought, what the child thought, everyone was important in this process." Iván's sense that *pobladores* were appreciated and respected in the Popular Unity period helped shape his concepts of participation and the importance he placed on community organizations in his future activity as a community leader.

Mónica Janet participated in a similar array of social activities when she was a teenager and the *población* was new. "We had a club called 'Friendship'...a youth

group where we played ball, where we got together . . . we had festivals, we sang."
Of special importance to Mónica Janet was the recreational area made from the
forest that had stood on the farmland La Bandera. "It was a beautiful park, it had
so many trees, a large gorgeous house. . . . I would go with a friend just to sit beneath the trees. . . . They offered lots of workshops, for which you didn't have to
pay." The availability of public space enhanced the proliferation of cultural activities and strengthened social relations between residents.

It is at this pivotal point of cultural identity and community organization that
one can see features that both connected and distinguished Frei's and Allende's
projects. As has been described, both administrations took place in a period of Chilean history that featured a strong role for the state. During their terms in office,
both presidents encountered an increasingly mobilized population, and both encouraged forms of social organization. Frei's Christian Democrat administration
sought to channel popular sector demands through government-organized centers
within the framework of *Promoción Popular*. Institutions like neighborhood councils
and mothers' centers encouraged residents' organized activity but simultaneously
upheld a capitalist economic system and assumed that local organizations would
receive direction from the state. In contrast, the Allende period challenged the
bases of capitalism and opened space for more autonomous political and cultural
activity in the shantytowns.

It was this level of organizational autonomy and the culture of popular protagonism that presented President Allende with a crucial dilemma. As historian
Peter Winn (1986, 6) notes in his book on textile workers, a wave of factory seizures forced Allende "to choose between his carefully controlled and phased
strategy for socialism and a confrontation with his central mass base." Allende's
intention was to back popular sectors and social movements. Yet his political project was rooted firmly within the formal democratic political system, which resisted
such mobilization. As seizures of countryside, factories, and urban land multi-
plied, they grew increasingly outside Allende's control, and mistrust intensified in
Congress. With workers and the urban poor expecting the state's support, but with
Allende's own position in national political institutions crumbling, Allende faced a
crisis in his presidency.

Political and Economic Troubles

Increasing national political conflicts meant that the time of heightened mobilization, declining hunger, and vibrant cultural activities that characterized La Bandera in the early 1970s would not last long. While the government had favorable
municipal election results in 1971, by the second year of the Allende administration Chile faced severe economic problems and social tensions. Propelled by rising
wages, inflation climbed rapidly, and the government went into debt to finance
public services. With the many takeovers of farms and industries, industrial production and agricultural efficiency fell, and Chile began to import food to meet increased demand.

In addition to the economic problems generated by his model, Allende's policies met with political resistance. Discontent was dramatically illustrated in December 1971, when upper-class women marched through the streets banging on pots to protest what they saw as the decreased availability of food in their neighborhoods (Winn 1992, 321). In the subsequent two years, opposition demonstrations escalated, and strikes by merchants and truck drivers threatened the economic viability of the government's program. Strong countermovements developed among the wealthy and the middle classes, businesspeople, and the political Right.

Conflict grew not only within Chile but also internationally. Anaconda and Kennecott, two American copper companies, fought the nationalization of their businesses by the Chilean state.[31] The Allende government had decided that although theoretically the companies were entitled to compensation, they actually owed the Chilean government money as a penalty for taking "excess profits" over the years. ITT, an American multinational firm facing expropriation, sought to involve the U.S. government in ousting Allende. The United States did not immediately dismiss the idea. In addition to economic threats to American business, the very symbolism of an elected Marxist leader infuriated then-president Richard Nixon. In the context of the cold war, the idea that a Marxist could be voted into (and, more worryingly, voted out of) office gave unacceptable legitimacy to socialism. As a complement to the money it had pumped into the Frei campaign a few years earlier, the United States now withheld loans and foreign aid to Chile in an intentional effort to destabilize the Allende government (Collins and Lear 1995). The Church Report by the U.S. Congress later documented the Central Intelligence Agency's role in supporting opposition groups in order to undermine the Popular Unity government.

Still, not all of the opposition to the Allende government was external, be it domestic or international. Within the Popular Unity coalition itself, disagreement prevailed. The Left split between those who, like Allende, favored the gradual electoral transition to socialism and those who advocated more revolutionary change. These fundamental philosophical and political differences within the coalition weakened the government. Debates continue over whether the demise of the Allende government was caused primarily by external or internal factors; whatever the ultimate cause, the conditions were present for both.

In La Bandera, the availability of food and the proliferation of cultural activities were short-lived. On September 11, 1973, the military staged a coup. As Mónica Janet remembers it, "Afterwards... all the people disappeared [from the cultural center in La Bandera]. They no longer attended the workshops.... My mom belonged to a mothers' center that was called Popular Unity. It never functioned again."

CHAPTER TWO

Military Rule

THE TERROR OF THE MILITARY COUP

By the early 1970s, there was ample precedent for military rule in the southern cone of Latin America. Brazil had already had a coup d'état in 1964, as had Argentina in 1966, and Santiago served as a refuge for intellectuals and activists exiled from neighboring countries. Yet despite periods of military intervention in the past, many interpreted Chile's history as one of enduring constitutional rule, strong democratic institutions, and a professional army. They expected it to be different from other countries in Latin America. Nonetheless, as political polarization heightened in 1973 and opposition to Allende intensified, many in the country began to support the idea of military intervention. The political Right was most receptive to this option, but centrist Christian Democrat politicians and elements of the Catholic Church also supported a coup. They believed that the armed forces could ward off communism, restore order, and quickly return Chile to democratic rule.

Events did not turn out as they had anticipated. On September 11, the military bombed the presidential palace with Allende inside. Billows of smoke rose toward the sky as the building burst into flames. Lest anyone missed the message, a warning from the Junta quickly followed: "The Junta of the Military Government hereby announces that, while having no intention to destroy, if public order is in any way disrupted by disobedience to its decrees, it will not hesitate to act with the same energy and decision which the citizenry has already had occasion to observe."[1]

The brutality of the days that followed still brings terror to those who remember them. Thousands of Chileans were detained, many of them interrogated, tortured, and executed. Among the dead was the folksinger Víctor Jara. His hands, which had once so movingly strummed his guitar, were reported to have been broken—as if to etch into his body the lesson that the country's military was cracking down not only on persons but also on the symbols and culture of the Left (Loveman 1988, 311).

The repression continued, so that

[b]y December, at least fifteen hundred civilians were dead—shot in confrontations, tortured to death, hunted down by vigilantes, or executed by firing squads. Thousands of detainees had been shipped to military prison camps, more than seven thousand had fled into exile after receiving safe-conduct passes, and the grounds of the Venezuelan, Swedish, Argentine, Italian, and British embassies were jammed with asylum seekers. (Constable and Valenzuela 1991, 19–20)

Families experienced the trauma of having their relatives disappeared: gone without a trace, presumably murdered, and never seen again. Others, the *relegados,* would be sent into internal exile in the far reaches of Chile. By 1974, responsibility for repression fell under the direction of the newly created Directorate for National Intelligence (DINA). As Chile's secret police, it was responsible for many acts of torture.

The military did not limit itself to persecuting individuals. It also targeted the political institutions of Chilean democracy. In the first few months, it closed the Congress, suspended electoral rolls, disbanded political parties, and censored the press. It took over universities and workers' unions, expelling those it considered subversives and replacing them with its own personnel. The military burned books. Throughout the country, rights of assembly, expression, and organization were suspended. According to the military, the actions were taken to eradicate "the chains of totalitarian Marxism" from Chile and thus bring liberty (Loveman 1988, 311). Ironically, the military government defended its actions as safeguarding democracy.

The intense violence led many former advocates of military intervention to oppose the new regime. The Catholic Church quickly rescinded its support for military intervention and declared its opposition to military rule. Soon thereafter, the church developed the central human rights organization Vicaría de la Solidaridad, which would shelter individuals, families, and social organizations for the next fifteen years. It would document human rights violations, hold handicraft workshops so women could make money and tell their stories through art, and serve as the one place where clandestine unions and social organizations could meet. Recognizing that they, too, were repressed and would not be returned to power any time soon, politicians from the Christian Democrat Party likewise retracted their original support for the military intervention. But by then it was too late.

In La Bandera, the first few days of the military period unfolded in a series of shocking events. On the morning of September 11, 1973, residents of La Bandera began to sense that something was amiss. Although Mónica Janet was only a girl at the time, and thus not old enough to understand everything that was going on, the images of that day are riveted in her mind. She recalled:

I remember that I got up, and my father arrived and said... "they overthrew Allende. And the shop over there on the corner... is selling all the groceries...." All the [merchandise from the] black market was out on the street. And I remember that my father went over there and brought lots of noodles, lots of sugar, all being sold....

And afterward he said, "I'm not going to work because this is starting to look ugly," and he didn't go [to work].

...at noon, one of my aunts arrived...crying... "they killed Allende. They killed Allende." Afterward on this street lots of women dressed in black went by, crying, saying that they had killed the *compañero*, that we had to go out onto the street. And then I remember my mother told us "Everyone inside!"...because this was at two in the afternoon and lots of soldiers started to come out... [This was the start of a curfew.] We felt gunshots, we felt bombs, we felt the explosions....And my father told me that here you could see the smoke from where La Moneda [the presidential palace] was burning.

Not surprisingly, given the high levels of mobilization and the politicized origins of the *población*, La Bandera was one of the areas most severely repressed after the military coup. Víctor Toro and Pelusa, two leaders of the land seizure 26 de enero, narrowly escaped into exile. Rumors circulated that La Bandera would be bombed because of its reputation as a bastion of communism.

For months after the coup, residents of La Bandera awoke to see corpses littering the open fields. As Iván described it, "For everyone it was a daily spectacle. At first the impact, the fright, on encountering the dead....But afterward it was like whoever got up first in the morning found dead bodies." These corpses were brought from other parts of the city and left exposed until they would be hauled off in trucks.

The appearance of corpses lasted three or four months, but police raids on houses continued. In massive raids, the armed forces ransacked the *población* house by house, purportedly looking for subversives and weapons. Mónica Janet recalled, "The first massive raid was terrible....I remember that a kid went to buy [cooking] gas and there were trucks, tanks, airplanes passing almost on top of the rooftops. And...he came...shouting, 'They are coming to kill everybody, they are coming to kill everybody.'"

Iván remembered the raids. too: "All the tanks filled Santa Rosa up to San Francisco where the *población* ends. Nothing but tanks. And afterward on the other side. And they went throughout the entire *población*....They looked in all the houses, took apart the mattresses with bayonets...broke the ceiling....They broke everything that caused suspicion immediately." The military forced all males over age fifteen to stand in the fields while they checked their records by calling in the data over the radio. "The men might be an entire day there without drinking water, without anything...all day on their feet. And anyone who protested was kicked hard," Iván recalled. "These were like small concentration camps but in our own *población*."

The forms of terror exercised in the initial years of the military regime illustrate how the space of the *población* was used as a location in which to punish and control. Military vehicles lined the four streets bordering the *población* and sectioned it off to cover it sector by sector, allowing no escape. Fields, once planned for public services, became places of detention and repositories for dead bodies. And even people's painstakingly built houses were ransacked by the armed forces. The space of the *población*, once carefully planned for community life and parks, had become a grid for exercising terror and was permeated by the power of the armed forces.

Repression extended not only to people's property and persons but also to the obliteration of cultural symbols. Residents of La Bandera told me that any feature the army interpreted as related to the Left—long hair on men, pants on women, clothing in the color red—could subject a person to arrest. In a crackdown on symbolic meanings, the military changed place-names. The wide road at the top of La Bandera called Manuel Rodríguez (named after an independence hero of the Left) became Américo Vespucio. The road known as Gamal Abdul Nasser became Almirante Latorre (after a nineteenth-century naval hero). Elsewhere in Santiago, the MIR-initiated *población* Nueva La Habana (New Havana) received the name Nuevo Amanecer (New Dawn). As people were persecuted both physically and culturally, fear permeated everyday life.

A principal consequence and intention of the repression was to "create fear in the people... terror." Mónica Janet recalled "that there were people who hid their cooking knives out of the fear that they [would be seen as] dangerous weapons.... It is like a psychosis of fear that they [the military] wanted to sow."[2]

The fear that infused the *población* had a chilling effect on social organizations. Community groups shut down as leaders were persecuted. Curtailed by near-constant states of "siege," "emergency," and "exception," in which constitutional rights were suspended, and constrained by repeated curfews, residents were afraid to leave their houses. The many cultural centers and social organizations that had filled La Bandera's early history were gone.

TRANSFORMATION OF THE ECONOMIC MODEL

The silencing of the opposition gave General Pinochet the opportunity to implement a new economic approach. As mentioned earlier, the prevailing economic model in place until the early 1970s was one of import substitution and state intervention. The Allende administration sought to bring the economy closer to socialism by nationalizing private enterprises, accelerating land reform, redistributing income, and strengthening public services.

The powerful Chilean countermovements against Allende, and the U.S. support of a military takeover, were based on a rejection of Allende's economic policies. The military coup was intended to reverse his economic approach. Soon after the coup, control over the country passed from a group of men constituting the junta to a single commander, General Augusto Pinochet. Pinochet's first task was to stabilize the economy, which had spiraled out of control, with the 1973 inflation rate reaching 1,000 percent. In 1973, Pinochet's economic approach had not yet congealed into a coherent program. Thus the first actions of Pinochet and his civilian ministers were a limited set of stopgap measures to control inflation which dramatically reduced real wages (Schneider 1995, 81).

The early efforts to bring order to the economy were soon followed by a more comprehensive economic plan. The "Chicago Boys," a group of Chilean economists trained in the economics department at the University of Chicago beginning in the 1950s, provided guidance to Pinochet. Schooled in free market economics, this group sought to reduce the role of the state and privatize the economy. These economists sought nothing less than the wholesale restructuring of the Chilean economy and, with it, the society.[3]

The restructuring the Chicago Boys had in mind went far beyond reversing Allende's program. It required transforming the entire economic model by replacing import substitution with free market economics. No longer would domestic industries be protected from international competition. To the contrary, tariffs would be lowered and borders opened to the import of foreign goods. Rather than sell to a domestic market, the country would generate income by exporting its goods. In the new economic era, raw materials (copper, as well as wood, fish, and later fruit) became the linchpin of the export economy.

With increased international competition, reduced tariffs on imports, rising interest rates, and the availability of cheap products from abroad, Chilean industries manufacturing for domestic consumption experienced a severe decline. The textile industry is a prime example. As it collapsed because of the proliferation of cheap imports from abroad, "over seventy-three thousand...workers lost their jobs" (Schneider 1995, 92). The impact of deindustrialization on jobs was especially severe in urban neighborhoods. As one writer explained,

> By 1974 wages averaged $.07 an hour...compared with the $.38 an hour they averaged the year before the coup....The working-class share of national income dropped from 65 percent to 40 percent...and unemployment doubled in the first three months, to 7 percent, and then continued to rise, reaching 13.3 percent in the first quarter of July. By 1975 the average income of the poorest family was 46 percent of its 1973 level. (Schneider 1995, 82)

By 1976, poverty rates in Santiago would climb to 57 percent, and the unemployment rate would reach 80 percent in some *poblaciones*. With wages down, unemployment up, and prices rising, working-class Chileans endured economic hardship scarcely known since the market crash of 1929.

Poblaciones like La Bandera experienced the brunt of economic restructuring. Deindustrialization in the 1970s meant that people whose parents had steady industrial jobs now worked in the informal sector. Without contracts, they found work in construction, occasional repair jobs, or selling candy and trinkets aboard buses or on the street. The results more than two decades later in La Bandera show the effects of these changes. Manufacturing work declined 30 percent between 1970 and 1992, from 42 to 29 percent of employment. With manufacturing in decline, other areas grew. For example, occupations that increased in prevalence included commerce (from 15 percent in 1970 to 20 percent in 1992) and financial operations (from .4 percent in 1970 to 4.7 percent in 1992).[4] These figures

TABLE I Structural Change in Employment
for *Población* La Bandera, 1970–92

	Owner/ Employer	*Self- employed*	*Domestic Worker*	*Salaried Worker*	*Unpaid Family*	*Total*
Agriculture, fishing	0.0	0.3	0.0	−0.1	0.0	0.3
Mining	0.0	0.0	0.0	−0.3	0.0	−0.3
Manufacture	1.5	0.3	0.0	−15.3	0.1	−13.3
Electric, gas	0.0	0.0	0.0	−0.1	0.0	−0.0
Construction	1.0	1.1	0.0	−0.8	0.1	1.4
Commerce, hotels, restaurants	1.3	−1.8	0.0	5.8	0.2	5.4
Transport	0.5	0.4	0.0	0.2	0.0	1.0
Finance, real estate	0.3	0.3	0.0	3.7	0.0	4.4
Services	0.8	−3.1	3.6	−0.2	0.2	1.2
TOTAL	5.4	−2.7	3.6	−7.1	0.8	0.0

NOTE: Data represent change in the proportion of the workforce in each area by employment status and sector of the economy. Small discrepancies in totals are due to rounding. *Source:* Instituto Nacional de Estadísticas (INE).

show that employment was shifting from industry to business services. Those people I knew in the early 1990s who worked in financial offices held subordinate jobs as clerks and office assistants, often part-time. Yet these clerk-type jobs were not the largest source of employment. Instead, the most common work activity for men in 1992 was construction—a job characterized by short-term employment and no benefits or contracts (26 percent of men in La Bandera said they were employed in construction in 1992, compared with 20 percent in 1970).

With men employed only sporadically and incomes low, women increasingly worked to bring in income. In 1970, 84 percent of men had salaried work; in 1992 that number had dropped to 75.5 percent. For women, the percentage with salaried work increased from 54 to 62 percent over that twenty-two-year period.[5] The largest work activity for women, domestic service (33 percent), required long hours and offered no benefits. Clothing manufacturing (11 percent) registered second as a job category for La Bandera's female labor force.[6] Because large-scale textile production had declined, this sewing often went on in small production sites, as piecework, or as homework at very low wages. In my observation, the jobs available to residents of La Bandera paid so little in the early 1990s that people, particularly women, often cycled in and out of them. They did the work when the need for income was most dire. They stopped when the costs of working—leaving their children unattended, leaving their houses unguarded, compromising their health, experiencing the humiliation of working as a servant, being castigated by their husbands for leaving the house, or paying a large portion of their salary for transportation—outweighed the benefits of a meager wage.

As they restructured the economy, Pinochet's economists claimed that their work was apolitical. After all, they pointed out, they were causing the state—and thereby political influence—to withdraw from intervening in the economy. Instead, economics would be guided by the invisible hand of the market. Yet privatization and the dismantling of the welfare state were deeply political acts, for they would have been impossible without demobilization of the massive social movements making demands for public services throughout the country. In Britain and the United States, elected right-wing national leaders were partially limited in their attempts to restructure the economy in the 1980s because of opposition in Parliament and Congress. In contrast, the Chilean military government was able to reshape the economy profoundly because it both eliminated elected institutions and repressed a politicized citizenry. Although the training of the Chicago Boys began in 1957, it was not until after the coup that these economists were able to implement their policy ideas in Chile (Valdés 1995, 13).

The repression exerted by the state reflects a paradox in neoliberal ideology. The Chicago Boys claimed that they were reducing the role of the state in the economy, and to a large extent they were. By the 1980s, public services would be dismantled, and national industries privatized. Yet from another perspective, the state played an active role in facilitating economic restructuring (Martínez and Díaz 1996, 66). For example, the crackdown on union organizing kept wages artificially low. This was not a natural outcome of the market and the free acts of individuals but rather the result of active intervention by the government.

Beyond repression, there were instances of direct economic intervention that were not as laissez-faire as they first appeared. "Through systematic changes to the exchange rate, interest rates, public tariffs, and agricultural prices," Martínez and Díaz (1996, 66) argue, "the state took an active role in determining the level of prices and profits in the economy." The state also intervened directly by bailing banks out of an economic crisis in 1982. Moreover, it compensated for the income inequality that the economic model had generated by employing the poor in public works programs and directing targeted subsidies in health, housing, education, and nutrition to the poor. The military itself was financed by revenues from the copper industry, made possible—ironically enough—by Allende's nationalization of that industry (Martínez and Díaz 1996, 66). Although neoliberalism operated under the ideology of reducing the state, and although to a large extent it did, Pinochet's government simultaneously intervened in selected ways in the economy.

In short, broad-based repression facilitated the implementation of neoliberal economics. As Chilean sociologist Tomás Moulian (1997) points out, repression was not the raison d'être of the military government, as some of its opponents have supposed. Rather, it was a means to an end. Pinochet needed to subdue grassroots movements and political opposition in order to implement his economic vision.

Given this goal, the dictator's tactics worked. In the first few years, social organizations and political parties were effectively disarticulated through repression. As the recession deepened and the state's cutbacks took effect, however, small groups of *población* dwellers organized collectively to survive economic privation.

REEMERGENCE OF ORGANIZATIONS

The repression that accompanied the economic model was so intense that, in order to reestablish community organizations, residents of *poblaciones* had to overcome their fear. Mónica Janet remembered the transformation she underwent early in the dictatorship when she began to shed her terror of the military. At first, she said, "I didn't go out the door at two in the afternoon because I was frightened." But over time she "lost this fear." She described the moment at which this happened:

> There was a clinic [located in a nearby house]....And I remember that it was my turn to bring [my baby brother] for his checkup....I was a child...fourteen years old....The soldiers [arrived].... They were looking for Pelusa [one of the leaders of the 26 de enero land seizure]....I was with the baby in my arms...and a soldier came to my side and...pulled my hair...And I began to cry because I was...still a child. They asked me, are you Pelusa...and I said no, and they pulled my hair like this....And from then on I began to lose my fear.

"*That* made you lose your fear?" I asked her. "Sure," she responded, then continued:

> I said why should they treat me like that if I haven't done anything?...I have to confront them, too. So I began not to feel fear of the soldiers. I think I was the only one in my household...because here everyone was afraid. And I never again felt that fear....I'm not afraid to go out into the street if I sense the soldiers, the police, I go out just the same to watch everything.

Mónica Janet not only overcame her fear but also became one of the most active participants in organizations emerging during the dictatorship. She attributed her motivation to join organizations to her growing outrage at the injustices she saw around her:

> I began to read, and I began to hear that there were people...disappeared without reason....They told me...about a day in which the soldiers arrived at a house... they were going to kill everyone—cut their stomachs—including the children. So I said, with what morality, for what meaning?...So all of this motivates you to...go out, finding out things,...to struggle for something of value. [For] the rights of each person.

The sense of outrage would lead her to be an active leader in her community.

Because of the destitution engendered by the economic model in poor neighborhoods, the first organizations to emerge in La Bandera during the dictatorship were oriented toward meeting basic needs. As early as 1973–74, children's dining halls *(comedores infantiles)* operated with the support of local parishes of the Catholic Church (Gallardo 1987, 179). A different kind of organization, *ollas comunes,* or "common pot" cooking cooperatives, responded to widespread hunger and unemployment. Unlike soup kitchens in the United States, where volunteers or paid staff provide food and the poor receive it, these were cooperative endeavors between the people affected by hunger. In these groups, women who could not otherwise feed their families would pool the small amounts of food they had—a bag of beans or a handful of noodles—and would request donations of vegetables in the market. Sharing the work responsibilities, they cooked a single pot of food and distributed it, one ladle per family member, to participating households. Women, responsible for the nutrition, health, and housing of their families, were central actors in these organizations.

As the work of Chilean sociologists has shown, participating in organizations such as common kitchens drew women out of the narrow world of their houses and demonstrated to them that their problems were familiar to others. Joining housing committees and cooking cooperatives reinforced lessons about the value of acting collectively (Frohmann and Valdés 1995, 281). These organizations sometimes generated conflicts between leaders and participants or fostered dependency on external institutions that supported the local efforts (Valdés and Weinstein 1993, 155). Nonetheless, they created social spaces where women could discuss their problems and share information (Winn 1992, 328–30).

In addition to *ollas comunes,* residents of poor neighborhoods began other organizations, including committees of the homeless and organizations of the unemployed.[7] These groups operated clandestinely for fear of repression from the state. One of the few places where local organizations could gain protection was the Catholic Church, which, through its Vicaría de la Solidaridad, was the main sheltering institution during this period. It documented violations of human rights and provided space for crafts workshops such as the *arpillera* tapestries Chilean women made to earn money and communicate the Chilean political situation to an audience overseas. Survival groups also received help from nongovernmental organizations whose financing came from abroad. In contrast to the emphasis on mobilization in the late 1960s, during this period the grassroots organizations did not seek to make demands on the government because the military regime had no mechanism for negotiating with popular organizations.

Organizations that residents of La Bandera became involved in were not simply concerned with day-to-day survival. Some of the people who became the leaders in community organizations and urban social movements received political education that they called *formación.* Sometimes this came from political parties, and at other times from nongovernmental organizations. Nongovernmental organizations, which had existed prior to the military coup, grew in importance during the military period. Professionals who had worked in the public health and education systems, or who had been part of universities, found themselves newly

unemployed once the state took over or drastically curtailed university departments and public services. Seeking new venues in which to continue their work,
they found refuge in nongovernmental organizations that ranged from institutes
dedicated to research, to popular education projects that sought to provide training and education to residents in poor sectors.

Valeria, who would later become the coordinator of Llareta, was first introduced to community organizations by another *pobladora*. Coaxing Valeria out of
her house, this friend brought her to a workshop sponsored by a nongovernmental organization that worked with women. Later, Mónica Janet and Sonia received
their *formación*—their personal development and political training—in this NGO
as well. Valeria described the group as meeting twice a week for two years, during
which time the budding leaders attended workshops with themes such as the
meaning of working in groups and the relation of persons to society. For example,
within the subject area of working in a group, the women would discuss what a
group was and then converse about topics such as how "to grow by participating;
giving and receiving together in a group; [and] changing negative attitudes."
Looking back at printed materials to jog her memory, Valeria outlined the subsequent components of the curriculum:

> We worked in a personal area where we spoke more about oneself, our life, of the
> feelings, of the communication and the relation with God and nature.... And after-
> ward, we did a family area and a social area.... After passing through all of those
> prior themes, you are finally going to understand what the social area is and what its
> use is in your life. Because you are always in relation with others. So you can under-
> stand who your neighbors are, what relation the family has with the society.

The training was organized to move outward from the individual to the society at
large, incorporating the concerns of the women's lives into political organizing.

Valeria felt that during those years of training she came to know herself as a
person, learned to reflect on her life, and was able to identify paths for action to
address the difficult circumstances in which she lived. Through this process, "I
achieved my internal liberty.... I feel that I broke...all my prejudices. I broke the
pain. I broke the myths, the beliefs. I [now] have things that are useful in my life
and that let me act. I don't have things that don't let me act." Because this intense
education happened over a two-year period, started with her personal life, dealt
with the things most painful and important to her, encouraged her to analyze the
society in which she lived, and inspired her to identify options for action within it,
Valeria says she was permanently transformed. She eventually left when she found
the organization too constraining. From her perspective, once she became a social
and political actor in her own right, the nongovernmental organization curtailed
rather than supported her activities. But because of the enduring personal growth
she had experienced within it, her participation in social organizations outlasted
not only her departure from the women's program but also, and more important,
the transition to democracy. She says the process transformed her "to the point in

which [I] arriv[ed] at a consciousness—where I decided to…continue fighting, and where I continue still. [After the end of the dictatorship,] I didn't go into my house. Because I acquired a distinct political consciousness."

Once people became active in one organization, they tended to join others. Mónica Janet first became involved through the same women's organization as Valeria. She explained,

> It was like a way of educating women. But it also showed you the hunger that already existed, unemployment, the disappeared. All these things. And [it showed us how] to organize ourselves. Afterward I entered the health group.…And from there, I began to organize myself with all kinds of people. I began to enter all the organizations that existed.…I was in common kitchens, we tried to form a union of the unemployed. [I was in] all of the organizations. Always.

Iván, too, became involved in a broad range of groups at that time. He recalled, "We formed the first union of the unemployed of La Bandera.…We had a cooking cooperative.…I also formed youth groups. I mainly participated in a group of human rights and in the antirepression committee…acts of solidarity." The survival organizations of the mid-1970s represented a new kind of *poblacional* organization—one tailored to the political period in which it arose. Unlike *población* organizations in the late 1960s and early 1970s, which were self-consciously part of a widespread social movement for broader social change, organizations emerging in the early years of military rule addressed *pobladores'* immediate economic needs. Nutrition, employment, housing, and human rights organizations became necessary for survival at a time when salaries had reached an all-time low and unions were illegal. Where economic needs became desperate, where fear kept people from operating openly, and where the state would neither negotiate nor provide public services, people organized clandestine survival groups. Although the organizations started out to ensure day-to-day survival, they would ultimately have a broader impact on the culture of the *población* and on its subsequent ability to mobilize.

FORCED RESETTLEMENT, FEAR, AND CRIME

While residents were grappling with surviving unemployment, hunger, and inadequate housing, the land use crisis in La Bandera was exacerbated by another set of arrivals. In the early 1980s, the military government uprooted people living in squatters' settlements in the upper- and middle-class areas of Santiago and relocated them to the poorest areas of the city. Under a program billed as providing permanent and solid housing for residents of squatters' settlements in Santiago, the military government forcibly relocated thousands of people.[8]

The district of La Granja, of which La Bandera was a part in the early 1980s,[9] was a major "receptor" area for these relocations. Many arrivals were sent to live in the tiny houses—nicknamed "matchboxes" to describe their size—deep in neighboring La Pintana. Between 1981 and 1983, a total of 1,260 families (representing 7,500 to 10,000 persons) were forcibly resettled (eradicated) to La Bandera,[10] creating an increase of approximately 20 percent in the population. Families came from seven districts and thirteen squatters' settlements. Their housing was built in the areas that the late 1960s blueprints had designated for public services and parks.

In implementing the eradications, the military government explicitly sought to "homogenize" the different areas of the city by social class. The following text, from a letter written in 1982 by the mayor of La Granja to the director of the National Service for Housing, illustrates how intentional this policy was:

> The squatters' settlement Roto Chileno, located at bus stop *[paradero]* 21 of Santa Rosa, occupies land that is the property of the national housing agency. These lands, because of their location, cannot be used for the construction of basic housing (low-income housing), but rather [housing of] a much higher level, in accordance with the population that exists in that area.
>
> In consideration of the above, I solicit of SERVIU the delivery of the lands that are located in the *Población* La Bandera.... In those mentioned lands the 400 families that comprise the current Squatters' Settlement Roto Chileno would be located.
>
> The proposed formula would signify giving a permanent housing solution to those families, and moreover, SERVIU would *recuperate a land of excellent location for the construction of housing for middle sectors* [emphasis added].[11]

As the letter demonstrates, the purpose of eradications was to segregate the city by social class. Families living at *paradero* 21 received housing in La Bandera not because their previous location was unsuitable for permanent housing but because authorities considered the land too valuable to house the poor. In the context of a free market economy and orientation toward an export strategy for growth, the state-led eradications intensified and accelerated the spatial manifestations of an economic policy that was increasing income inequality and magnifying the differences between a modern city center and an impoverished urban periphery.[12]

The effect of relocation on the families resettled in La Bandera was powerful. As in earlier city planning, people were settled by *manzanas*, blocks of housing arranged back-to-back. Because of this design, families from completely different parts of the city, located in different *manzanas*, faced each other across narrow passageways. In many cases family members and former neighbors found themselves scattered over a range of locations throughout Santiago. Although solid, the houses they received were unfinished and small, a condition that produced immediate overcrowding. Furthermore, after living in places with adequate or excellent public facilities, the newcomers found themselves in locations with the worst services in health, education, and transportation.

As new arrivals received smaller and smaller plots of land, La Bandera became more crowded. And as empty areas became filled with housing for the relocated families, grown children of the original residents had nowhere to build their homes. They continued to live *allegado*—overcrowded—in their parents' small yards. Social tensions increased as people from vastly different parts of the city, with different experiences of social organization, were settled against their will in a *población* that, in turn, did not want them.

The arrival of resettled families immediately changed the spatial and social organization of La Bandera. The eradications essentially doubled the number of homes in the area of the fourth sector by surrounding a previously isolated set of houses with densely populated communities on three sides. The relocations put much greater pressure on limited local services, especially a health clinic called upon to serve far more residents than the number for which it had been designed.

Work patterns changed as well. Once close to sources of employment, the new residents now had to travel over an hour to reach their jobs in the upper-class area of Las Condes as tennis ball boys, golf caddies, night watchmen, and maids. Doing casual work like washing cars became impossible, and looking for work such as domestic employment became a full day's activity. New and unusual bus routes reflected these changing work and residential patterns. Although one had to switch buses to reach the *población* La Pincoya in the northern part of Santiago, buses now went directly from La Bandera to the wealthy *comuna* of Las Condes.

Angélica and her extended family were relocated from a squatters' settlement in Las Condes in 1982. Angélica, who later became a member of Llareta, had grown up in a rural area but came to Santiago at age fifteen to work as a live-in domestic in the house of professors. Raised by a mother who had fought actively for left-wing presidential candidates and the right of women to vote, Angélica became active in party politics, organized other domestic workers, and worked for the election of Salvador Allende beginning with his electoral campaign of the late 1950s. Having married a man who grew up on the farmland near her childhood home, she moved to a squatters' settlement on the banks of a river in Las Condes. Living in the *barrio alto* provided an opportunity for her political work because it enabled Angélica to teach other domestics about the concept of class consciousness and their rights as workers by using the difference in living conditions between themselves and their employers as examples. When Angélica was forcibly relocated to La Bandera in 1982, the experience was difficult, but what helped her adjust was the sense of class consciousness and a solidarity with other poor people that she had developed over decades of political *formación*. Resenting the disdain with which she was treated in wealthy parts of the city—the suspicion directed at her in shops, the infantilizing use of *tú* instead of the respectful *usted* when she was addressed—she felt more comfortable living near people she considered more like herself.

Angélica's brother-in-law Rodolfo, who was also moved to La Bandera along with the rest of the extended family, did not so fully come to terms with his new location. He remembered his old home vividly and with great fondness, often dreaming that he was back there only to find himself, upon awaking, in La Bandera. Although he had lived in a wooden house on the banks of a river that constantly threatened to overflow, he recalled never having any fear of violence. Most important to him was the sense of community he and his neighbors had built during a lifetime in Las Condes. For him, being relocated to La Bandera was a nightmare. He remembered his reaction when he first heard the news:

> I didn't even want to come and see it because I had worked distributing books for a bookstore during those five years, and I had to travel outside along Américo Vespucio. I saw this and I never, never would come to live here.... Plus in the news when we heard the news of death, that there had been assaults, it was all in La Bandera. For us it was...very bad to think of coming to live here.... We came here by force.

The arrival of people from other parts of the city immediately provoked tensions in La Bandera. Rodolfo described the irony of disturbing people in a place to which he did not even want to go:

> I remember that they told us on this day you'll go. The day before that we had to take apart our houses made of wood, take off the roof... it was hard work to take it all apart, very hurried because they only told us at noon. The following day, early in the morning, came municipal trucks.
>
> It was quite sad to arrive here.... People that had lived their entire lives here [in La Bandera], that had dreamed of having their house like this one, constructed [of solid materials], that had more right than we did.... I never had wanted this house, [and] we came to take away the possibility from them.... For this reason we had more difficulty at the beginning. The people robbed us, all those kinds of things.

Rodolfo interpreted the violence he and his family faced as a kind of vengeance enacted on them for taking housing that rightly belonged to longtime residents. He described the fear and violence that he and relatives experienced during their first years in the *población:* "Soon after we arrived, my brothers came home late from a party...they were assaulted, beaten up...[The attackers] were on the point of doing more harm. Thank God it didn't go farther than that, they only robbed some things. But it was traumatizing for us. Later, in fact, they robbed us. ...The fights and gunshots in the nighttime were tremendous." Except for traveling to work, Rodolfo and his family remained inside their narrow passageway, not venturing out. Many of Rodolfo's neighbors told me they never walked beyond the ends of the block except to go to the outdoor market or the corner store. One of Rodolfo's ideas for creating a sense of connection with his neighbors was to join efforts in constructing tall metal gates at both ends of their street. The eradications had helped create a fractured *población.* Divided from each other and mistrustful of their neighbors, people were unlikely to leave their houses or blocks, much less organize.

The *erradicados* were not the only ones to experience fear of crime. Young men whom neighbors called *delincuentes* controlled the space and borders of the *población* and monitored movement within it. "[During] the protests you had to pay [a toll], ...to pass from one street to the next," said one woman who had to travel to work as a cleaning woman in a middle-class neighborhood. "If...for example, you were going to take a bus toward Santa Rosa, there [a group would tell you], 'No, you're not passing. Pay up, or you don't pass,' or 'I'll take your jacket or I'll take the radio, I'll take what you're carrying.' Or they stab you." Another woman, who worked within the *población* in the minimum wage program, didn't have to travel as far. As she recalled, "We had to go to the municipality...standing in line all day long, so that they would give us the money [wages] they had to give us...and...the package of groceries. Then, at the exit, [were] the *delincuentes*. We had to exit in groups so that they didn't take the packages of food." Although this woman and those who worked with her avoided the *delincuentes* by walking in groups, for many, particularly women, fear of *delincuencia* kept them trapped in their homes, without interpersonal contact. I was told by a woman in the early 1990s that she virtually never left her home, for fear someone would rob it while she was gone. Such isolation made social organizations more difficult to sustain, since people would not go to meetings. And with hardly anyone outside, the streets became even more dangerous.

Residents of La Bandera with whom I spoke believed that the presence of crime was not a random social occurrence but the product of an intentional strategy by the military government to keep people in fear. They held that the military maintained and fostered *delincuencia* in an effort to undermine relationships between people. Valeria's husband, Jorge, speculated that wine and *pisco* (an alcoholic beverage) were kept cheap during the years of dictatorship to keep people in the area drunk, with the implication that they would become violent and out of control. Other residents of La Bandera explained that police would round up young men, check them for political records, and then release those not identified as political subversives. In addition to capturing anyone involved in politics, this kept *delincuentes* out on the street, and neighbors in fear.

The military's efforts to turn people against their neighbors became most intense during a period known as Allá Viene, Allá Viene (there they come, there they come). During the 1980s, rumors circulated that people from different sections of the *población* were going to attack one another. As one woman described it,

> All the *poblaciones* were alarmed at this. That the *[pobladores]* were going to attack each other. They were going to take...the houses, they were going to destroy everything, everything, everything....So what happened? Every night all the neighbors from here [placed ourselves in different spots], all of us guarded our *población* so they wouldn't destroy it, waiting for them to come from over there....
>
> ...Some nights, I didn't sleep at all. Because one had to lie down dressed...for the fear. To guard the things, the television, guard...the money.

The rumors further heightened the mistrust that already existed. This woman described it as being like "a sudden pest, like a sickness, from one day to the next and they began throwing pamphlets saying that the *pobladores* were going to kill each other." In the end, "It never happened. This was a...false rumor that [Pinochet] ran....what [that] gentleman intended was that the *pobladores* kill each other. At least the *pobladores* were intelligent and we didn't harm each other." The fact that armed groups roamed the streets breaking windows on houses lent credibility to the rumors. But according to her, residents eventually came to realize that these groups, which traveled in vehicles, were people from outside the *población*. She described the early meetings in which people from different sectors of La Bandera began to discuss the rumors and realized that no one had any plans to harm their neighbors. They concluded that it was a scheme initiated by the government. It was this process of finally coming together to talk that enabled neighbors to see how the military used fear as a divide-and-conquer strategy.

Beyond using *delincuentes* to fragment social relationships and discourage organization, leaders reported that police also used them to break up the political rallies that surged in the 1980s. Community leaders describe having to fight the young men physically to keep them from ruining political events by attacking participants or stealing cameras from visitors. I was told in 1992 that one of the reasons I could work in La Bandera unharmed was because the community leaders I knew best had physically fought the *delincuentes* to gain their respect. And indeed, although assaults, muggings, and robberies were occurring in La Bandera in the early 1990s, I was never harmed in the time I lived in the *población*.

Police also used *delincuentes* to inform on activists. According to local leaders, during the years of protest, *delincuentes* routinely passed information to the police. The resulting sense that anybody could be a spy created substantial distrust between people, precipitating a range of clandestine behaviors that permeated not only political activities but also daily events. For example, in 1991, the first piece of advice I received upon arriving in La Bandera was never to ask anyone's name. If I did, said my host, no one would trust me. "Why?" I asked, as I tried to imagine another way of greeting people. To him the reason was clear: It's not that they're afraid you will actually learn their name—you won't, because they will use an alias anyway. But by asking, you'll give the impression you are a spy. After all, who else would want that kind of information? I was also advised not to ask a person's address—instead, information would be apportioned on a need-to-know basis. Going to find friends at their houses, I learned to stand outside the gate and call *"aló"* rather than shout their name, so that a passing plainclothes policeman would not overhear and discover the identity of the inhabitant. What remained unmentioned, but lurked just below the surface, was that one wanted to avoid knowing names and addresses in case one was interrogated under torture. Under those circumstances, it was better not to know. That these practices were active in 1991 shows how deeply ingrained fear and clandestinity had become.

The habit of not using real names fostered a range of creative cultural solutions. Young men on the street had *sobrenombres* (nicknames) that vaguely described their personal appearance: Fatso, Grandpa, Baldy. Politically involved youth used *chapas* (aliases), often drawn from the names of revolutionary leaders. While such precautions protected individuals and political organizations from repression, and could create bonds between people using the same codes, it also made it all the more difficult to create an open political culture and connections between people in the *población*. "Even now [after the end of the dictatorship], we still find situations of distrust," said Serena's brother, a youth who had participated in the protests. "The organizations were always clandestine... and being clandestine, they worked in groups... of people who were known to you.... And we still have this vice of working only with groups of friends." In 1991, people who had worked closely for years in opposition to the dictatorship, and risked their lives together, were for the first time learning each other's real names. While for many the fear created by *delincuencia* and the constant presence of spies reduced interpersonal interaction and social organization, others were able to create strong organizations based on a culture of clandestine communication and action.

THE ECONOMY REVISITED

The "shock treatment" instituted in 1975 to curb inflation finally began to bear fruit in 1977. Inflation fell, and the economy experienced powerful growth. The years from 1979 to 1981 came to be known as the "Chilean Miracle" and gained Chile international praise in financial circles. Exports of fruit, fish, and forest products flourished. The availability of loans and an overvalued peso combined with reduced trade barriers to create a boom in consumerism. Some of the prosperity reached the *poblaciones*, where families began to acquire television sets and other cheap imported electronic goods.

Amid the confidence in the economy, Pinochet's economists accelerated free market measures. They privatized public utilities such as electricity and telecommunications. And, under their direction, the state sold off banks and companies, deregulated industries, and created conditions favorable to foreign investment (Collins and Lear 1995, 30).

On the coattails of his economic success, Pinochet introduced the famed "seven modernizations." These were policy changes that brought free market principles to seven key areas: labor, agriculture, education, health, social security, justice, and public administration (Oppenheim 1993, 156). Responsibilities in many of these areas would be transferred from the state to the private sector. In public services, for example, the military government replaced the national health system with private health insurance (ISAPRES), the pension system with private retirement accounts (AFPs), and the public school system with subsidies to private schools. Those who could not purchase services on the private market would attend schools and health clinics managed by municipal governments.

Housing provides a good example of the state's new role. Unlike Frei and Allende, who promised to build houses for the poor, Pinochet redefined housing from a "right" to a "good" allocated through the private real estate market. The state did not entirely retreat from facilitating access to housing, but it limited its role to providing vouchers for those who could least afford to purchase homes on their own. This practice of targeting subsidies to the poorest of the poor was described as "subsidiarity": rather than offer public services and redistribute income downward, the state directed limited funding to those families most excluded from access through the private market.

Some of the free market measures, like the privatized pension system, became models for countries around the world, and the Chilean regime had some successes with respect to the poor. For example, the targeting of health care to mothers and children resulted in a significant drop in infant mortality. The regime used that decline to publicize the success of its policies. But beyond these isolated examples, privatization heightened inequality and reduced the accessibility and quality of public services such as health care and education in the *poblaciones*.

In the euphoric moments of the miracle, few believed that Chile's economic success would prove chimerical. But toward the end of 1981, perceptions changed as the economy came tumbling down. The "boom" had been based on speculation, not production. Amid an international debt crisis, banks and private companies became financially unstable. And with a recession in the United States and Europe (primary markets for Chilean goods), Chile, too, experienced a severe recession. What had once been celebrated as a miracle was now characterized by increasingly desperate economic times, the worst economic crisis since the Great Depression of the 1930s.

In the *poblaciones,* the economic situation deteriorated rapidly, so that "by 1982 more than half of the labor force (53.3 percent) was either unemployed, in emergency work programs, or in the informal sector" (Martínez and Díaz 1996, 139). Hunger became severe (Raczynski and Serrano 1985).

One of the ways in which the military government dealt with the crisis was by establishing emergency work programs. These originally had been created in the mid-1970s, at another moment of economic recession. Now, in the early 1980s, the government operated programs called PEM (Programa de Empleo Mínimo, or Program of Minimal Employment) and POJH (Programa Ocupacional de Jefes de Hogares, or Occupational Program for Heads of Households). These work programs hired the *población*'s unemployed. The workers were paid one quarter of an already low minimum wage.[13] Most of the jobs involved maintaining public infrastructure, for example, by paving roads and planting grass.

Mónica Janet's father and many of her neighbors worked in these programs. "POJH [paved] this street," she told me, pointing out a window. She remembered the anguish of the work: "I saw all the men here in the hot sun—a sun that burns you. With shovel and pick, chopping the street in order to construct the road. For a very low salary... about fifteen hundred pesos every two weeks. It was a pittance.... PEM paid even worse. It was about four hundred pesos every two weeks that they paid." Angélica also remembered watching the PEM and POJH employees at work. What struck her was how demeaning the activities were. She recalled: "They occupied the men and the women, sweeping streets, cleaning plazas, planting grass in the parks, and paying a minimum. It didn't cover anything. And moreover they used anyone: ladies of seventy or sixty years old, it seems, with white hair. And a little old chubby one.... I would see her digging the ground in Américo Vespucio.

Figure 6. Mural on side of a house depicting the public works program under the dictatorship. Photo: Gordon Whitman.

Across from the municipality." Imagine if I, at my age, with a bad back and all my health problems, had to be out there with a pick and shovel digging up the dirt, Angélica said to me. Both she and Mónica Janet were emphatic that the problem with PEM and POJH was not only the low wages, which they considered miserable, but also the humiliation and indignity that workers endured—an indignity that they, as health promoters, were trying to overcome. Jorge was most infuriated by the purposelessness of the activities. He remembered being hired to build roads, but at times he was ordered to do what amounted to busywork, hauling rocks from one side of the street to the other, only to be told to move them back again. Years later, people who participated told of how the public works laborers burned down a municipal building. It had once been the landowner's house and later operated as a cultural center under Salvador Allende, but during the dictatorship the building was used to store tools belonging to the public works programs. By the time that event occurred, urban neighborhoods throughout Chile were involved in protest against the military regime.

THE CREATION OF AN OPPOSITION

From the perspective of social organizations, 1980 was a turning point in the political history of Chile. In that year, General Pinochet called for a plebiscite to ratify a new constitution. Drafted by him and modified by a constitutional commission, the Constitution outlined the schedule for a transition to civilian rule. It also contained provisions that would enshrine Pinochet's institutionality into the future. As one commentator put it, "The Constitution of 1980 was a fundamentally undemocratic document whose purpose was to prolong Pinochet's rule, institutionalize military oversight over civilian policy-making, increase the president's power at the expense of the legislature, severely limit popular participation, and permanently exclude Marxist parties from participation in politics" (Oppenheim 1993, 136). The decision to authenticate the constitution by popular vote showed how crucial legal legitimacy and international approval were to Pinochet's regime.

Attempting to block ratification of the new Constitution proved to be an opportunity for the opposition—which until that time had been weak and divided—to build its strength (Oppenheim 1993, 136). The opposition united in an effort to bring about a NO vote in the plebiscite. They lost, for the Constitution was approved handily by popular vote. That Pinochet should have won the referendum is not surprising, given the conditions posed by a military dictatorship: restricted rights to assembly, unequally distributed access to the media, and the absence of an electoral registry, making it possible for individuals to vote multiple times. The vote was later condemned as fraudulent by international human rights organizations. But although this NO campaign went down in defeat, the occasion marked an opportunity to organize, leading to a resurgence of the opposition. After 1980, organizations began to act more publicly.

In La Bandera, organization was also rebuilding. In 1980 the first land seizure to occur in Chile under the dictatorship happened in La Bandera. Settlers took land in a field across from a neighborhood council. The land occupation was rapidly disbanded, and the squatters, who by then had nowhere else to go, lived for months in the yard behind a church until space for housing could be found. Although the La Bandera land seizure was dissolved, other land occupations were more successful. In the early 1980s, two land seizures—Fresno and Cardenal Silva—took hold. While few in number, they were massive in quantities of participants. The number of squatters in the two sites equaled the total population involved in the numerous land seizures that had taken place in the 1960s and 1970s combined. As the land seizures demonstrated, social organizations had begun to gain power and visibility, even under military rule.

Although the opposition to the military regime became more visible beginning around 1980, it was after the economic crash of 1981–82 that protest against the regime intensified dramatically. By this time, dire economic circumstances had created discontent throughout Chile. Moreover, international pressure to respect human rights had generated a mild political opening, which was rapidly filled by social movement activity. While taking on a distinctively local and popular character, the protests in *poblaciones* like La Bandera were coordinated at the national level. The first national day of protest, in May 1983, followed the Confederation of Copper Workers' proclamation of a one-day general strike (Collier and Sater 1996, 376).[14]

But direction of the protests soon passed from labor unions to political parties, which were regrouping after years of repression. Two major coalitions with different strategies and ideologies emerged. The Democratic Alliance, dominated by the centrist Christian Democrat Party and including the renovated Socialists, small parties such as the Humanists and the Radicals, and a moderate segment of the right wing saw the protests as a path to a negotiated transition (Collier and Sater 1996, 377).

The Democratic Popular Movement, led by the Communist Party and including left-wing Socialists,[15] the Christian Left, and the MIR, centered its strategy around mobilizing networks of activists in urban neighborhoods and universities for protest against the regime. According to observers, the Democratic Popular Movement mobilized "hundreds of thousands of shantytown dwellers, trade unionists, women, professionals, and students" in the streets of the city center and the *poblaciones* (Petras and Leiva 1988, 97). In the center of Santiago, middle-income professionals like teachers and health workers took to the streets, marching during the daylight hours. In the *poblaciones*, in contrast, especially at night, *pobladores* threw stones, lit bonfires, and chanted slogans into the evening sky. Their protests had a different, more popular, flavor. The coalition banked on using mass mobilization to overthrow the military regime.

In part, the strategy of the Democratic Popular Movement built on the strengths of its component political parties. The Communist Party, at the core of the coalition, had strong roots in the *poblaciones* as a result of its long history of grassroots organizing through committees of the homeless in the late 1960s and its support of survival organizations in the 1970s (see Schneider 1995). Despite repression, the Communist Party had continued to function throughout the military years. In the mid-1980s, when the party sought to rejuvenate social movements, the labor movement had already been weakened by targeted repression and constraining labor laws. Thus the Communist Party focused its organizing efforts not on unions but on urban *poblaciones*—the places where workers and their families lived (Roberts 1995, 503).

Despite the political parties' pivotal roles in the coalition, the Democratic Popular Movement was not directed by parties alone. While some grassroots leaders were themselves party militants, many *poblacional* organizations, like Llareta, remained autonomous—neither initiated, run, nor controlled by the political parties. Amid party factionalism at the national level, grassroots organizations were able to create unity across the Left by weaving together persons from various political trajectories into large-scale mobilization and an active social movement. In coalition, the parties supporting the Democratic Popular Movement and the grassroots organizations that joined them fostered widespread political and social activity in the *poblaciones*.

Although organizations began to emerge slowly and clandestinely under military rule, by the early and mid-1980s La Bandera was the site of some of the most active protests against military rule. The people who a year later would become founding members of Llareta were already involved in a variety of community organizations and as leaders were instrumental during the protests. Valeria recalled initiating La Bandera's first march by using the same form of expression—banging pots—that wealthy women had used in their demonstrations against Allende a decade earlier. She remembered expressing her impatience to one of her nieces, Cristina's daughter Marilén:

> I said to Marilén, "I can't remain quiet [any longer]. Let's make noise…and walk with the pots." Marilén said to me, "Let's." [So] I grabbed my little kids, the three of them, and we went out with a pot. "Pah, pah, pah." All the little kids from next door followed me. The youth went out. Marilén went out. All the people on this block left their houses, following me.…I am never going to forget it because I made it happen. …Nobody, nobody was doing anything, and I went out into the street, grabbed my pot, and went out banging it outside…in the middle of the street, alone. With Marilén. And with the little girls. And the people started to leave their houses.…We covered all of La Bandera walking. And with chants. Against Pinochet. Against hunger.

Thousands of people in La Bandera joined Valeria and Marilén as they traversed the four sectors of the *población*. Later that night, the march took on a life of its own, with a fight occurring when the crowd neared the police station. Many other marches occurred in the following months.

As the protests gained momentum and coordination, strategy in La Bandera revolved around controlling space: creating a free zone from which police could be kept out. Leaders did this by controlling roads and blocking traffic at the borders of the *población*. Marcos, whose sister Serena participated in our history workshop, was a youth leader in the 1980s. He remembered, "At the beginning, they marched through the streets, they stopped the traffic…and the idea always was that the buses not run. Because if the buses didn't run and there was a stoppage…there wasn't any production. And this fundamentally affected the regime." The centrality of roads in both control and rebellion politicized all the boundaries of the *población* and made Américo Vespucio, La Bandera's northern boundary, a central arena of conflict. Those who ran the protests hoped to battle police at the periphery while maintaining the internal area free for cultural activities. In Marcos' words,

> At ten in the morning…people started to…go to Américo Vespucio.…People began to gather to protest… to occupy the streets.…And inside it was a different atmosphere. It was like…a holiday.…There were people who were playing ball, there were *compadres* that were playing guitar…while those who wanted to fight…could go to Américo Vespucio.…And they also organized a series of *ollas comunes*…to have a recreational afternoon.

Highly organized, the protest days involved a series of linked events, including street theater, volunteer work, and political graffiti, attended by those who could not get to work because of the blocked roads and stopped transportation. The activities drew La Bandera's many organizations into a coordinated strategy.

Although a broad segment of the residents participated in activities during the day, it was in the evenings that the youth went out to the large road Américo Vespucio to burn barricades, seal off the *población*, and battle with police. On these nights, the banging of pots, the noise bombs, and the shouting of slogans ripped through the night air. The sounds of protest were matched only by the noise of repression from the military: tear gas, water cannons, detentions, and live ammunition. "When they came to stop the protests [and] the bonfires, the military and the police...arrived shooting," said Marcos's girlfriend Marisol, who was a university student at the time. Participants in the protests took risks in hopes of ending the military government. They expected that by ousting the dictator they would resolve many of the problems they faced. "The people didn't have [anything to lose], since they already didn't have anything to eat," said Marisol. "And there was born another slogan: 'On only bread, on only tea, that's how we are with Pinochet.' And it was true. All of us felt identified with that slogan because bread and tea, bread and tea, that is what we ate.... There was a lot to protest about." The link between their economic hardship and military rule seemed clear.

If the entire three-year period was known as the *protestas,* the strategy and character of the activities changed over the years. Marisol described the difference between 1983 and 1986 as the "degree of organization." In 1983, "the masses went out into the street...because they had a lot of anger. And they went out without anything. They went out just to shout.... And one grabbed whatever was on the way—grab a fence, grab a stone, and put it in the street." In 1986, in contrast, community organizations anticipated the protests. Marisol explained, "And so they organized. You go there, you go here, in this house we'll gather, we need this, we need that,...we have to bring a doctor. In the human rights commission... they have a telephone nearby to call the doctors, we need to have a radio to know what is happening on the other side."[16] "That's the fundamental difference," she concluded. It was the degree to which they were organized. Not all of La Bandera's residents participated in these activities. However, the massive numbers of people out on the streets engaging in protest were sufficient to give La Bandera a reputation as one of the most highly mobilized *poblaciones* in Santiago.

CONCLUSION

Chapters 1 and 2 have shown that the history of the *población* La Bandera was structured by collective action. From land seizures to popular organizations to protests, La Bandera gained a reputation for being a highly mobilized *población*.

But if collective action permeates the history of the *población*, the *forms* collective action took shifted as the political context was transformed. In the late 1960s, the chief avenues of organization were housing committees and land seizures. Under an economic model of import-substitution industrialization and the compromise state, organizations put pressure for public services on a state that had the intention, if not the wherewithal, to fulfill some of their needs. Political parties of

the Left were key vehicles for these movements. In the Frei and especially the Allende years, broad-based social movements gave cultural emphasis to the idea that
pobladores were protagonists in Chilean society.

All that changed with the onset of the military government. In the context of
severe hunger and poverty arising from the new neoliberal economic model, residents created survival organizations such as common kitchens and groups of the
unemployed. These organizations operated clandestinely because of repression
and fear. They also needed to function independently of the state, with financing
from international solidarity organizations or nongovernmental organizations, or
with locally generated funds, because the state had retreated from spending
money on social services. The organizations were not oriented toward making demands on the state, since the military government had no mechanism for negotiating with popular sectors.

When economic conditions became desperate and the opposition began to
gain some strength in the early 1980s, the old survival organizations took on a new
significance. Here, cultural centers, community kitchens, and human rights
groups became nodes in a network of organizations bringing people out on a mass
scale to delegitimize the regime. The networks were coordinated city- and nationwide. Knowing they would not be able to get adequate responses from a military
government, leaders sought to destabilize the regime through widespread rebellion. The form of organization, and the strategy, had changed once again.

The health group Llareta exemplified these processes. When the group began
in 1984, its members were initially interested in providing emergency health services, at a time when the state had retreated from public health expenditures and
people in poor urban neighborhoods were being repressed. But its role went beyond offering immediate aid as its purpose transformed. Amid the protests of the
1980s, the leaders in the health group became part of a massive movement to fight
the dictatorship. Over time the group reduced its emphasis on social service provision (though this remained part of its activity) and oriented its activities toward
providing education about public health and launching a critique of political
economy. Through their activities and education, health promoters came to believe that not just the organization of public health services but the neoliberal economic model itself affected their own and their community's well-being.

Having looked at the shifting strategies of grassroots organizations from the
1960s to the 1980s, it is time to examine the transition to democracy. How did national politics change in the movement toward political democracy? And how did
the strategies of La Bandera's community organizations transform? To answer
these questions, it is necessary to look closely at the end of the protest period and
the onset of the negotiated transition.

CHAPTER THREE

Transition to Democracy

April 16, 1991
Población La Bandera
Marisol's house, second meeting of the history workshop

We continue to discuss the periods into which we might divide La Bandera's history. The exercise becomes particularly difficult as we debate how to understand the late 1980s.

Gordon: Are you saying that after 1987 was one period or more?

Serena: I'm going to [say] one long period. Of dialogue, more than anything. From '87 on.

Julia: Dialogue.

Diego: It started like that. . . . Already there wasn't such a direct fight, like a demonstration by the people against the dictatorship. The people already began to be pacified, and the armchair politicians. . . of the Left began to create a campaign, began to form committees, of the large organizations. Where there were political parties of the Left, they began to make themselves more visible, they began to come to agreements with the government, with the ministers and things. They began to seek agreements, arrived at by way of the very same [Pinochet's] constitution. And they began to see that there was the plebiscite of YES and NO. Afterward they produced this thing of rejection *(rechazo)* and afterward the presidential elections. Now we are with the Aylwin government.

Julia: So are we now in the same period?

Diego: No, it's changed. It's changed, not totally, but. . . it's complicated.

. . .

Laura: It's that—look. It's as if in '87 . . . was when you most saw the possibility of change. Because we were going to change the government. . . . But now, no. Because now we are in the '90s, and it's another period.

Julia: When did this period start?

Laura: When [Aylwin] took office....

Julia: In 1990.

Laura: In 1990.

Serena: Right. I think the people...now are more calm. [They] think that with the government of Aylwin everything was solved. So now there aren't so many demonstrations...now there is only work for the organized people.

Diego: It's...mostly the people of the *población* whom the dictatorship didn't affect, they [feel] relaxed, understand? My very own parents, we have never had problems....a brother held prisoner, a brother dead, or me, or my dad, nothing, understand? So...my old man and old lady are pacified....They go along with...the changes.

[The politicians] found a way, and they arrived at an objective. That is what we're in now. But there were many other paths that they proposed at the time. Different paths, but more complicated to analyze. But now we are in a period that is not really like that. There are still a lot of problems. And above all for the people that the dictatorship really affected. That is, those who have *compañeros* who are prisoners, those who have *compañeros* who are dead, those who have *compañeros* who are arrested, disappeared, executed, all of that. All these people are the ones that still continue fighting. So [you] speak with people that couldn't care less *(no están ni ahí)* and you say to them, "What do you think of those who are dead that they found in some place [wrapped in] plastic?" [here he is referring to the corpses of the executed and disappeared found in mass graves]. "Ayyyy, *no estoy ni ahí*, they go around making nothing but trouble in the city center those people," [they say]. And now that we are in the government of Aylwin, and now that we have everything, it's like they've covered their eyes. That [with] Aylwin everything is beautiful. It's over.

Laura: It's as if they all go around fighting to get rid of the dictatorship, and now it's like we're left with nothing but this.

Diego: One begins to ask oneself, What happens from here on out? We are in a government of transition to democracy and everything. But what happened before this? You can't forget what happened....On paper the truth is written, in the Rettig Report. An official truth. But...they died and you [can't] forget. We have to, I don't know—we have to do something for those persons.

Gordon: And what appeared to be taking out the dictatorship appears now as the opposite....We've heard this a lot. That what was previously seen as a success...to get rid of the dictatorship, now seems like a continuation of the same system.

Laura: What they want is what they have always said. Forgive and forget.

Julia: So here we have '80 to '83 as preparation. '83 to '86 as the very strong protests. '87 to '90 dialogue. And '90 and on?

Diego: Transition. Supposedly.

Laura: In quotation marks.

Diego: The protected democracy.... Protected in the sense of rights.... Protected...because the *compadres* are all trying to hide themselves, those who killed...they are trying to... [get] pardon. So it's not an open democracy, understand?

Gordon: Limited...

Diego: Restricted. A democracy with[in] limits.

DEMOBILIZATION

By the time I arrived in La Bandera, the land seizures of the 1960s, the survival organizations of the 1970s, and the protests of the 1980s were mostly memories. In 1991, the *población* was littered with the remnants of former community groups: old murals cracking and fading along outside walls; closed doors of cultural centers that no longer functioned; the noteworthy absence of any commemoration, like a *velatorio* (candle lighting along the streets) on anniversaries of important events. Women recalled days when they had been so busy participating in organizations that they spent little time at home or with their families. For the first time in many years they were now paying attention to their medical problems, earning some money, learning a vocation. In the words of community leaders, those who withdrew from social organizations had "returned to their houses."

To say that community organizations had closed and collective action declined is not to imply that organizational life had shut down completely. In the early 1990s, newly elected boards of the neighborhood councils took office, displacing a directorate that had been appointed by the authoritarian regime. Social organizations such as senior citizens' clubs functioned in the neighborhood council building; a collective kitchen continued to operate; and in the Catholic chapel, the nun ran a reflection group and a Christian base community continued to meet weekly. Anniversary celebrations for La Bandera took place in January 1991 and 1992, with the exiled 26 de enero leader Pelusa returning from Spain to visit on one occasion. These events and some community organizations continued to function.

Nor did the decline in organized activities mean that in 1991 there were no signs of social life in La Bandera. In the dirt open squares of the fourth sector, one could find old men playing cards, children dancing in circle games, or young people kicking a soccer ball. In the evenings, people of all ages gathered to watch children play volleyball on a lighted court, and nearby, teenagers crowded into a room to play pinball and pool. During the summer, when the heat made it unbearable to go out before sundown, people congregated outside in the evenings. On those long summer nights, a woman on one of the blocks fried potatoes over an open fire in her front patio, and teenagers gathered, chatting as they waited for the food to cook. On three summer evenings in 1991, preteenagers held outdoor performances. Imitating their favorite stars, they lip-synched rock lyrics while dancing on a hand-built stage. Adults and children gathered to watch and applaud.

But when summer had passed, the dirt roads were nearly empty at night, as families stayed in their own homes watching television. At night, young men roamed in groups, drinking and carrying knives, disappearing over fences and into houses at the sight of police. On those nights when I came home late, I walked up the road quickly and hurried into the house. During the daytime, one could see people outside going and coming from their obligations. Women made their way to the market carrying their white bags empty and returning with them weighted down with purchases, children in their blue uniforms walked to school, cutting across littered fields, and adults waited at the curbs of large avenues to take buses to work. Aside from the young men standing on the street corners, the long roads were mostly traversed, not used for socializing. A sense of public activity in the streets had diminished, according to residents, and despite the small groups that continued to meet or the efforts by community leaders to jump-start activities, La Bandera's culture of collective action had declined.[1]

In addition to the lack of public events and the waning of collective activity, the kind of street mobilization shown in the protest era was also absent, with one notable exception. On an unforgettable evening in 1991, residents of La Bandera poured out of their houses into the streets. Teenagers set fire to dozens of tires scattered along the roads, and thousands of people advanced en masse toward a major intersection at the edge of the *población*. En route and once at its destination, the crowd shouted slogans and waved banners. When a pharmacy was broken into, police dispersed the crowd with a barrage of tear gas, sending people running in all directions. After four relatively quiet years, when mass mobilization was not common, it was remarkable to see a reenactment of the protests of the 1980s: the pouring of people into the street, the lighting of tires and blocking of traffic, the battle with police. The event showed that even after the political transition, residents of La Bandera had retained the capacity for massive action, the cultural practices of ritualized expression, and the collective memory of what it meant to mobilize.

While this demonstration resembled the protests of the 1980s in some respects, it also differed in fundamental ways. This was not a political protest but a celebration of a Chilean soccer team's victory in the Latin American championship. While the game went on, teenagers would run into the street after every goal, jump into the air and chant team songs, then run back into their houses to see the rest of the game on television. After Colo Colo (the Chilean soccer team) had won, hundreds of people crowded outside, filling the street from curb to curb, hopping on top of cars, jumping up and down with their arms around each others' shoulders, and singing the Colo Colo cheer.

The Colo Colo celebration demonstrated that forms of shared expression cultivated in earlier periods were still embedded in collective memory and practice. Coalescing around popular events like the soccer victory, these forms of collective action had become detached from an overtly political movement. The Colo Colo celebration contrasted with public reaction to key political events such as the presentation of the Rettig Report (the government investigation on human rights violations), the eighteenth anniversary of the military coup, and International

Women's Day. On those occasions, few people went outside, and the only lights visible in La Bandera were from the glowing televisions in every house. No candles were lit, and no marches traversed the *población* streets.[2] A lone exception in years of demobilization, the Colo Colo celebration underscored the fact that in the post-dictatorship period, moments of massive collective expression only rarely occurred.

Residents of La Bandera—both community leaders and the nonorganized—commented on the lack of activity in the 1990s compared with La Bandera's politically vibrant past. To my surprise, in La Bandera—a place that experienced severe repression under the dictatorship—in the 1990s I noticed much nostalgia for the military years. Community leaders remembered the 1980s as a time when people had cooperated and shown solidarity with each other, and when they felt as if their lives had a purpose. They remembered the dictatorship as a time when the opposition commanded respect, and when the urban poor had taken part in social action. They recalled the military years, too, as a time when the link between the government and the economic model was evident, and when the political goal—overthrowing the dictatorship—was clear. After the change to an elected civilian government, in contrast, community leaders explained that they felt abandoned by political parties, disconnected from broader social movements, and isolated from their neighbors. They reported feeling that their lives had less meaning and that they experienced a sense of loneliness and lack of purpose. For people who were not community leaders but who had joined in the cultural activities during the protests, democracy brought isolation, individualism, and no small degree of boredom.[3] Both leaders and community members who had been active during the dangerous period of dictatorship looked back wistfully on the years of military rule.

These feelings of nostalgia for the past could be heard in the words of Isabel and Marta, two young sisters-in-law who lived in La Bandera. The women, their husbands, their children, and their in-laws shared a three-bedroom house in the *población*. In the early 1990s, neither Isabel nor Marta participated in any community organizations. They rarely left their house, it seemed, except to visit relatives, take their children to school, and work at the *feria* (outdoor market).

When they described the street and their activities during the 1980s, both women portrayed a social life in the *población* and a sense of their own activity within it that contrasted with their current reality. "I wasn't as quiet before. I also went out," said Isabel. She described the street activities during the protests: "We made campfires out here in front, we made tremendous bonfires; we burned sticks and chairs.... So the cops arrived where they saw the bonfires and a group, and started to throw [tear gas] bombs.... All of us crying ([because the bomb] makes you cry),... eating lemons, putting on salt, a handkerchief, or wetting it, and breathing.... It was great." "Great?" I asked her, picturing the stinging and gasping sensations produced by tear gas, the deafening sound of noise bombs, the fear of being shot by police. But Isabel insisted, "I liked to go out to the protests." "Mostly to enjoy myself," she said. "For fun," added Marta.

Marta explained that the appeal of the protests was not only the enjoyment of socializing but also the sense of solidarity that emerged among neighbors: "I did it because my mom and various neighbors were there, so we were all the same.... if something happened—all of us united.... if a person bought a drink, we drank it between all of us here, even if it were a little....everyone had some." Marta characterized the mid-1980s as a time when social relations in the *población* were strong, when residents shared their meager possessions, and when there was a sense of equality and an ethic of solidarity among neighbors. She contrasted that to the present. "Now...no," she continued, "because now a person buys a drink and you drink it alone and that's it." In her view, the sense of mutual support that had characterized the protest years had disappeared by the early 1990s.

The solidarity they experienced was not only informal—expressed, for example, in sharing a drink—but also actively organized. The women remembered community meetings in which neighbors gathered to talk through their problems, register their children to receive Christmas toys from the *unidad vecinal,* and plan meals *(onces)* out on the street. As Marta described these events, she again contrasted the activities during the 1980s to the lack of organization in the 1990s. "Here, before, [neighbors] closed the...three corners [of the street],...they put a number of tables outside, and they gave *onces* to each child: a cup of milk...with bread or a piece of cake or a cookie...Now this isn't done." Like the community *onces,* even assisting neighbors in need was organized. Marta explained, "Before... [people] helped the people that didn't have...I remember that sometimes the people were in very bad shape; they didn't have anything to eat...so everyone had a meeting and we got together things for this person, be it a little bit of groceries, or a little clothing." "But now, no," she continued. "Now, all the people are [like] ...it doesn't matter what's happening to the neighbor." These forces supporting community organization in the 1980s overcame some of the distrust and individualism present in that period. They were strong enough to involve in community events even women who were otherwise politically uninvolved and who, a few years later, would rarely leave their homes.

While nonorganized women like Isabel and Marta missed the protest era because of the social relations they had enjoyed, community leaders like the members of Llareta had their own reasons for longing for aspects of life during the dictatorship. Health promoters could plainly see that in the 1990s, as before, they and their neighbors faced a host of problems. Hunger, low incomes, unemployment, inadequate housing, and insufficient health care persisted from the days of military rule. But while living conditions remained miserable, the political climate for organizing had deteriorated. Popular organizations had closed down or continued to hang on by a thread, and overall mobilization was low. With the lack of robust organizations, there was less collective power with which to address ongoing harsh realities.

Health group member Sonia was impatient with the lack of public outcry against poor living conditions and inadequate public policies. She voiced her frustration at the absence of publicly expressed anger toward events that impacted the *población.* When I asked her if the protesting during the dictatorship had succeeded in lowering the prices of food, she conceded that it had not. Residents knew that, under a military regime, their protests would not affect government policies. But the shouting had another significance, she said. It was an opportunity for people to express their outrage. Her words suggest that the ability to publicly and collectively articulate anger had a more enduring importance than momentary emotional expression. Implicitly, it affirmed the premise that the poor had the right to a decent quality of life, it solidified their collective identities as *pobladores,* it sustained the ability to engage in coordinated mass action, it claimed the space of the *población* as an arena for political action, and it held out the hope of someday achieving change. In the 1990s, when people no longer expressed their frustration collectively and publicly, these other elements, too, had been lost.

The declining mobilization evidenced in La Bandera and articulated by these women reflects contradictions inherent in military rule. On the one hand, the dictatorship had created the conditions for distrust and division: it cultivated fear, a sense of surveillance, and the uncertainty of not knowing whom to trust. As described in chapter one, during the years of military rule, many people stopped talking to those they did not know. Residents, particularly women, described being afraid to leave their houses. The years of military rule were also a time when individualism born of consumerism flourished, especially during the economic boom. On the other hand, in a *población* like La Bandera, which had a long history of mobilization, the dictatorship generated conditions for revitalizing a culture of collective action. There were times during military rule when women worked together in *ollas comunes,* teenagers held summer camps *(colonias urbanas)* for young children, cultural centers operated, and political parties were active. Ironically, to a certain extent the dictatorship created the context in which a sense of common purpose among residents could thrive, and relationships could develop among neighbors.

In contrast to the years of military rule, collective action appeared to decline in the 1990s. The closing of community organizations and the decline in public activities occurred at a time of purported political opening, when freedom of expression and politics might be expected to resume. This paradox is central to contemporary Chilean democracy. It compels us to ask: What kind of democracy was installed in Chile such that it would lead to reduced social interaction and diminished political activity in the post-dictatorship period? Why would a political system that would presumably open space for political expression oversee its demise?

Answering these questions requires first considering the political context of the transition. In the mid-1980s the military regime came under pressure not only from popular protests but also from powerful international forces, including the U.S. government, and some in the Chilean business sector. These interests shared an analysis that a formal transition to democracy would both limit social conflict and help sustain the economic changes undertaken during the dictatorship. In fact, the maintenance of the basic economic model was a key feature of the transition. By the 1990s, after the economy had already been fundamentally restructured and the labor movement debilitated, the economic program instituted by Pinochet's regime gained legitimacy from being administered by an elected government.

To identify political and economic continuities between the military and civilian periods is not to say that nothing changed; nor is it to say that dictatorship and democracy are essentially equivalent. It is to argue, drawing on Sally Falk Moore's (1987a) processual approach to ethnography, that movement over time does not necessarily signify change. Instead of transforming, things may well be kept the same. The operative verb here is *kept*, for it is important not to attribute lack of change to mere continuity. Rather, what appears to be stasis may in fact be the result of active processes of maintenance. In the case of Chile, changes in political regime—the movement from dictatorship to an elected-civilian political system— have been used to maintain economic and political structures.

That the neoliberal economic model was maintained after the military period does not mean that Aylwin's economic policies were identical to Pinochet's. As mentioned previously, Pinochet's economic project itself was transformed during the seventeen years he was in power. Upon taking office, the Aylwin government increased social spending in certain areas, particularly health and housing. These expenditures ameliorated some of the harshest free market measures taken by the military regime. The period from 1987 on also saw a significant decrease in the percentage of people in poverty as Chile's economy recovered from economic crisis in the early and mid-1980s (see Ruiz-Tagle 1996). However, the basic characteristics of the economic model—such as its reliance on export-generated income and foreign investment—were retained. As a consequence, the degree of inequality in Chilean society remained largely unchanged.[4]

In this context, the obstacles faced by community groups were not mere byproducts of political transition. Rather, demobilization was an intentional outcome of a transition negotiated between elite opposition politicians and the military. Their project of sustaining the economic model was premised on keeping both labor and neighborhood social movements—groups that might create demands for housing, public services, or higher wages—in check. The transition process was based on *"concertación,"* agreement and consensus, not with social movements (although this was initially stated as a goal) but with business, Chilean political elites, international financial institutions, and foreign trading partners. As social movements receded from their role as major social actors and were replaced by political elites, their demands receded from the public stage.

Because the political democracy was rooted in a framework devised by the military government, and because the politicians of the Concertación sought to limit mobilization, the new political situation presented community organizations with unprecedented and largely unforeseen dilemmas. In the 1980s citizens had demonstrated against the military regime. But after the inauguration of an elected government, it became difficult to protest. How, after all, could one attack officials one had personally voted into office? Furthermore, once the political figure blamed for widespread misery (Pinochet) had receded from center stage, against whom exactly would one protest? It now became more difficult to challenge the economic model because to do so would be to confront not key political figures but the anonymous bureaucrats and faceless technocrats who made administrative decisions. Given ongoing poverty and an elected political system in which the poor had little voice, the question for social organizations still functioning in the early 1990s became how to reformulate their approaches to politics. In the post-dictatorship period, what kind of strategies would be most effective for the type of political system that had emerged?

To understand the nature of the new political system, it is necessary to examine the processes that resulted in a negotiated transition in the late 1980s. This discussion requires us to look beyond local events in La Bandera. To gain insight into the transition, we must redirect our focus to political elites, the actors who displaced popular movements in bringing about political democracy. To that end, my historical narrative resumes where it left off: at the end of the protest period. That historical moment would be followed by a plebiscite, elections, and the official change of regime. It is this historical account of high-level negotiations that can begin to explain widespread demobilization and at the same time show the roots and character of contemporary Chilean democracy.

TRANSITION TO DEMOCRACY

When the national protests first began in 1983, mass mobilization had seemed to most opposition politicians across the political spectrum to be a viable approach to destabilizing and overthrowing the military regime (Puryear 1994, 79). Although party leaders in both coalitions initially supported the national protests, they did so for different reasons and with different outlooks for the future. The Democratic Popular Movement considered mass mobilization to be a viable process for over-throwing the dictatorship. In contrast, the Democratic Alliance viewed the protests as a tactical step. It hoped to use mobilization to pressure the military regime into negotiating a transition to democracy.[5]

Over time, the Democratic Alliance modified its perspective on mobilization. As the protests took on a life of their own, outside the control of politicians, they were seen not merely as a tactic but also as a threat. The protests had become concentrated in the *poblaciones* and universities, while professionals and members of the middle classes grew more mistrustful. To political party elites, the protests were not accomplishing their goal but were growing dangerously out of control. From this perspective, popular mobilization potentially had consequences beyond hastening a negotiated transition. The protests demonstrated that social movements had their own momentum and demands. They could constitute a power that could shape the resulting political system under democracy and challenge the economic status quo. The Democratic Alliance began to question what might occur after the military regime was supposedly defeated by a protest strategy.[6]

The failed assassination attempt on Pinochet in 1986 and the repression that followed convinced leaders of the Democratic Alliance political opposition to shift strategies. Sociologist José Joaquín Brunner, of the Nuñez branch of the Socialist Party, was central in articulating the new approach. In a memo written in September 1986, Brunner "sharply criticized the social mobilization strategy and proposed cutting ties with the hard-left Popular Democratic Movement, shifting emphasis from conflict to negotiations, and recognizing the conditions for transition established by the 1980 Constitution" (Puryear 1994, 107). The time had come, he was arguing, when mobilization no longer reaped political benefits. Indeed, it could be a detriment to achieving political change. The time had come to create a negotiated settlement with the military government.

Brunner's memo provoked heated debate among opposition politicians and eventually led to widespread criticism of mobilization strategy. In September and October 1986, political elites in the Democratic Alliance broke with the Democratic Popular Movement, purposefully distancing themselves from a popular rebellion strategy (Petras and Leiva 1988, 97).

The decision to abandon social mobilization dovetailed with pressure from Washington: Robert Gelbard, undersecretary of state for inter-American affairs, told political party leaders in August, after being in Chile during national mobilizations in June, that the Reagan administration "did not favor the tactics of 'social mobilization'" (Petras and Leiva 1988, 99). By October, therefore, the Reagan administration, the Pinochet dictatorship, and much of the oppositional parties' political elite were all convinced of the undesirability of popular mobilization.

With major opposition figures shifting approaches to ending the military regime, it became clear that the political transition would proceed not through the activity of broad-based social movements but through a series of negotiations among elites, ironed out within the military's constitutional framework. This decision to accept the military's constitution would prove to be decisive both for inaugurating the transition to democracy and for determining the kind of democracy to emerge.

Changes inside the Chilean Socialist Party that developed since the coup played an important role in the shift in strategy around the protests. So-called renovated sectors of the party would go on to play an important role in shaping the character of the transition. During the Popular Unity period, the Chilean Socialist Party sustained at least two competing ideologies. Salvador Allende backed an electoral strategy for bringing socialism to Chile. Given his commitment to working within political institutions, Allende had a contradictory relationship with social movements. On the one hand, occupation of land by urban squatters, seizures in the countryside by peasants, and takeovers of factories by workers fulfilled his goal of building "popular power." On the other hand, Allende needed to constrain these movements in order to preserve his political support in Congress. This ambivalent relationship with social movements constituted a central dilemma of his presidency (Winn 1986). In contrast, the left wing of the Chilean Socialist Party backed popular rebellion outright. It advocated armed revolution to bring about a socialist society.

From the mid-1970s into the 1980s, the landscape of Socialist Party ideology changed and the common ground between its factions deteriorated. In 1979, the party split in two. During the protest era, the Socialist Party–Almeyda joined the Democratic Popular Movement in supporting popular mobilization to end the dictatorship. It sustained a trenchant critique of the economic model in Chile. In contrast, the Socialist Party–Altamirano (or Socialist Party–Nuñez) took a very different stance. It came to reject Marxism-Leninism and set its sights on political democracy (Walker 1991, 453). These "renovated socialists," as they called themselves, had reworked their political and economic ideas sufficiently to back a negotiated transition strategy by the mid-1980s.

The process of rethinking the past and reconsidering strategies for the future began at the time that exiled Chilean intellectuals and politicians formed party networks in the European countries in which they had sought refuge. Focused on sorting out their frightening experience of torture and human rights abuses in Chile, they deliberated recent Chilean history and debated the causes of the 1973 military coup. Over time, many of the exiles came to interpret the military takeover as not simply a brutal act by fascist political opponents but the result of strategic political mistakes made by their own party during the period of Popular Unity. They faulted Allende for not safeguarding the support of the middle classes while the popular sectors radicalized, for creating an economic plan that heightened inflation and sent the economy into chaos, and for not taking advantage of opportunities to strengthen a relationship with the Christian Democrats while there was still a chance of saving the political system. This self-blame, the reflection on the causes of the coup, and willingness to question their own past paved the way for a dramatic transformation in political ideology.

While they were debating Chilean history, the exiles also were observing the societies around them. Chilean socialists exiled in Eastern Europe (mainly the USSR, Romania, and East Germany, where the Chilean Socialist Party had its headquarters) quickly grew disillusioned with the very political systems they had once idealized (Silva 1992, 10–11). While Socialist Party members living in Eastern Europe were critiquing actually existing socialism, Chilean exiles living in Western Europe were becoming intrigued with European-style social democracy. These Chileans, living primarily in Italy and France, credited European social democracy with improving living conditions of the working classes (Silva 1992, 11). They began to embrace the idea of creating a mixed, rather than exclusively socialist, economy (Silva 1992, 19–20).

It was through these experiences in European countries and reevaluations of Chile's authoritarian period that exiled Socialist Party leaders fundamentally transformed their political ideology. The change in thinking constituted a major paradigm shift. In the words of Chilean political scientist Manuel Antonio Garretón, they came to believe that "the real choice was not between 'socialism' and 'fascism,'" as they had held before, "but rather between military dictatorship and a political democracy" (quoted in Walker 1991, 452). Now the primary categories were no longer economic but political.

The shift is starkly evident in the changing language of Socialist Party statements. A resolution from the Socialist Party Congress of 1971 exemplifies the philosophy that prevailed before the military coup: "The Socialist Party reaffirms its *class-based politics* and stresses the need of the leadership of the working class in the *battle of economic and social liberation* which the working masses and other *exploited, oppressed sectors* are now deploying *against the bourgeoisie and...imperialism* [emphasis added]."[7] In this statement from the Popular Unity period, "class-based politics" and "economic...liberation" against exploitation by the "bourgeoisie" are the central preoccupations. It is a politics rooted in (Marxist) economic analysis.

By the late 1970s and early 1980s, renovated Socialists were framing their politics not as an economic project but as a political project that repudiated all kinds of dictatorship, be it of the Right or the Left. Significantly, they included in this category not only Pinochet's authoritarian regime but also the "dictatorship of the proletariat" implicit in the Marxism-Leninism their party had long advanced.

The critique of Marxism and the focus on human rights led the renovated Socialists to hold political democracy as their primary goal. Those who had once dismissed formal democratic institutions as "bourgeois" now prized them as an end in themselves. They redefined socialism to mean the "*profundización* (deepening) of political democracy" (Walker 1991, 455). While many would hold that democracy required the eradication of poverty, the leveling of inequality, and the provision of social services, the Socialist Party's project was now centered on the creation of formal democratic institutions. These principles were articulated years later by prominent Socialist Jorge Arrate (1991, 52): "We are fully committed to Chilean democracy, to the *reestablishment of a full democratic system in Chile. That is the main principle* under which we place the other purposes or objectives of the party [emphasis added]." Achieving political democracy, with its formal institutions, had become the centerpiece of Chilean socialism.

When renovated Socialist Brunner and Christian Democrat Aylwin urged their fellow coalition members to discontinue a popular mobilization strategy, they had an alternative political approach in mind. These politicians were increasingly convinced that the way to end the dictatorship and achieve political democracy would be through negotiations with the military itself.

When it started negotiating in 1983, the Democratic Alliance had a relatively ambitious agenda. It called for "the end to exile, legalization of political parties, bringing back those in internal exile, end to the detained-disappeared, [and] access to television" (Otano 1995, 16). The Democratic Alliance politicians presented political demands that aimed equally high. They insisted that the military dictatorship come to an immediate end, that a "provisional" government be installed, that a "Constituting Assembly" draft a new constitution, and that there be free elections for president and all members of Congress (Moulian 1997, 307). By proposing

Pinochet's immediate exit and reform of the Constitution, the Democratic Alliance politicians were taking a firm stand—one that Pinochet could and would easily reject. Opposed to any change in the Constitution, the general refused their proposal outright, and the first negotiations ended abruptly.

As time wore on and Pinochet did not budge, the Democratic Alliance adopted a set of agreements that accepted Pinochet's constitution and created a political system deeply embedded in Pinochet's own institutionality. This fact is crucial, for the later agreements—the ones that stuck—shaped the subsequent political system known today as Chilean democracy. The critical decision made by the Alliance was to stop rejecting the Constitution and debating its legitimacy. Instead, opposition politicians accepted the Constitution as a fact, and decided to try to take advantage of opportunities for political transition embedded within it.

On the basis of this change in position, the Democratic Alliance resolved to forgo hopes of direct elections in 1988. Instead, it decided to participate in the schedule laid out in the 1980 Constitution, which provided for a plebiscite on a single candidate. The plebiscite became a nationwide referendum that would determine whether Pinochet was to remain in power for another eight years. If the SI (yes) vote for Pinochet were to win, Pinochet would retain the presidency. But if the NO were to win, the Constitution stated, Chile would hold free presidential elections. Opposition politicians decided to take the gamble. Perhaps by running an effective political campaign, they could convince more than half the Chilean population to vote NO in the plebiscite, which would give them a shot at winning the presidency in free national elections. Maybe, just maybe, they calculated, they could beat Pinochet at his own game.

The decision to participate in the plebiscite was not heralded universally on the Left. Members of the Democratic Popular Movement initially objected to this idea. They saw the electoral campaigns as legitimating the military's constitution and perpetuating Pinochet's institutions. Yet they were also influenced by the new electoral ethic sweeping the country. The ambivalence can be seen in the changing stance of the Communist Party, which initially asked its adherents to annul their vote in the plebiscite by marking the lines for both "approve" and "reject" on their ballots.[8] As the plebiscite drew nearer, and after sustained debate and influence by polls showing that the NO could win, the party changed its position and instructed its members to vote NO against Pinochet.

Disagreement and shifting positions on the Left not withstanding, political events were rapidly moving toward a plebiscite as a means to a negotiated transition. In February 1988, the political opposition created the "Concertación de Partidos por el No," an entity that "linked more than fifteen parties and movements (not including the Communists) in a common effort to win a 'no' vote in the impending plebiscite" (Collier and Sater 1996, 379). This was a historic first in Chile, for the Socialist Party was now in an electoral coalition not with the Communist Party but with the Christian Democrats, thereby creating a strong center-Left. Still potentially outlawed from participating in congressional elections by a constitutional provision that prohibited parties that advocated class conflict, and not wanting to give official recognition to the 1980 Constitution, the Socialist Party created an "instrumental" party, the Party for Democracy (PPD), to participate in the elections. The political parties of the Concertación were united in the belief that a coalition held together by consensus and *concertación* could create a stable transition.

The highly creative NO campaign bore fruit. To General Pinochet's surprise and alarm, the opposition won the plebiscite—although the fact that Pinochet received 43 percent of the vote indicated that he continued to have significant support. In the following year came the long-sought free elections for president. Three candidates ran: Pinochet's finance minister, Hernán Büchi, on the Right, businessman Javier Errázuriz ("Fra Fra") for the Union of the Center Center, and Christian Democrat Patricio Aylwin as the head of the Concertación coalition. In virtually the same proportion as the Concertación had received in the plebiscite, Aylwin won with 55 percent of the vote. The opposition had succeeded in voting the dictator out of office under his own rules of the game. For the first time in seventeen years, Chile had an elected civilian president.

Yet the following months would reveal deeply entrenched characteristics of the military regime still embedded in the new political system. This should have been evident to anyone who had watched the transition process closely, but at the time it was hard to see amid the ebullient celebrations of an official end to military rule. Political democracy had been achieved through negotiations with the military, within the military's own constitution, and by sustaining its institutions. Although Aylwin formally replaced Pinochet as president, Pinochet's legacy continued to shape Aylwin's presidency.

One of the best ways to understand the continuities between dictatorship and democracy is to listen to the words of Socialist José Joaquín Brunner, who, as noted earlier, was an architect of the negotiation strategy. In one article, Brunner (1990) suggested that rather than being seen as a single process, the transition should be understood as a series of interlocking pacts between the opposition and the military regime.[9] They include a *constitutional pact*, in which the political opposition accepted Pinochet's 1980 Constitution; a *party pact*, in which the Concertación agreed to work within Pinochet's institutional framework; an *electoral and governmental pact*, in which groups would compete for the presidency and congressional seats within the unfavorable electoral laws established by Pinochet; and an *institutional pact*, which guaranteed the armed forces that the transition would occur within existing institutional arrangements. Rather than foster substantial change, each pact maintained aspects of the military's institutionality within the subsequent political democracy.

Because of these pacts, the regulations and institutions under which democracy would operate were to a large extent shaped by the military regime itself. Before leaving the presidency, Pinochet named members to the Supreme Court, designed electoral laws to favor his candidates, appointed senators (Pinochet himself would become a senator-for-life in 1998), and made the Constitution especially difficult to change. The Concertación government was formally constrained in the kinds of laws it could advance, limited by the votes of nonelected senators who, along with the Right, constituted a majority in the Senate, and curtailed by the constitution from straying from Pinochet's path.

Not only would Pinochet's institutions live on, but the former dictator himself would play a central role in the new political system. He would remain head of the army until the year 1998. In this ongoing capacity as military leader, Pinochet guaranteed that policies favorable to the armed forces, business, and the political right wing would succeed by keeping ever-present the threat of military intervention. For example, in response to accusations against his son's financial activities, in December 1991 General Pinochet declared an *acuartelamiento*, in which he placed the armed forces on alert. I vividly recall Concertación politicians appearing on television that evening. Looking nervous, they assured the public there was nothing to worry about, that everything was under control. The military threat sent repercussions around the world, and the European news media reported that a coup had occurred in Chile. These reports were wrong: no such thing had taken place, and the crisis soon ended. But the incident made the indelible point that former dictator Pinochet retained a powerful position in the country. Later that point was reinforced when the military appeared in the streets in May 1993 following calls for trials of perpetrators of human rights violations. Although Pinochet had allowed himself to be elected out of office, and although formal democratic institutions were installed in the country, his institutional arrangements were perpetuated by political agreements and backed by threat of military force.

For all the continuities in Pinochet's institutional framework and his own ongoing presence in political life, perhaps nothing better secured the legacy of the dictatorship and shaped the ensuing political system than a fifth pact, a *pact of national development*. In this final pact, opposition politicians agreed to leave the basic economic model—characterized by an export-driven open economy, private and foreign investment, regulation by the market, an independent Central Bank, and protection of private property—intact. Under the pact, macroeconomic policies would be preserved, and neither domestic nor international investors would feel threatened.

Given the "pact of national development" at the basis of the negotiated transition, the economic model itself never became an explicit and contestable issue in the presidential election. Unlike Argentina, where the army went out in defeat (as the result of a military debacle in the Falklands Islands) and the economy was in shambles (gripped by hyperinflation), the Chilean economy was being described as an economic miracle in the late 1980s. Far from exiting in ignominy, Pinochet was credited with successfully transforming the Chilean economy into a leader for the world. Noting the economy's success, all three presidential candidates supported the existing economic model. Although their precise policies and frameworks varied—the Christian Democrats promised "growth with equity," for example—all of them sustained similar economic ideas: they backed neoliberalism, an export-oriented economy, and a free market economic approach.

To a large degree politicians supported the economic model because the fundamental changes had already taken place. The privatization of public services (education, health, social security), the selling off of state enterprises, privatization of publicly held land, deindustrialization, and the export of primary resources were by now deeply entrenched in the Chilean system. These practices were reinforced by international lending institutions such as the International Monetary Fund and the World Bank, hailed by the United States, and rewarded with foreign investment. When I told a sociologist in a Santiago research center in 1991 that I was thinking of attending a seminar on neoliberalism, he was quick to discourage me. Don't go, he said. That topic is boring; that debate has already passed. By the 1990s, the neoliberal economic system was securely in place. It had receded from public discourse as an issue of debate.

What was most striking was not the seeming entrenchment of the model and its solidification in pacts but the passion with which Christian Democrats and Socialists defended it. Some of these same figures and their political parties had been ardent critics of the model during the 1980s, when critiquing Pinochet's economic strategy had been a way to discredit his regime. Their critiques usually centered on the inequality the model had wrought. While macroeconomic indicators might show stunning success, they argued, there was an "underside" to the miracle, an "other side [to] modernization" (Tironi 1988, 11).

Yet by the 1990s, Concertación politicians' support for a neoliberal economic model—the same one previously faulted for producing inequality and poverty—was striking. The turnaround in economic principles was especially vivid among renovated Socialists, who, after rejecting Marxism-Leninism and supporting political democracy, had now become advocates for free market capitalism. A statement by prominent Socialist Party member Enrique Correa expresses the changes the political party went through: "The Socialist Party...represents a new way to be leftist...: The Socialists are moderate, democratic, *trust in the rules of the market*...no longer believing in statism and centralism, but rather in *a state which has only a regulating function and in an increasingly privatized economy* [emphasis added]."[10] The critique of capitalism that the Socialist Party had sustained in mobilizations during the late 1960s and early 1970s, and that it had used to discredit Pinochet's neoliberal project in the 1980s, was now supplanted by a very different economic vision. Renovated Socialists came to accept the free market, foreign investment, and international trade. Party members continued to call themselves Socialists, but their embrace of neoliberal economics gave the party a new economic and political ideology.

By 1990, then, the economic model had largely been pushed outside of the political arena. Because pacts and the constitution ensured continuities, what was on the table to vote on—what was open, therefore, to democratic contestation—had been circumscribed. Privatization—achieved by imposition under the military, not by democratic vote—had already taken place. Through privatization, decision making on important policy questions had largely moved to private firms and therefore outside the jurisdiction of state policy. The fact that international lending institutions conditioned foreign loans and investment on structural adjustment exacerbated the draining of economic decision making away from state, and therefore citizen, control. And the fact that Chilean politicians across the political spectrum had reached a consensus on economic matters meant that these issues were not contested in the elections. Combined, these processes meant that precisely when Chile and other Latin American countries were experiencing transitions to democracy, many of the crucial decisions that affected people's lives were not accessible to the influence of citizens. This fact fundamentally limited the scope and meaning of democracy.

DEMOBILIZATION REVISITED: THE TRANSITION IN LA BANDERA

In 1991 organizations in the *población* faced the challenge of not only redefining their work and analyzing the post-dictatorship reality but also sustaining participation by members facing pressures in their personal lives. The economic strains they faced at the time were not entirely new, but, combined with new political conditions, they made sustaining community organizations a challenge in the post-dictatorship period.

It was April 1991, a month after the end of summer vacation. Llareta had scheduled a meeting to plan a particularly important event: a training seminar for a new team of health promoters in the *población*. Because this would be the first time the health group had cosponsored a training program with the municipal health clinic, the health group's meeting was crucial to the seminar's success.

On the afternoon of the health group meeting, Valeria, Llareta's coordinator, walked to the scheduled meeting place—a small room in the Catholic chapel. Gordon, who participated with the health group that year, had also arrived, as had Eladio, Llareta's adviser from EPES. The time for the meeting came and went, but none of the other health promoters showed up. Eladio deliberated, then decided neither to cancel the meeting nor to hold it without everyone there. Instead, he suggested that they walk through the *población* looking for the health group members. When they got to each person's house, they would ask the health promoter to explain why she or he had not attended. As a popular educator, Eladio viewed this as an opportunity to situate the personal problems of each health group member within the political, social, and economic reality he or she was experiencing.

As they started their walk, Valeria, Eladio, and Gordon spotted Iván returning from an event with another community group. Talking with him, they determined that he had few problems attending health group meetings. With a steady job as an office clerk in an international church organization, supplemented by work as a food vender in the outdoor market, he was able to support his family. Involved in many grassroots organizations, he found that his biggest obstacle to participating in any given activity was time.

The situation for others in the group, all women and many of them heads of households, was quite different. Sonia invited the small group into her house when they arrived and offered them seats on the couch. Sonia, who was separated from her husband, had three children living at home and no permanent income. In order to care for her children, she had been doing piecework in her house. She had been sewing from noon to 3:00 A.M. for about twelve hundred pesos (four dollars) a day. In theory, contracting garment assembly out was an economic opportunity for women who could do it at home, in their "free time," without a fixed work schedule. Companies found it profitable because of low costs and the ability to hire workers only as needed. But in practice, Sonia found herself working long hours for little money and with no job security, benefits, or contract. She stopped sewing because her back hurt her and she considered the pay to be miserable.

What had the greatest impact on Sonia was the tension between her obligation to earn money and her commitments to participate in community organizations. In her view, she needed to work in the afternoons in order to feed her children. But she also needed to participate in the health group. She described the dilemma to Valeria, Eladio, Iván, and Gordon as if she were weighing the two obligations, trying to come to the right balance. It was a powerful statement about how important social organizations were to these community leaders, because what Sonia most wanted to do was be active in the health group. Yet despite her strong commitment to the group, and even though she had stopped working, on this occasion she could not attend the meeting. "It is bad enough when your children are hungry, but it is worse when they're hungry and you're not with them," she told the others. "I could not leave them here in the house alone."

Having left Sonia's home, the small group walked around the corner to Lili's house, a wooden structure in the shape of an "L," constructed over a dirt floor. Lili, her husband, and their sons slept in a single bedroom attached to the house they shared with other branches of the family. The bathroom, one of the *casetas sanitarias* built by the government with money contributed by the family, was detached and located across the dirt patio. The patio became soaked in the winter, creating a trail of mud as the children brought their wet feet back to bed.

Lili was home and, after welcoming the health group members in, explained her situation. She worked from four in the morning until three in the afternoon six days a week, selling vegetables at the outdoor market. When she was done, she had to be home to cook, clean, and care for her children, which made attending meetings difficult. But her obstacles were not just time and other obligations. Her husband had forbidden her to participate in the health group, and on those occasions when he discovered she had gone, he would beat her. She attended the meetings when she could but did so at the risk of inciting his rage.

Nearby, in a house set back from another dirt road, lived Ana, a young woman who also had problems with her husband, from whom she had separated. He provided no financial support for her and her five-year-old son. Meanwhile, Ana lived overcrowded with relatives, waiting for another housing site. Without any other source of income, she had taken up work doing surveys, which precluded her from regularly attending the meetings of the group.

Listening to these stories, Valeria reflected on her own situation. Her husband, Jorge, a bus driver, was unemployed. Without any steady income, the family of five often went without food; they lived on tea and bread when they could get them. Jorge spent long days looking for work—traveling to the houses of bus owners to seek employment, standing on line to get his documents renewed at the municipal building, studying for long-distance driving exams or a job as an auto mechanic; borrowing ties, shoes, a shirt, and disposable shavers on the rare occasions when he got interviews. When job prospects for bus driving were dim, he took whatever jobs he could find, walking the city for hours to get work installing heaters, doing carpentry, or fixing plumbing. When prospects in even the informal labor market were particularly bad, Jorge would sit in the back room of the house sewing soccer balls, work that ran in his family and that he found degrading, for it symbolized his failure to find work that used his skills. Valeria, meanwhile, was in school full-time, trying to eke out time for studying and attempting to stretch a limited scholarship to cover transportation and tuition. At the time, she was the only health promoter to be finishing her high school degree.

A number of health promoters were not home as the members of Llareta proceeded on their walk. They had medical problems in addition to economic obstacles. Angélica, burdened by chronic illness, had just gone into the hospital for an operation. Her husband was one of the few who had steady work. An *erradicado*, he commuted to the wealthy part of Santiago, where their squatters' settlement had been, to work as a guard in a building. Sandra, a single woman raising her niece, suffered from mental health problems. When she was not sick, she worked in a pharmacy. Mónica Janet had the most severe health difficulties of all. She was in the hospital, on the verge of dying of kidney disease complicated by a pregnancy. Her unborn baby was sure to be underweight. She considered the hospital conditions appalling, especially the rats running through the garbage scattered beneath the hospital's foundation. Mónica Janet and her family had to bring food, sheets, clothing, syringes, and medicine to the hospital, since those supplies were not provided. Mónica Janet had seen other kidney patients in her ward die of neglect and lack of medicine. Despite her illness, she had often walked long distances to get to health group meetings, but now it was not clear when she would be well enough to leave the hospital.

As Eladio, Valeria, Iván, and Gordon finished their trip around the *población*, they discussed the situation, concluding that the economic strains families were under had forced many women into low-paid work, created long-term health problems, and left little time for participating in community organizations. Economic conditions might not be as desperate as they had been during the peaks of economic crisis under the dictatorship, but on a day-to-day basis hunger and poverty persisted. Of course, most of the pressures that made participation difficult were not new to the 1990s. The expansion of low-wage, informal, flexible work was a key characteristic of the economic model developed under the military regime. But it had remained and in some ways intensified under the elected government.

The health group's analysis of its members' impediments to attending a meeting highlighted the economic and health constraints experienced by members. But there were political factors unique to the post-dictatorship period, such as the withdrawal of political parties from activity in popular sectors, that also contributed to the decline in social organizations in La Bandera. Parties of the Left had helped coordinate collective action throughout La Bandera's history. Appearing first in the land seizures and housing committees that formed the *población* in the late 1960s and early 1970s, they reemerged as important forces in the protest era of the 1980s. In the 1990s, however, the political parties that had formed the Democratic Popular Movement weakened significantly or lost their close connections with the grass roots. The MIR barely continued to exist, the left wing of the Socialist Party had split into competing factions, and the Communist Party, although not fully accepted by the Concertación coalition, had entered the realm of elite politics, straying far from its *poblacional* "base."

At the same time, few other political parties were making their presence felt in the *población*. Ironically, the one party with a grassroots organizing strategy was the right-wing Independent Democratic Union (UDI), which launched a number of land seizures around Santiago in the early 1990s. The *campamento* that health group member Ana finally became a part of after her *comité sin casa* gained land in 1992 had an Independent Democratic Union member as president. Concertación parties of the center and Left, in contrast, had distanced themselves from popular sectors. The Democratic Alliance's rejection of a mobilization strategy in the 1980s resulted in distance between political parties vying for power at the national level and social movements in urban popular sectors. In the new political scenario, local communities were useful to the extent that they could be depended on to vote, and in the 1990s political parties showed up in the *población* mostly to offer patronage jobs. For example, Diego, who participated in our local history workshop, found work in the central post office through the Socialist Party. One member of the health group was asked to work for the Party for Democracy (part of the Concertación), an offer she turned down. Grassroots organizing was not a priority for Concertación parties, which were more interested in "governability," "stability," and "consensus" at an elite level than in promoting social organizations. Having left organizing behind them, when political parties of the Concertación did appear in the *poblaciones*, it was to make small inroads into incorporating residents into their ranks.

Health group members also attributed people's retreat to their houses in the 1990s to the kind of organizational strategies chosen to overthrow the dictatorship. Although the first organizations to emerge after the onset of military rule were survival organizations, the types of actions taken during the 1980s are better characterized as "reivindicative" in that they placed demands on the state and denounced it for not meeting those demands. Organizations had been reivindicative in the late 1960s and early 1970s as well, as the movements for housing described in chapter 1 attest. But in that period, the state had a capacity to negotiate with popular social movements and found it in its interest to meet some of their demands. Moreover, strong political parties, active labor unions, local cultural centers, and vibrant ideological currents provided the opportunity for widespread political education.

In contrast, because the military regime would not negotiate with social movements, *poblador* organizations in the 1980s used demands for a different purpose. By making claims they knew would not be fulfilled, they sought to demonstrate the inadequacies of the state, assert people's rights, delegitimate the government, and contribute to overthrowing the dictator. This strategy was suited to the task of destabilizing a military regime, for it articulated discontent as a generalized experience and diminished the credibility of the regime internationally.

But the strategy of large-scale mobilizations and denunciation also had an impact on the long-term culture created in the *población*. In particular, it affected the kind of personal and political development people would carry with them after the military period came to an end. Valeria observed: "When you...do work that is...reivindicative, the only thing you wanted is...'Ah, we're going to march,... we'll denounce, we'll create a campaign.' But...now...we see that...we overthrew the dictator and these people went into their houses." Because political action during the military years was oriented toward getting masses of people into the streets for demonstrations, the political training that many individuals received was minimal. Moreover, because the goal was political democracy, once elections had come and gone the purpose of continuing to be active in organizations became unclear.

Valeria contrasted the limited political education that many residents of La Bandera received during the dictatorship with her own *formación*. She felt that she had been permanently transformed by her participation in popular education workshops and popular organizations. Since it was this political *formación* that health group members felt was missing in the neighbors who had retreated into their houses after the protest era, they sought to achieve it in their day-to-day practice of post-dictatorship organizing with women in the *población*.

Both Mónica Janet and Valeria were convinced that they needed to reach out to other women and bring them through a similar process of training. They saw this as especially vital because of the many ways in which poor women were beaten down: by the humiliation of working as servants, by domination by husbands, by disrespect in the society, and by economic hardship. It was a kind of organizational work that Valeria called *trabajo de hormigas*—as slow and steady as the work of ants—work that started with women where they were: with their pain, the violence they had experienced (particularly domestic abuse), their experience of humiliation, and their struggles with living in poverty.[11] The organizations would then work through those issues with them until they were able to transcend the forces beating them down and become actors.

These health group members believed that this kind of work would transform women, so that they could stand up for their rights and make demands in larger social and political systems. Because this was sure to be a slow process, it would require having long-term goals for social change. From Valeria's perspective, it might create some hope of achieving "in...fifteen more years...a government with popular support."

CONCLUSION

The beginning of this chapter posed two questions: What kind of democracy was installed in Chile such that it would lead to reduced social interaction and diminished political activity in the post-dictatorship period? And why would a political system that would presumably open space for political expression oversee its decline? This chapter has argued that by the 1990s change had occurred, but it was a change embedded less in a simple movement from dictatorship to democracy than in changing forms of power through which elements of the military's own economic and—to a degree—political project could be maintained. Sustaining that project required the demobilization of social movements, something that, ironically enough, could be accomplished more effectively by political democracy.

How, then, do we understand the ways in which power operates in the post-dictatorship political framework? What less brutal but equally compelling forms does power take? And how do social organizations in the *poblaciones* craft a response to these new forms of power?[12] It is with the goal of answering these questions that the next chapter examines the cultural and symbolic correlates of economic restructuring.

PART TWO

Ethnography of Democracy

Part one of this book gave a historical view of how political power had transformed over time and how the strategies of social movements had shifted under different political circumstances. Part two brings that question to bear on the post-dictatorship period in Chile. I ask how power operated in the early 1990s, when repression was not its key expression and when demobilization had seemed to take hold in Chile. In this context, I examine how the health group Llareta deliberated about and experimented with strategic responses to the transformed political scenario.

The question of changing forms of power and varieties of resistance was not my question alone, nor was it a purely academic one. In the early post-dictatorship years, the health group members were critically examining the *coyuntura política*—the political characteristics of the moment they were living through. Such discussions were going on within neighborhood organizations, as well as within the nongovernmental organizations with which they worked.[1] It was within this atmosphere of critical reflection and political analysis by community organizations that I initiated my ethnographic fieldwork. In this context, the Chilean transition to democracy was not simply an object of study for me, but rather, like "the third" described by Marcus (1998), an idea whose critical examination forged a relationship between myself and the health group. While our analyses converged, they also differed, for the immediate goals and the forms our analyses took were distinct: the health group, like other organizations in Santiago, sought to innovate new forms of collective action appropriate to the new era. My study broadened into an analysis of the subject effects and forms of power operating during the political transition.

Given these preoccupations, the chapters in part two include detailed ethnographic accounts of the health group's debates, dilemmas, and experiments with social action in democracy. Ethnographic accounts of the health group's work—a meningitis campaign (chapter 4), a cholera campaign (chapter 5), and a district health seminar (chapter 6)—show how Llareta was trying to comprehend the dynamics of the new political context and attempting to formulate effective strategies for these conditions. The chapters also offer a theoretical approach to the specific mechanisms through which power operated during political democracy. Chapter 4 uses the notion of "marketing democracy" to situate contemporary Chilean democracy in relation to international economics and to foreground the ways in which the idea of democracy has been strategically deployed by a variety of actors to moderate or propel social movement activity. Chapter 5 examines the discourse of "participation" and the attendant concept of civil society as a language and set of practices used to channel the energies of social organizations and minimize government expenditures. Finally, chapter 6 looks at the health group's critique and appropriation of expertise as a kind of strategic resistance to the forms of power emerging in the post-dictatorship period.

CHAPTER FOUR

Marketing Democracy

May 17, 1995
Philadelphia

The conference room at the Society Hill Sheraton is already filling with people when I arrive: mainly middle-aged men and some women with leather portfolios, sleek attaché cases, and conservative business suits. The attendees sip coffee and peruse the day's schedule as they wait for the program to begin. This event, called "Forum Chile: Going for Growth," has been arranged by the Chilean and American Chamber of Commerce of Greater Philadelphia and the United States Department of Commerce. Designed for "senior and middle managers," it seeks to promote opportunities for American companies to do business in Chile by providing information and generating contacts. The printed program I hold in my hand announces the day's activities: reports on Chile's commercial and economic status, briefings on import regulations, rules for banking and finance, "legal aspects of doing business in Chile," foreign investment, trade relations, and approaches to promoting business. The Chilean ambassador to the United States will provide a political perspective on hemispheric free trade, and at the luncheon, the U.S. ambassador to Chile will update the audience on Chile's prospects for joining the North American Free Trade Agreement. Following lunch, attendees will meet one-on-one with the mostly Chilean professionals who have given presentations in the morning.

Later in the session, I wander into the hallway where the coordinators have placed a table displaying brochures. The publications include "Survey of Political and Economic Trends in Chile" with an opening message from President Frei, a tourism guide, and a booklet from the Chilean airline Ladeco. One brochure in particular catches my eye. Produced by the Chilean Export Promotion Bureau, Pro-Chile, it opens to reveal a vista of Santiago set against the spectacular Andes Mountains. Glossy photos showcase Chile's primary exports: ripe fruit, giant cuts of lumber, fish caught fresh from the sea, wine in barrels and bottles, a tall factory to represent manufacturing, and the broad expanse of a copper mine. The brochure

Figure 7. Cover of a brochure promoting trade and foreign investment in Chile. PROCHILE.

presents Chile as an exceptional place to do business: a country with an excellent consumer market and an environment well suited for foreign investment.

But what most impresses me about this brochure is the intermingling of politics and economics. After opening with "Chile: It's not just a country. It's a new world of opportunity," the text goes on:

> Imagine a country where American partnerships are established every day; an economy that has grown at an average rate of over 6% per annum for ten straight years; *a government that offers stability and democracy.*... This is Chile, where the country, its

economy, government, and people are all poised to be the new world of opportunity in the decades ahead [emphasis added].

Democracy and stability: the political conditions that make the economic ones work. Political democracy combined with the relative absence of civil disorder: lures through which American entrepreneurs might be convinced to invest.

In 1991, Llareta was grappling with how to understand the new political period it was living through and struggling with how to reanimate community organizations. In this context of diagnosis and deliberation, one story—about two meningitis campaigns—came to have iconic status among health promoters in Santiago. Members of Llareta and the staff of EPES told it repeatedly to highlight the frustrations of dealing with the elected government. I reproduce the story here because I believe it crystallizes how, in the post-dictatorship era, the idea of democracy was used strategically by government officials with effects that could dampen mobilization and by social organizations trying to define their role in the post-dictatorship political system.

A TALE OF TWO MENINGITIS CAMPAIGNS

In 1985, while Chile was under military rule and experiencing national protests, meningitis broke out at a community center in La Bandera. Seven neighborhood children died of the disease. Llareta, which had come into existence only the previous year, responded to the emergency. In an essay of political analysis prepared subsequently for a new journal (which was never published), Valeria and Iván explained the health group's efforts to prevent further deaths:

> We made instruction sheets with the symptoms and preventions for this sickness....
> we carried out an assembly of *pobladores* that sent letters to the health authorities, to the clinics, to the chiefs of the areas, to the ministry itself, to the communication media. We organized health workshops in schools, committees of the homeless, and kindergartens, so that they would know what to do in case the symptoms presented themselves. (Grupo de Salud Llareta 1991b)

Aware of the limits on what a community organization could do single-handedly, the health group made demands on political authorities: "What we requested, as a group and as nonorganized *pobladores,* was that they close the community center [the source of the contamination], that the contagious people get priority medical attention, that they put specialized personnel in the local health clinic, and that they...respond to the fear people had of...the illness." Despite the health group's many appeals, its demands went unanswered. Iván and Valeria continued, "[T]he Director of the Health Clinic...did not give any concrete response. She ignored what was happening." And the national Ministry of Health remained impassive, telling the health group that "there had to be twenty deaths for the sickness to be declared an epidemic." Valeria and Iván wrote, "The authorities were not interested in the problem. In truth, they were not interested in the health or death of our children." Although the health group mobilized large numbers of people in its public assemblies, officials dismissed its demands.

The lack of response during a military dictatorship is consistent with the type of regime in place at the time. General Augusto Pinochet's free market experiment had cut budgets for public health services and relied on the private sector to cover health care needs, while targeting limited funds for specific causes like maternal-child health care. Within the neoliberal economic model, it was not the state's responsibility to guarantee health. Moreover, in the context of national protests during the mid-1980s, the authoritarian state's approach to *población* community organizations was one of repression and control, as grassroots organizations rebelled against the regime. Pinochet's government was oriented toward neither negotiating with nor meeting the demands of popular sector organizations.

In 1990, just after the transition to an elected government, meningitis again broke out in La Bandera. As they had five years earlier, members of Llareta distributed information sheets, held educational workshops, and sent letters to public officials. "[We] mobilized ourselves rapidly," Valeria and Iván later wrote, because "now, as a group, we were not going to wait for our children to begin to die."

This was a very different political moment—the first year of political democracy—and this time the group's efforts were not ignored. Instead, representatives from the Ministry of Health invited Llareta and other Santiago health groups that were organized into the Metropolitan Coordination of Poblacional Health (Coordinadora Metropolitana de Salud Poblacional) to a meeting at the ministry. There, a doctor welcomed the community leaders, congratulated them on their work, and praised them for distributing educational literature. But when the health promoters requested that the government take action to prevent the spread of the disease, the doctor told them in a cordial tone that no funds were available to deal with the problem.

Here one can see similarities and differences between conditions under dictatorship and democracy. In contrast to the military regime's response, the civilian-controlled Ministry of Health actively invited and politely welcomed the health groups to a meeting. After all, political democracy was known for dialogue and negotiation. It gave a special place of honor to organizations of "civil society," and it encouraged "participation." But if the welcome was warm, the response was similar: no resources would be allocated. The claim that the state lacked the financial resources to provide medical services reflected the fact that the political democracy had inherited and maintained the economic system devised by the military government. Although the Concertación increased overall health expenditures, health services remained privatized, government expenditures had already been cut, and public health services had been decentralized to municipalities.[1]

When the doctor refused their request for resources, health group members informed him that they were prepared to take action: "We suggested that if there were not an appropriate response by the authorities, we as a health group would have a demonstration, like the march in the center of Santiago that we had held in 1985, because the responses of today [1990] were the same as then: 'there aren't resources'" (Grupo de Salud Llareta 1991b). Upon hearing the threat of a demonstration, the minister became adamant. He told them not to hold the march and accused them of being traitors (Calvin 1995, 167). Health promoters at the meeting understood him to be saying that if they proceeded with the march, they would be considered disloyal to the elected government and would potentially risk destabilizing the new democracy.

This story suggests that while the privatized economic model (expressed here in the continued lack of resources available for public health) had persisted into the post-dictatorship period, the government's strategy in confronting citizens' pressure had changed. Rather than make repression or neglect a primary form of control as the dictatorship had done, officials in the elected government tried to convince popular sector organizations not to march by attributing to them the responsibility for upholding the national project of democracy.[2] The doctor's response to the health groups marked one way in which the idea of democracy was being invoked in the post-dictatorship period: as a symbolic glue that might make the nation cohere despite an unequal distribution of economic resources.

Such a rendition of democracy also reflected a characterization of politics circulating in Santiago in the early 1990s: one that saw political systems as falling into two main camps—democracy or dictatorship. This logic held that actions taken by politicians were by definition democratic because the politicians had been elected. Citizens were obligated to support the government and its actions because to do otherwise was to invite what was considered the only other alternative: authoritarian rule. Such a formulation of political options left little room for debate about the quality and characteristics of democracy itself.

This vision of democracy did not go uncontested, for the health promoters who went to the Ministry of Health had their own definitions. They told the doctor that it was precisely to preserve and enact democracy that they planned to march. In their view, democracy meant having their opinions taken seriously, preserving their rights to free expression, and being able to hold the government accountable. They asked the doctor if he expected them to watch their children die of a preventable disease in the name of democracy.

Unable to obtain the resources they sought, the health promoters held the march. Yet the government's strategic invocation of the concept of democracy succeeded in creating confusion and division within the health organizations and ultimately limited the strength of the demonstration. Whereas hundreds of *población* residents had assembled in 1985 despite threats of repression, in 1990 far fewer people showed up to march in the city center. According to EPES staff, the citywide leadership of the health groups had become divided, with some leaders (from groups other than Llareta) convinced that they did need to support the government.

These leaders concurred with officials that dissent could destabilize the elected government and threaten the ongoing survival of democracy.

THE NO CAMPAIGN AND POLITICAL MARKETING

The strategic use of the concept of democracy to limit social movement activity, as illustrated by the 1990 campaign against meningitis, takes place at an intersection of politics and economics that I call the "marketing of democracy." I intend that phrase to have a double meaning. First, I use it to refer to the way the free market economic model provides the context for and to a great extent shapes the characteristics of contemporary democracies. In the current globalized economy, policy decisions are strongly oriented toward transnational market considerations that foster an export model of development, rely on attracting foreign investment, and saturate societies with imported goods. Sustaining this model requires political stability, which is advanced through the moderation of social movement activity and enhanced by the widespread stimulation of consumerist behavior.

By contributing the material and semiotic infrastructure, the saturation of politics by the market lays the foundation for practices that constitute a second meaning of "marketing democracy." Here I refer to a kind of political marketing that draws on the techniques of advertising and market research, and the logics of desire and consumer choice, to create images that sell the idea of democracy to both citizen-consumers and foreign investors. While the marketing of products and the marketing of candidates, political platforms, and national imagery are not identical, political marketing is based on a logic of gauging, targeting, and creating desire among voters similar to that which commercial marketing directs toward consumers (O'Shaughnessy 1990, 4).

The notion that political ideals can be transmitted through the techniques of image making borrowed from commercial marketing is most commonly associated with the campaigns for individual candidates in electoral processes, though it has also been used by authoritarian regimes that seek to strengthen their rule by promoting nationalist ideals through visual and verbal imagery. In this chapter I focus not on the marketing of candidates nor on national image making but rather on how the idea of democracy itself has been promoted and sold. I show that *democracy* is a term to which a multitude of meanings have been attached as it has been strategically used by a range of actors to differing ends.

Understanding the debate between government officials and the health group over the meaning of democracy requires examining the uses of the concept in the early years of the political transition. As discussed in chapter 3, the 1988 plebiscite was a pivotal moment in Chilean history because it would determine the nation's future governance. As indicated in the 1980 constitution, a win for the YES would mean that General Pinochet would continue in power for another eight years. A victory for the NO would result in presidential elections. Although the political opposition to Pinochet had initially rejected the plebiscite on the premise that participation in it would constitute a tacit acceptance of what they considered a fraudulent constitution, in 1986 opposition leaders made a strategic decision to change their course and attempt to end the dictatorship by winning the plebiscite. Efforts to register citizens and capture votes included a range of techniques such as door-to-door visits and massive demonstrations. Opposition leaders developed a sophisticated political marketing strategy that included extensive opinion polling and focus groups and made unprecedented use of television advertising.

Scholars have traced the rise of political marketing to the television and radio campaigns of U.S. presidential candidates in the 1950s and 1960s and attributed its development to the confluence of electoral politics and proliferating media technologies (Maarek 1995, 7–11). A similarly propitious coincidence of political and media conditions occurred in Chile in the late 1980s. General Pinochet's changes in television financing in 1975 (McAnany 1987, 58) meant that the mixture of state and private funding that had characterized television in Chile until that time was to be replaced by revenue from commercial advertising exclusively, presumably stimulating a proliferation of companies skilled in publicity over the subsequent years (McAnany 1987, 58; Piñuel 1990, 135). At the same time, and as a result of the influx of cheap imports of electronic goods following the reduction in trade barriers in the 1970s and 1980s, access to televisions increased dramatically, so that by 1987 nearly all Chilean households possessed a television set (Piñuel 1990, 136). In La Bandera specifically, according to census data, more than 80 percent of families had televisions in 1982, up from only 2.5 percent in 1970. The focus of programming changed during this time as well. President Salvador Allende (1970–73) had promoted educational and cultural programming, which under the dictatorship was largely replaced by imported entertainment shows (Fuenzalida 1984, 178; cited in McAnany 1987, 59). The military government, which controlled the content of news reports and announcements throughout the dictatorship, had mostly eliminated spaces for political dialogue and debate (Piñuel 1990, 136). By the late 1980s, when competition for leadership of the country had begun, the conditions (in terms of access to TVs, television viewing habits, and a history of government involvement in programming) were present for widespread use of televised publicity in politics.

The military regime, which had control over the mass media and resources to hire advertising talent, aired a series of twenty-minute television spots beginning in January 1988 (Piñuel 1990, 146). Along with leaflets and other print media, the publicity celebrated Chile's economic progress and national development under Pinochet. Later, in response to the NO campaign's propaganda, it warned of a return to the violence and chaos associated with the Allende period if the electorate voted NO in the plebiscite, and it mocked the NO campaign's slogan that claimed happiness was coming.

In September 1988, both the YES and the NO campaigns were allotted fifteen minutes of television time daily leading up to the plebiscite vote on October 5. Lacking the financial and media resources available to the state, the opposition

Figure 8. Flyer in support of the YES campaign. Emphasizing economic progress under the military government, the flyer shows Pinochet surrounded by graphs that indicate progress in such areas as seafood exports, foreign investment, overall exports, inflation, adult literacy, forests, and the percentage of the fiscal budget directed toward the poorest people. The caption points to "the force of the deeds/facts" and notes: "Pinochet: If he governs, you govern." Department of Rare Books and Special Collections, Princeton University Library.

also faced the delicate challenge of convincing a population to vote against a dictatorship under which it lived. During this period, professionals from the United States traveled to Chile to teach poll taking, focus groups, media use, and other political marketing techniques. Chilean advertising executives, social scientists, and politicians organized themselves into "creative," "editorial," and "production" committees to design a strategy (Piñuel 1990, 142). Their activities included identifying undecided "swing" voters, eliciting citizens' views in focus groups and surveys, and designing a media campaign. Their slogan, "Happiness is on its way," sought to create an upbeat atmosphere and persuade disaffected Chileans that change was possible.

Juan Gabriel Valdés, one of the Chilean political scientists who helped design the opposition's publicity campaign for the NO vote, described the teams' work as an effort to "sell" (the quotation marks are his) symbolic themes to voters. In the following, he identifies the values imparted by specific televised images.

Figure 9. Promotional material for the YES campaign. Playing on the NO campaign slogan, this material reads: "Chile, Happiness Is Already Coming" (top illustration, right) and "The happiness of the UP [Popular Unity government]" (bottom). Implying that voting Pinochet out of office will return the country to conditions under Allende, it offers two images of that time: violence (presumably as a result of communist insurrection) and people waiting in line because of food shortages. The flyer concludes, "You'll laugh till it hurts" (back cover, top illustration, left). Department of Rare Books and Special Collections, Princeton University Library.

QUIENES ESTAMOS POR EL **NO**

Nos comprometemos

A mejorar la salud pública

Hoy día el sistema de salud es deficiente. El número de personas cubiertas por este beneficio es muy inferior al de principios de los años '70. Las largas colas que Ud. ha hecho en los consultorios, el alto precio que Ud. ha pagado por los medicamentos, son una muestra del desamparo en el que viven millones de chilenos.

¡Es una verdad!

COMANDO NACIONAL POR EL **NO**

Figure 10. Flyer for the NO campaign. The front side of the flyer (top) says that those promoting the NO vote commit to improving public health. The man on the gurney says, "Vote NO and it will change your life." The reverse side of the flyer (bottom) decries the state of the public health system. Department of Rare Books and Special Collections, Princeton University Library.

> Our program employed all the modern techniques of publicity and marketing to
> *"sell" products* like *social solidarity* (the theme of Señora Yolita), *reconciliation and justice*
> (the solitary *cueca* dance of the family members of the disappeared), *recuperation of the*
> *true patriotic values* (the march of Chile), *education* (Gabriela Mistral and Pablo Neruda),
> *reconciliation and identity* (the cop and the stick) [emphasis added]. (Valdés 1989, 99)

Here, values (like justice) were encapsulated in televised images (like the dance by
family members of the disappeared) and became the products that political marketing could sell. In this sense, a business model was operationalized in politics.
Each time that values like reconciliation and justice were invoked, it was actually
democracy that was being marketed, for it was democracy that was credited with
bringing those other things about. Democracy emerged as a flexible, multifaceted
term that at once captured all that was missing during dictatorship as well as a
changing array of other values and meanings.

Two particular television spots mentioned by Valdés demonstrate how democracy can be embodied in images and invested with multiple meanings. The first
example, "Señora Yolita," a spot in which an old woman goes into a store to buy
bread and tea, links democracy with economic betterment. The second spot, "the
cop and the stick," in which police beat a civilian, is—at the explicit level of its
spoken narrative—about national identity and reconciliation. At the level of its visual imagery, it offers a different set of meanings in that it implicitly positions democracy as the opposite of a violent dictatorship.

The following is my own description of the "Señora Yolita" spot based on a
viewing of the ad on video:

> The old woman walks slowly, steadily, and pushes open the creaky door. The glass
> panes of the little neighborhood store have yellowed with age. As she enters, a
> young woman stocking items on the shelves to her left calls out a greeting, and Se-
> ñora Yolita nods to her and says, "Good morning, my child." Her knit hat and long
> scarf keep her warm, but her bag is empty. She approaches the counter. "Good
> morning, Anibal," she says to the owner, who is attending customers from behind
> the counter. "Good morning, Señora Yolita," he replies. The store is filled with typi-
> cal grocery items—the pump of oil, the stacks of bread, the container of little
> cookies. The woman sets her wrinkled hands down on the counter. "Give me two
> pieces of bread," she says. "Why not?" says the owner, and he pulls a brown sheet
> of paper from the counter and wraps the small rolls. He speaks tenderly, "Here is
> your bread. Something else?" Breathing in with studied discipline, she gathers her
> strength. "I'll have tea as well." He nods, smiles warmly. "Why not?" he says and
> begins to pull two tea bags out of a box. But then he hesitates. "Two bags?" he asks
> her. She looks at him, then down, and then slowly opens her purse. Her fingers
> probe as she peers inside, but she does not find the necessary coin. She raises her
> eyes to him. "Just one."

This scene was well known to many Chileans: an old woman who could not afford
even a second tea bag, much less a slice of meat or a little jam to eat with her

bread. It was an experience of hunger and humiliation to which the poor in San-tiago could easily relate and which the ad attributed to the dictatorship.

The campaign spot went on to offer a solution. After the scene, a narrator's deep voice came on. "All of us have a reason to vote NO," says the announcer, as the old woman takes the single tea bag from the owner's hand. "No more misery. For this reason, the NO wins." The image switches to a hand marking a ballot "NO," and the NO campaign theme song plays in the background: "Happiness is already on its way." The image of poverty shown in this television commercial was accompanied by a hopeful message: voting Pinochet out of office could bring an end to hunger and misery. Whereas poverty was attributed to dictatorship, de-mocracy was associated with economic betterment.

Bringing an end to misery was just one of the meanings attributed to democ-racy during the plebiscite campaign. The second television spot I will consider ad-dresses reconciliation. It depicts police beating a man who had fallen to the ground. The spot uses slow motion, voice-overs, and other special effects (including on-screen circles to highlight various actors) to dramatize the horror of conflict and the promise of national reconciliation associated with democracy.

Once again, the following narrative is based on my transcription of the voices and description of the ad captured on videotape.

Narrator 1: For too many years, Chileans have suffered the pain of disunity in a country artificially divided.

As military police drag a man across the ground, a circle envelops the head of a soldier.

Narrator 2: This man desires peace.

As the man struggles on the ground, his head is now surrounded by a circle.

Narrator 2: This man desires peace.

The circle returns to the soldier as he wields his stick.

Narrator 2: This man is Chilean.

Again the circle returns to the man who is being beaten on the ground.

Narrator 2: This man is Chilean.

The circle returns to the military figure.

Narrator 2: This man fights for what he believes in.

It returns to the man being beaten.

Narrator 2: This man fights for what he believes in.

The sequence is shown again in slow motion.

Narrator 2: These men have the right to live in peace and have the right to work for what they believe in. The country will be great when no Chilean has fear of another Chilean. Chile will be great when all have a place in the fatherland…

The soldier's stick smashes down on the man's head.

…so that this never occurs again.

The full beating recurs in real time.

Narrator 2: In war, everyone has fear. Peace is achieved in democracy.

Narrator 1: We will seek reconciliation because all of us are Chileans.

This ad provides two glosses for democracy that differ from the focus on economic betterment advanced in the "Señora Yolita" television spot. At the overt level of its verbal narrative, and reinforced by the lines encircling each participant, the ad is about equality of Chileans and the national reconciliation that can be achieved through democracy. In this explicit verbal explanation, the spot omits reference to the fact that one man has the power of the state behind him, ignores the fact that there is more than one policeman beating only one civilian, and leaves out any reference to why the civilian might be justifiably protesting. In so doing, the text of the commercial sidesteps reference to power inequalities, instead portraying the two parties as symmetrical in the sense that both are Chileans, both desire peace, and both are defending causes they believe in.[3] As equals in Chilean society, the men need to overcome their differences and reconcile in a national unity that will be brought about by democracy.

At the level of visual imagery, the spot sends a different message. It depicts the military as brutal aggressor and the man being beaten as victim of that violence. In this visual narrative, democracy is set in contrast to dictatorship and is depicted as the condition that will bring violence to an end.[4]

In the NO campaign ads, the term *democracy* was given at least three different meanings—one associated with economic betterment (in the Señora Yolita ad), one linked to the unity and identity of the nation (in the explicit verbal narration of the cop-and-the-stick television spot), and a third dedicated to the end of military-sponsored violence in the visual imagery of the cop-and-the-stick ad. Several years later, in the 1990 meningitis campaign described at the beginning of this chapter, different actors drew upon available discursive resources foreshadowed in the NO campaign's portrayals of democracy. In its health campaign, the health group posited democracy as the right to march and hold the government accountable. It made a claim to health care resources that recalled the premise of the Señora Yolita television spot—that democracy should bring substantive economic improvements. For his part, the doctor at the Ministry of Health asserted a vision that positioned democracy as the opposite of dictatorship, a version that was more closely aligned with the visual message of the cop-and-the-stick television ad, while drawing on a version of its verbal message of reconciliation. The reference had a new meaning, however, for while the visual elements of that ad position the cop as beating the protester, in the doctor's argument, it was as if the would-be protesters (the health group) were viewed as provocateurs and therefore, in the context of political democracy, seen as responsible for any military backlash that might ensue as a result. In short, the attribution of multiple meanings to the concept of democracy at the moment preceding the plebiscite generated resources that after the transition to democracy could be used strategically by a range of actors to a variety of ends.

THE USES OF DEMOCRACY

During the early post-dictatorship years, a contradiction emerged from how democracy had been presented during the plebiscite. Democracy had been portrayed as the opposite of the dictatorship it was replacing, but strong continuities in economic policies persisted between the two regimes. In part, this was the result of factors beyond the will of any particular Chilean politician. Transnational forces of globalization, the requirements of international lending institutions, and the perceived lack of alternatives in the post–cold war era all played their part. Yet maintaining neoliberalism in the absence of the population's explicit consent (given that economic restructuring had taken place under an authoritarian regime and was for the most part off the agenda by the time elections occurred in 1989) required the "marketing of democracy" in the second sense of the term—an intentional and carefully calculated promotion of images of democracy that could legitimate an economic model imposed under military rule. This worked in different ways internationally and domestically.

Internationally, democracy served as a mechanism to legitimate neoliberal economics for foreign investors and for countries seeking their own political transitions and free market openings. This is illustrated by a 1993 article from the *Wall Street Journal* reflecting on Chile's political transition:

> A few years ago, heaping praise on Chile was unthinkable. Its economic success was overshadowed by the political horror story of the dictatorship of General Augusto Pinochet, whose 17-year rule was marked by massive human rights violations, including at least 2,025 deaths or disappearances. But President Patricio Aylwin, confounding predictions that his democratic election in 1989 would lead to a wave of populism, has stayed the course of austerity and economic reform. (Kamm 1993, 1)

Highlighting economic continuities between the military and civilian periods, the article notes that the democratic government helped legitimate the economic model by disassociating it from human rights violations generated under authoritarian rule: "Suddenly, Chile switched from pariah to model, attracting many Latin Americans and Eastern Europeans for crash courses on how to combine democracy and free markets."[5]

Fernando Mires (1993) has noted that a model cannot exist outside the context of its history. That is to say, there would have been no economic miracle without an authoritarian regime because dismantling the welfare state could not have been accomplished without the violent silencing of the political opposition. Given that fact, promoting Chile as a model through which countries could combine free markets with democracy required a set of cultural practices that could disassociate capitalism from authoritarianism and locate free markets within political democracy.

Legitimation of the economic model was an important product of Chile's political transition. Brought about through a series of pacts negotiated between opposition politicians and military officials, the transition was a complex process outside the control and intentionality of any single set of actors. Once in office, politicians in Chile's first elected government made the legitimation effects of democracy part of their political strategy. One Chilean commentator has made this explicit, paraphrasing Edgardo Boeninger, secretary general to President Aylwin, as saying that "the Aylwin Government fulfilled the mission of 'legitimating' the economic model imposed in the years of dictatorship" (Fazio 1996, 25). In Boeninger's own words: "'Without this legitimation…the model of an economy open to the exterior, based on private property and the market, would not have developed in Chile. We have legitimated the past …on the basis of this being part of the reality of Chile in the present and future.'"[6] Legitimating and thereby fortifying the neoliberal economic model through promoting images of Chile's political system abroad was thus a strategic use of the flexible and multifaceted concept of democracy.

If internationally the Chilean government could use democracy as a legitimating mechanism for attracting international investment, domestically it used the symbolic resources generated through the transition to help overcome the contradictions of a democracy deeply shaped and still influenced by the prior military regime. The terms of the pacted transition made it difficult for former human rights violations to be punished and ensured that the military would continue to play a major role in the government, with a number of senators appointed by Pinochet, and Pinochet's own tenure first as head of the army and later as senator-for-life. The idea of reconciliation foreshadowed in the cop-and-the-stick plebiscite spot was used to facilitate social peace by creating the image of a profound rupture between the past and the present, and therefore between the dictatorship and the democracy. It also was used to overcome divisions by creating a sense of national unity. The publicizing of these ideas on television and their arrival in the *población* reveal the way in which suppression of memory was needed to symbolically disconnect democracy from dictatorship.

On the evening of March 4, 1991, Valeria and I sat talking in her house in La Bandera. Near nine o'clock, we pulled up chairs around the round wooden table in the dining area and brought the television in from a bedroom to set it high on a shelf. Then we turned the television volume down low and tuned in the radio to get the clearest sound. The familiar product ads appeared on the television for a few minutes, but soon the program we were waiting for began. Waterfalls, the Entel tower, and other symbols of Chile flowed across the black-and-white screen.

Then President Patricio Aylwin appeared, seated beside the national flag, and began to deliver his speech.

Aylwin was on television that evening to present to the Chilean people the *Report of the National Commission of Truth and Reconciliation*, also known as the Rettig Report after the commission's head, Raúl Rettig. It had been written by a presidentially appointed committee given the task of interviewing thousands of relatives of the disappeared to determine the circumstances of reported deaths. Aylwin had ordered the study despite objections of the military and the political right wing, which were not ready to acknowledge, much less accept responsibility for, the deaths. The commission had spent months gathering the testimony that would identify the Chileans disappeared and killed at the hands of the military. Its product—a 1,350-page report—documented over two thousand cases of human rights violations resulting in deaths or disappearances committed between 1973 and 1990 under military rule. This evening was a momentous occasion, for it was the first time the government officially acknowledged the military's role in killing Chilean citizens.

While the task of the commission was to inform Chileans about past abuses of human rights, Aylwin used the occasion to send a seemingly contradictory message. Ironically, he framed the presentation of the Rettig Report as a moment to end the preoccupation with the history of human rights abuses. As he presented the report, President Aylwin said, "Many compatriots think that it is time to put *punto final* [period, end of discussion] to this issue." With these words, Aylwin emphasized not grappling as a country with the legacy of the deaths, nor bringing the perpetrators to justice. Instead, he urged Chileans to move on and put the theme of human rights abuses behind them. "For the good of Chile," he said, "we should *look toward the future that unites us more than to the past which separates us.* There is much that we have to do to construct a truly democratic society, advance development, and achieve social justice, *to waste our energy in scrutinizing wounds that are irremediable* [emphasis added]." By saying that it was time to put *punto final* to the discussion, Aylwin suggested that the point of the Informe Rettig was to close, rather than inaugurate, a national discussion about human rights.

The key concept Aylwin advanced in his speech and in the report was reconciliation. Quoting Pope John Paul II, who had visited Chile in 1987, Aylwin said: "And we remember the words of his sanctity John Paul II on his visit: 'Chile has the vocation of understanding, and not of confrontation. It is not possible to progress while deepening the divisions. *It is the hour of pardon and reconciliation*' [emphasis added]" (Aylwin 1991, 10). The term *reconciliation* reflected in the title *Report of the National Commission of Truth and Reconciliation*, contrasted with the name of human rights reports in Argentina, Brazil, and Uruguay, where accounts of human rights abuses had been entitled *Nunca Más*, Never Again (Margaret Crahan, personal communication). That title implied a historical vision—the idea that the society was remembering the violations of human rights in order to prevent them from being repeated. In contrast, the title of the Chilean report emphasized the healing and reconstitution of the nation, through the burying of the past.[7] The nation and its future became the centerpiece of identity.

On Palm Sunday, a few weeks after the president's presentation of the Rettig Report, I walked in the early morning hours toward the main Catholic chapel near the center of La Bandera. The streets were remarkably quiet at that hour—people worked on their fences or stood outside talking to neighbors. The morning sun flickered in the dust hovering above long stretches of dirt road.

Two women were playing guitar and singing on the porch of the church as I arrived. Within the sanctuary, sunlight filtered in through the windows, illuminating some locations and leaving other places dark and cool. A white cloth covered the table at the front, and on it sat two goblets of wine, each with a linen cloth settled gently above. I had seated myself outside to reflect on the scene, when I was startled from my reverie by the ringing of a church bell. Outside, the quiet morning had filled with a large group of people singing, walking en masse into the sanctuary, and waving palm branches.

The crowd moved inside, and as the service progressed, the priest spoke briefly but movingly, linking religion to politics. He raised the theme of human rights violations by drawing a parallel between Jesus' experience of crucifixion and the torture and disappearances that had occurred in Chile. Then, near the end of the service, four parishioners walked up the aisle holding before them the white volumes of the Rettig Report. They presented the report to the priest as an offering "in the spirit of truth, of reconciliation, and of pardon." Having been introduced by the president on television a short time before, the report was now backed in La Bandera by the weight of the Catholic Church. It had entered the *población* at a space of encounter of a great many people and in the context of spirituality, worship, and the ethical principles of Jesus himself.

The penetration of the Informe Rettig into La Bandera through the Catholic Church continued after the Palm Sunday ritual. In the following weeks, the church coordinated a march through the streets of the *población*. The march was attended by workers at the Vicaría Sur (the southern zone branch of the Vicaría de la Solidaridad that had worked with victims of human rights violations during the dictatorship) and many residents of La Bandera. It included a speech by one member of the Rettig Commission itself.

In addition to the march, the church held workshops in which *pobladores* were taught how to pardon. In these forums, residents of La Bandera engaged in a process of reworking emotions and overcoming difficult memories for the purpose of national reconciliation. In seminars and workshops, in church services and in conversations, the idea of reconciliation advanced on national television became a real and present force in the *población*. At the same time, other community leaders and residents in the *población* decided not to participate, and they even held counterdemonstrations calling for an end to impunity. Nonetheless, while the effort to bring the Retting Report to the *población* generated discussion and often disagreement about pardon and reconciliation, it ultimately served as a symbolic

Figure 11. Ceremony in La Bandera marking the completion of the *Report of the National Commission of Truth and Reconciliation*. A Catholic priest holds the microphone for Iván as a member of the Rettig Commission looks on. Photo: Gordon Whitman.

substitute for punishment of human rights abuses or resolution of Pinochet's ongoing role in the post-dictatorship period.

I have argued above that sustaining the economic model internationally and maintaining civil order domestically entailed strategic use of a variety of meanings for democracy, some of which had been publicized during the NO campaign. The idea that the concept of democracy could be strategically deployed to consolidate identities and limit popular mobilization in the service of economic restructuring is not merely an analytic observation on my part. It follows from a programmatic suggestion made by advisers to the Chilean government. An advocate of this position is Eugenio Tironi, a sociologist and political strategist in Chile who became director of the Office of Communication and Culture in the Aylwin government. With the end of the welfare state and the corresponding transfer of public services to the private sector, Tironi argues, democratic governments have had to grapple with how to unify ("integrate") a population increasingly divided by economic inequality brought about by neoliberal economics. He writes, "The possibility of regressing to the old Welfare State not being open, democratic regimes are obligated to look for forms to compensate for the tendencies toward *social* segmentation maximizing the use of factors of *political* integration" (Tironi 1990, 257).[8]

Tironi asks how the state might achieve the "integration" of society. To this admittedly Durkheimian problem, he offers a Durkheimian solution: the creation of collective representations. The postwelfare state democratic regimes, he writes, compensate for economic divisions by finding new forms of integration. Chief among them are the "re-creation of national symbols." Tironi offers France's celebration of its bicentennial as a model for symbols that can create national integration. In Chile, the idea of reconciliation demonstrated in the cop-and-the-stick ad in the plebiscite, spelled out in the president's presentation of the Rettig Report, and brought to life through seminars in La Bandera can be seen as a similar attempt to create a single national identity.

The programmatic suggestion that the state create symbols to make the nation cohere, thereby overcoming inequalities that threaten to rend it apart, elucidates the Health Ministry's admonition to health groups not to demonstrate for resources to prevent the spread of meningitis in their *poblaciones*. The doctor asked health promoters to contain their demands in order to support democracy. In so doing, he offered the idea of democracy as a symbolic substitute for economic redistribution (in this case, resources for public health). Here, reference to democracy was incorporated into a political strategy for reducing mobilization, ultimately complementing and sustaining the economic model.

POWER EFFECTS: POLLING AND PUBLIC OPINION

If democracy had a multiplicity of meanings, it also had a variety of technologies through which to operate. These practices, particularly opinion polls, constituted particular mechanisms through which a kind of power unique to political democracy was exercised.

In the early 1990s, members of Llareta were trying to understand the reasons for low levels of social organization. They noted that whereas residents of poor neighborhoods had protested economic and political conditions under the military regime, during the first years of democracy many popular sector organizations had folded or remained barely active, despite the ongoing existence of poverty.[9] In an interview in 1992, Sonia contrasted her neighbors' silence in the 1990s with their vociferous protests during military rule: "It makes me angry because before we went out to shout when the price of bread and other things rose. We would yell, complain, protest. Now they raise the price of bread, sugar—they raise the price of everything on you—and we have to remain quiet. We don't even speak— nobody does a thing. Nothing nothing nothing nothing. . . . nobody does anything."

I asked Sonia why people said nothing when the prices rose during political democracy. "Because the people already don't believe in it," she told me. "[They think] that although we complain, nothing is going to happen."

Sonia's neighbors' perceived skepticism that the political system would respond to their demands accurately reflected some aspects of the institutional structure following the dictatorship. From one perspective, Chile had successfully undergone a transition to democracy because its government, including a civilian president and (most of) the Congress, had been chosen through elections. On the other hand, the post-dictatorship democracy differed markedly from the pre-1970 democracy, which featured a wide array of political parties, a politicized population, and elections that generated enormous popular participation. In part to avoid the ideological conflict characteristic of that era, the negotiated transition instituted mechanisms to insulate the government from direct public influence. These included nonelected senators (including, after 1998, General Pinochet himself), which gave Pinochet's followers effective veto power over new legislation; a complex binomial voting system designed to channel support away from ideological extremes and into two centrist blocks; a constitution (very difficult to modify) that had been written during the dictatorship; and the relocation of the Congress from Santiago, the capital and largest city, to Valparaíso, some distance away. These features of the political system give institutional grounding to Sonia's neighbors' speculation that their attempts to hold the government accountable to their interests were unlikely to be effective.

There were additional pressures on social groups not to engage in protest. Institutional factors included the restructuring of nongovernmental organizations, the decline in international funding to them, and the channeling of remaining funds through a new government office. But Sonia's subsequent comments raised another possible explanation for observed demobilization. They suggest that the government was difficult to resist precisely because people had given their consent by voting. Sonia summarized her neighbors' logic in this way: "'Against whom are we going to shout? Didn't we want this government?' 'Why [should we shout]? We ourselves elected it.'"

From Sonia's perspective, the demobilizing effect of democracy operates by convincing people that they themselves have participated in electing the government and therefore should not protest it. Whether or not people actually believed that by voting they had authorized the policy decisions of elected representatives, the act of voting conveyed a sense that citizens were complicit in the government they had elected. This premise of incorporating citizens' opinions operated not only through voting but also through the expanded use of public opinion polls.

In Chile, the use of polling in political campaigns coincided with the beginning of the transition from military to elected-civilian rule in the late 1980s. Before that time, surveys were used mainly for social science research. They were first introduced to Chile in the late 1950s, when Eduardo Hamuy imported "such U.S. methodological advances as scales and polls" in the service of developing a scientific sociology (Puryear 1994, 14). He later used the methodology to garner voters' political attitudes in order to predict electoral outcomes.

During the military period, surveys served additional purposes. Businesses employed them for market research, and the military drew on them to assess its public reputation. Opposition think tanks used public opinion polls for social science investigation.

But it was not until the late 1980s, when politicians were devising their approach to a negotiated transition, that opinion polls were incorporated into political campaigns. In preparation for the plebiscite, opposition leaders drew on internationally tested political campaign strategies. Political scientist Juan Gabriel Valdés, a leader of the NO campaign,[10] sought information about political marketing from private survey research companies in the United States (Puryear 1994, 139). Later, as part of an effort to promote a transition to democracy in Chile, the United States' National Democratic Institute for International Affairs (NDI) coordinated the efforts of volunteer consultants from U.S. organizations who "offered technical advice in polling, computerization, media and organization to a gifted group of Chilean campaign organizers and strategists" (National Democratic Institute 1988, 6).[11] Drawing on diverse skills, Chilean social scientists, opposition politicians, and technical experts experienced in media and market analysis collaborated to conduct research and produce publicity materials for the NO campaign.

By tying social science to politics, the NO campaign inaugurated a new use for survey research in Chile. Whereas previously Chilean scholars had collected data in order to describe political situations and predict election results, in the 1988 campaign, politicians and intellectuals used surveys less to anticipate the results of the plebiscite than to achieve particular electoral outcomes. Survey research thus took on not just a descriptive but also a strategic role (Puryear 1994, 138).

But despite the fact that survey research was used to affect results, politicians garnered credibility for polling by emphasizing its legitimacy as a scientific tool and its history of operating in a primarily descriptive manner. They portrayed public opinion polls as information-gathering mechanisms that gave political elites direct access to the interests and desires of citizens. Eugenio Tironi is one intellectual who expressed this view. "Modernization of politics is inevitably linked to 'marketing,'" he wrote.

> The fear that this raises in some circles, comes from a reductionist vision, that identifies it with the manipulation of public opinion by an elite. Nonetheless, why not take it in the inverse sense, that is, as *a vehicle by way of which the society brings its aspirations to bear on the elites* [emphasis added]? From this point of view, the "manipulated" would be the elites, not the citizens. (Tironi 1989, 4)

Polling, from Tironi's perspective, gave political elites direct access to citizens' preferences, thereby enabling the elites to represent those interests as they made political decisions. By appearing to express the will of the majority, polls in Chile were positioned as a manifestation of democracy. Opinion polls allow politicians to legitimate policy decisions by representing them as the product of citizen choice.

The aggregate "public opinion," however, is not necessarily an underlying reality transparently revealed through surveys, as Tironi seems to suggest. Rather, as poststructuralist theorists have argued, public opinion is constructed through the concept and procedures of polling itself. Jean Baudrillard (1988, 209) holds that the doubts frequently raised about opinion polls (do they manipulate public opinion? do they distort democracy?) are moot, because the questions confuse two different systems of knowledge. According to Baudrillard, "An operational system which is statistical, information-based, and simulational is projected onto a traditional values system, onto a system of representation, will, and opinion."

That is to say, although residents may answer questions on a survey, purportedly expressing their will, the aggregate "public opinion" is not something they control or that emanates from them. As a statistical construct calculated from results of a population survey, it does not embody people's desires. Rather, public opinion is a phenomenon people watch, as spectators, on the television news. Through polling, public opinion is not listened to but produced.

My own observations show not only that aggregate polling results do not reflect "representation, will, and opinion" but also that the actual experience of an individual giving information to a pollster does not do so either. A key reason polls are not able to reflect people's desires is that they use a limited-option format that precludes expression of people's concerns on their own terms. The following story illustrates this point.

One afternoon, a survey taker came by Valeria's house before the children had returned from school. Valeria was out at a meeting, and her husband, Jorge, went to the front gate. After jotting down Jorge's name, address, and other information, the poll taker began asking questions.[12]

One of the questions required Jorge to name the television channel he watched most frequently. None of Jorge's attempted answers fit the investigator's required format. "I just flip through the channels until I get to a show I like. I never pay attention to which channel it is," Jorge told the poll taker first. The interviewer rejected this answer. "Which do you prefer? Channel 4, 7, 9, 11, or 13?" he asked. When his first answer wasn't accepted, Jorge tried again. "Which channel we choose depends on who is watching TV—my daughters, my wife, or me alone," Jorge told the man. The survey taker rejected this answer as well and read the list of channels again. Finally, Jorge chose a channel, seemingly at random. The questioner wrote it down immediately and went on to the next question. He was clearly uninterested in getting information about Jorge's preferences for watching television. He only wanted to fill in the form.

The need to acquire information that fits the interview schedule is a characteristic of knowledge unique to electronics in what Mark Poster has called the "mode of information." Analog encoding of information attempts to produce direct imitations of material. So, for example, an audio sound track or a map aims to reproduce the contours of some sound or geography that exists in reality. In contrast, the digital encoding of information that is used in databases and polls aims to eliminate "noise" and all forms of ambiguity by reducing information to a binary of 0 versus 1 (Poster 1990, 94). Limited-response questionnaires such as that which Jorge answered exclude what is meaningful to him (his experience of watching television) and the actual practices through which he functions (his actions in choosing TV channels). None of this information was admitted into the survey. Because Jorge apparently chose it at random, the answer recorded on the questionnaire was, arguably, meaningless.

Despite the poor reflection of opinions they purport to record, polls are exalted as scientific because they produce quantifiable and comparable information (Poster 1990, 94). The mismatch between Jorge's qualitative response and the quantitative answer recorded is invisible in the final product. What is visible, and what ultimately gives the poll meaning and stature, is its ability to compile the responses of a vast number of people and generate an average or percentage breakdown of response.

The explicitly political questions on the same questionnaire were yet harder for Jorge to answer because they raised ethical and safety concerns. In what had been a highly politicized neighborhood in which people had been imprisoned and killed for their political beliefs over a seventeen-year period that had only recently ended, it was hard to expect someone honestly to answer the question "Which of the following political parties do you like the best?" Jorge, schooled by this time in choosing one of the options on the questionnaire's list, quickly selected a prominent center-Left political party that he and his family held in low esteem.

Jorge's guarded answer about party politics revealed that, in the 1990s in Chile, two forms of knowledge creation—and two forms of surveillance—intersected and overlapped. Technologies of knowledge such as opinion polls coexisted with police surveillance in a state whose secret service had not been dismantled but rather transferred from the government into the military. Plainclothes police gathered information secretly, while pollsters gathered it overtly, with the consent of local residents. Unlike covert intelligence gathering, polls do not make people mere objects of study. Rather, they engage respondents in a form of "participatory surveillance" (Poster 1990, 93) in which people themselves provide information to researchers. Yet how the data gathered on questionnaires would be used remained ambiguous, especially since the poll taker had recorded the respondent's name and address. Jorge's decision to lie about his political preferences revealed much about his perception of ongoing repression. It also calls into question how accurate polls can be as a measure of political preference.

As this example suggests, people's responses to questionnaires are influenced by the format of the questions and the political context in which they occur. This phenomenon leads us to ask, What might people's desires be if the conceptual options were posed differently? I thought about that as I listened to another of the questions asked of Jorge: "Do you believe that in Chile national reconciliation has been achieved, or that it has not yet been achieved?" There was no space in that question to say "I believe that violators of human rights should be brought to justice." Nor could one say, "I believe the subversives should be eliminated." Regardless of the answer he chose, by responding to the question Jorge was affirming that reconciliation was a desirable goal. By merely giving an answer, he was lending credibility to the poll's conceptual framework. In this instance, as in many others, the poll constructed the reality it purported to describe.

If polls do not allow respondents to provide answers that fit their preferences, why do people cooperate with them? It is significant that Jorge decided to answer the questions even though doing so meant giving false information, risking exposure of personal details, and listening to questions that were alienating, if not offensive. Why might he have agreed to respond?

It is my impression that responding to surveys offers a certain satisfaction. There is an attraction to thinking that for once your opinions count, that someone may be listening. That idea is linked in many people's minds with democracy. As mentioned in the introduction to this book, community leaders in La Bandera defined democracy as having their ideas taken seriously. For this reason, polling has an appeal because it is one of the few instances in which the urban poor are asked their opinion, much less listened to. This gives polling a certain legitimacy as a manifestation of democracy.

The incident described here shows, however, that the experience of being questioned does not necessarily meet those expectations. Given the fact that Jorge's answers were so distant from his desires, it is unlikely that by the time he finished responding to the questionnaire he thought the poll would result in public policy designed to meet his needs. This was not a situation, to use Tironi's words, in which "the society brings its aspirations to bear on the elites." It was a situation in which public opinion, far from being an accurate translation of reality, was constructed through the process of polling itself.

By circumscribing the alternatives through which respondents can reply, polls do more than narrow the field of possible answers. They also create certain kinds of subjects. Foucault has argued that power operates not only in a negative capacity in that it restricts, oppresses, or coerces, but also in a positive capacity in that it produces certain kinds of subjects, be they delinquents in the prison, slow learners at school, or mental patients in a clinic. Opinion polls, too, produce particular types of subjects: they construct respondents as choice makers.

One of the most fundamental impacts of the military regime and its economic policies on Chile was the permeation of consumer culture throughout the society. The opening of the Chilean economy to the world market brought an influx of imported goods, including clothing and electronics, and created booms and busts that led to periodic surges in consumer spending. Market research carried out in the 1980s by private companies both reflected and extended the expansion of consumerism. Commissioned by producers of brand-name products, these surveys were conducted in neighborhoods across the socioeconomic spectrum, including the poorest sections of Santiago. Marketing and market research helped construct Chileans as consumers.

The experience of Ricardo, a young man who grew up in a *población* in the northeastern hills of Santiago and earned money conducting consumer surveys, illustrates this phenomenon. Because Ricardo was newly hired and inexperienced (and probably also because of his own class background), he was often sent to the lowest socioeconomic communities, where interviewers were paid less for each completed survey. Reading from the survey form, Ricardo would ask people a series of questions about what products they used on a regular basis. Their answers were used not only to generate aggregate data on consumption but also to provide information that companies could use to follow up with direct marketing of products. Ricardo often suspected that when respondents said they did use a product, they were not telling the truth—that they were claiming to be consuming items that they actually could not afford. After he wrote down their answer, he would sometimes ask them if they really did use the item. Some respondents admitted they did not but told him to leave their positive answer, since he had already written it down. Ricardo interpreted their response to the survey question as an effort not to feel humiliated about their social status.

One day in 1987, he was sent to administer a questionnaire in La Bandera. Frightened of crime (for which La Bandera had a reputation), he asked a woman he was interviewing if he could step inside her house to fill in the questionnaire. Inside, Ricardo was able to compare the woman's responses with her living conditions. One set of questions asked her to identify which hot beverages she regularly consumed. The woman said she drank coffee. Looking around her kitchen, Ricardo could see that the shelves were bare. An old coffee tin was visible on a shelf, but it looked as if it had been bought years before; with the coffee long gone, the jar was being used as a container for other items. Ricardo knew from experience that nearly everyone in the *poblaciones* drank only tea, and sometimes they could not afford even that. The questions in this survey constructed the respondent as an agent of options and a consumer of products, if only in the imaginary space of an interview that presumed her ability to buy things she could not afford.

In positing choices, the survey constructed a particular type of subject. It construed the individual as having options, in this case between coffee and tea; in the case of the opinion poll administered to Jorge, among political parties. This sense of being able to choose is a fundamental property of both electoral democracy and the market. It fits the political-economic formation of a capitalist democracy, in which individuals are positioned simultaneously as citizens and consumers (see also Yúdice 1995).

The confluence of citizenship and consumption reflects the interweaving of business and politics that earlier I called "marketing democracy." Opinion polls bridge the needs of political democracy and neoliberal economics, blending the techniques of politics and business, as well as social science. Respondents may be unable to distinguish whether it is universities, private corporations, or political organizations—or the intellectuals and businesses that cater to politics—that sponsor the polls to which they respond (they also may be uninterested in doing so).

Choice making enacts a very distinct kind of power that activates respondents as agents in their own subjection and may contribute to demobilization. Market research positions respondents as part of a feedback mechanism: by asking questions of potential consumers of their messages, politicians know how to publicize themselves and their issues, and businesspeople know how to sell their products. In the NO campaign, opposition political leaders used focus groups to identify the aspirations of youth and, based on that knowledge, to create messages most likely to inspire them to vote NO (Weinstein 1989, 19–25). When they voted in the plebiscite, these youth presumably experienced their vote as a product of their own volition, even though (or precisely because) they had participated in creating the very televised simulations designed to capture their vote. In a similar way, opinion polls elicit respondents' views in order, later, to inform the population about what it thinks, desires, and feels.

The idea that the power enacted through polling might produce certain kinds of subjects raises the question of what kinds of resistance might emerge to challenge opinion polls. In his writings on polling, Baudrillard (1983) suggests that people resist in ways strategically suited to the form of power being wielded. He maintains that this is different for a repressive versus a "participatory" form of power. When people are treated as objects, he holds, they respond—they resist—as subjects. They construct identities, defend their rights, and voice demands (Baudrillard 1983, 107). This characterization well describes what happened during the protest era of the 1980s, when social movements fought back against Chile's repressive military regime.

But contemporary forms of power exemplified through opinion polls operate not by repression but rather by "participation." In Baudrillard's terms, they maximize "the word and meaning." Here ideas are purportedly welcome. In mechanisms such as elections and opinion polls, people are asked to express themselves "at any price, to vote, produce, decide, speak, participate, play the game" (Baudrillard 1983, 108). Baudrillard argues that, under such circumstances, speaking one's opinion, even in protest, would only reinforce the kind of power that these mechanisms enact. Rather than rebellion, he suggests, the resistance strategically suited to this kind of power consists of "a refusal of meaning and a refusal of the word" or, alternatively, "the hyperconformist simulation of the very mechanisms of the system, which is a form of refusal and of non-reception" (108).

In this context, rather than speak out and protest, people may refuse to respond. They may decline to vote or choose not to answer an opinion survey. These actions have generally been interpreted as political disengagement: the citizens' apathy that is said to plague contemporary democracies. But one might argue that it is a response strategically tailored to the form of power articulated in opinion polls, in which people's thoughts are constantly solicited, without necessarily bringing about desired results.

Alternatively, respondents may acquiesce to power's very mechanisms by playing the game. Like Jorge choosing a television channel, and like the señora who said she liked to drink coffee, they give answers to opinion polls, watch televised campaign ads, and turn out to vote. But their responses so conform to the system—so fit into its limited-answer procedures—that the results ultimately do not reflect a preexisting reality. By giving inaccurate information (often the only kind of information the survey allows) or entering the survey's imaginary space, they empty out the significance of the information-gathering form.

Despite its appeal, however, the poststructural concept of hyperconformity is limited when it comes to addressing the ways in which people respond (or refuse to respond) in elections and polls, because it erases both collective action and agency. People do not always conform to polling by participating in an individual and empty gesture; they may actively and collectively manipulate the results. An example of what might be viewed as hyperconformity to the formal electoral system, for example, was the percentage of voters who annulled their ballots, left them blank, or were themselves absent from the polls (in a system where voting is mandatory for those who registered) in Chile's 1997 congressional elections. Along with those who had never registered, they totaled 40 percent of the eligible population, causing a potential crisis of political legitimacy in Chile, where elections had regularly had high participation from the population. The choice not to vote was not just a minute and individual decision. At least some portion of the "lost vote" in 1997 was the outcome of organized campaigns in which flyers urged voters to annul their ballots in the upcoming elections.

CONCLUSION

This chapter has shown that years after their broadcasting in commercials during the plebiscite campaign, the various meanings attributed to democracy were picked up and strategically reappropriated by a variety of groups to different political ends. At the same time as it generated symbolic resources, democracy entailed a set of mechanisms through which power was exercised. Both political marketing in general and opinion polling in particular were—like the elections they facilitated—publicized as expressions of democracy in that they allowed politicians to hear and respond to the public's wishes. Chilean politicians positioned polling not only as a research method but also and primarily as a form of citizen involvement that was central to a modern democracy. By asking for people's opinions in questionnaires and using the results to construct public opinion, these mechanisms made the respondents complicit in the outcome, thereby tempering mobilization because they imparted the sense that people were themselves participating in the system.

My argument is not that this is a locked system to which no resistance is possible: the marches held by the health group and the organizing to convince people not to vote are just two signs of social movement activity that operated outside of the boundaries of such a logic. Indeed, the health group was able to use the concept of democracy for its own purposes in asserting its rights to march. However, the proliferation of polling and political marketing techniques and the strategic uses of concepts of democracy help to explain some of the demobilization that the *población* experienced in the post-dictatorship period.

To say that forms of power facilitated demobilization is not to say that all local organization was discouraged in post-dictatorship Chile. The beginning of this chapter described how the Ministry of Health praised Llareta for handing out educational materials on meningitis. As that case exemplifies, the state was actively encouraging certain forms of citizen involvement. It is these new kinds of participation that are the focus of the next chapter.

CHAPTER FIVE

The Paradox of Participation

I am exuberant and slightly nervous as the crowd fills the Lutheran chapel in La Bandera. The smooth wooden walls display decorations and information—a tapestry of the Last Supper, a bulletin board announcing church activities, and Chilean *arpilleras*, colorful scenes made of fabric scraps. Below a large cross in the front of the chapel, I hang a sheet of brown paper describing my agenda for the evening, a discussion of my work with La Bandera residents. It is two weeks after I presented my work to Llareta, and the health promoters have helped me organize this larger event. Sonia has spent the day shopping and cooking, and as I prepare to talk, she enters through the back with large plates of food—miniature sandwiches and homemade potato chips and pots of cooked and fruited wine that we will serve at the celebration afterward. During the week, María Eugenia from EPES typed up invitations and an agenda, and members of Llareta distributed them to people in the *población* who had had a personal connection to my work. Now, as I adjust my tape recorder and hang up my visual aids, I can see people entering: a woman whom I had interviewed about the 1970 land seizure 26 de enero; Cristina, who had told me about the committee of the homeless she led in the late 1960s; and her daughter-in-law, who had sat outside on a curb with me, explaining what it was like to be a young mother trapped by domestic responsibilities at home. The neighborhood council president who early on had challenged me to make a contribution to the well-being of the *población* has arrived, formally dressed as always in a dark suit, vest, and tie. The young people from the Lutheran youth group are here, as are health promoters from other *poblaciones*, staff members of EPES, workers and clergy from the Lutheran church, and the health promoters' children. By the time we are ready to start, the crowd is standing-room only—over sixty people fill the room.

My presentation this evening is similar to the one I gave to Llareta two weeks ago. I discuss my ideas about the legitimation of knowledge, the political transition, and the paradox of participation in the new democracy. As in my presentation to the health group, I use a time line to explain my analysis of political periods and forms of organizing in Chilean history. Now, however, I have added visual aids to capture the interest of a broader audience. I begin my presentation with a twenty-minute video Gordon and I made: it combines photographs of the *población*, music, and excerpts from interviews with *pobladores*. Many of the voices are of people in the room tonight. In the video, those interviewed reflect on political organizing in the early 1990s—that moment three years ago, at the end of the dictatorship and the beginning of democracy. During my discussion of a 1992 health seminar, I show slides of health promoters Valeria and Mónica Janet giving their speeches, and I display the graphs and illustrations they used in their presentations. And during a discussion about the legitimation of knowledge, I ask members of Llareta to speak from their places in the audience, telling stories in their own voices about how they were thrown out of a school when they had been invited to give a presentation on meningitis, and how they were treated with disrespect when they brought their own children to the health clinic.

The agenda specifies that at the end of the talk we will split the audience into small groups to discuss the ideas and debate a few questions. Then, in a "plenary," we will return to the large assembly to hear each group's views. But by the time I finish speaking, the hour has already grown late, so instead, we open the floor to discussion. I suggest that in addition to their own commentary, people respond to the central strategic question raised by the talk: "What kinds of resistance might community groups use toward the government's discourse of participation in the 1990s?" It is a question that opens this forum to public discussion of social movement issues.

The discussion is energetic as people reflect on cultural changes following the end of the dictatorship, their own interactions with the municipal health clinics, the difference between the years I had done the fieldwork (1991–92) and the present (1994), and their opinions on the discourse of participation. Listening to this discussion, a woman who works in a shoe factory, and whose son is one of the few *pobladores* on his way to college, tries to change the subject. I don't want to talk about the health group and community organizations, she says. We can do that anytime. I have never before seen anybody present a book in this *población*. Let's talk about the book.

We are in the middle of an animated debate when Cristina—Valeria and Sonia's older sister—raises her hand. Now in her late forties, Cristina was one of the first people to arrive in La Bandera, having been a leader in the committees of the homeless that acquired land in 1968. But since that time she has distanced herself from community organizations and is often critical of her sisters' involvement, fearing that their political activity might get them imprisoned or even killed. Having listened to my talk and the health promoters' comments, Cristina now stands to speak.

I came [this evening] because I was invited, [and] because my sisters participate. But I never have participated. Because I really don't see the help for the people. I see that you [members of Llareta] participate among yourselves, you have your group, you participate to the extent that you make posters, but in practice it's not seen. Occasionally a health group helps. But it's hard to get them to do a Pap [smear], [or] to give injections.

Cristina contrasts the health group's organizational activity with her own and her brother's direct provision of medical care:

In the time since we arrived here at the *población* La Bandera, my brother and I have never participated in any group. Nor have we worked in an organized way like you all. But we have helped. I have attended thirty births in La Bandera. Without being a midwife, without having degrees....My brother...gives injections—he's always willing. And without a salary. So I think that helping the people is better.

I can see the tension rising in Valeria's face as she considers how best to respond. When her sister finishes speaking, Valeria takes the floor. Health promoters do treat illnesses and give first aid, she tells the audience, "[Cristina] knows that... we give injections, take [blood] pressure, do cures. She has seen our campaign in the market. We have done a series of things and nonetheless, she doesn't see help." In addition to providing these services, Valeria goes on, members of the health group seek to educate their neighbors so that they can protect their own health. Here she mentions the health group's goal of making knowledge available to people who are not professionals. Valeria's first defense acknowledges Cristina's notion of health care as providing services, while the second affirms Cristina's proposition that one does not need a formal education to help. But the crux of the tension is that Llareta has a view of the role of community organizations not shared by her sister—the notion that rather than being service providers, grassroots organizations need to hold government officials accountable for ensuring the population its right to decent health. Valeria says, "There is a confusion in terms of what is the contribution that the social organizations have to make within the *población*."

At the top of Llareta's agenda in 1991 were environmental problems in the *población*. Fields littered with trash were potential sources of illnesses like hepatitis and typhoid, but the effort to get them cleaned spoke to issues far beyond garbage removal and the spread of disease: it encapsulated the challenges and dilemmas of post-dictatorship organizing.[1] Facing a municipal government that was unresponsive and a national government that continued to limit public spending, the health group was searching for new ways to get governmental officials to respond to citizens' needs.

Around this struggle arose a battle about the meaning of participation. As it tried to organize in the post-dictatorship period, the health group was confronted with the dual approach of the Aylwin government toward grassroots organizations. On the one hand, the government had little use for the organizations that had mobilized against authoritarian rule. But the government also had an interest in promoting participation in certain types of grassroots organizations. As the story of the meningitis campaign in the previous chapter showed, community organizations that extended municipal services and educated the public in preventive care served a useful purpose. In a time of limited public resources and government cutbacks, they could deliver some of the services the public sector would no longer provide. While the idea and mechanisms of democracy described in chapter 4 *legitimate* economic restructuring, the discourse and practices of participation *subsidize* it as well.[2]

CIVIL SOCIETY

Civil society has become a cornerstone of both those managing and those studying transitions to democracy. The recent revival of the concept has been attributed to the political and social transformations of countries in Eastern Europe in the 1970s and 1980s. Opposition intellectuals and activists in Eastern Europe argued that because totalitarian regimes operated by crushing independent organizations and controlling the economy, creating a vibrant civil society outside the influence of the state was the essential task for moving from communism to democracy and a free market economy (Fedorowicz 1990). Later, the discourse circulated to places such as China, where "many...reformers and dissidents of the 1980s...saw themselves...as building a civil society, a realm of social organization and activity not directly under state control" (Calhoun 1994, 195). Similarly, amid dictatorships in Latin America, "the resurrection of civil society" (Oxhorn 1995,

15) appeared to open the possibility of freeing citizens from state dominance and possibly overthrowing military rule.

The celebratory cast of civil society in these political contexts has spilled over into academic debates, where scholars have made the analytic concept into a normative ideal. Maxwell Owusu, an anthropologist who has consulted for a government-appointed committee working to create Ghana's new constitution (1997, 126), sees the "revival and proliferation of activist development oriented civic organizations and mutual-aid societies based on village, town, ethnic, family membership, and similar affiliations" (1995, 158) as integral to a "grassroots participatory democracy" that could become a model for other African countries. In the United States and Western Europe, civil society has been heralded as a key component of democracy by scholars who for the most part have lamented its decline (see, for example, Putnam 1993).

While ideals of "grassroots participatory democracy" and liberation from oppressive state rule have undeniable appeal, the concept of civil society as it is currently used merits far greater scrutiny. Connected to notions such as "good governance," "empowerment," and "partnerships," the idea of civil society has been integrated into the policies of international lending organizations. The Inter-American Development Bank (IDB), for example, sees itself as a "catalyst for civil society participation" and has developed a State and Civil Society Division that has "designed a program to strengthen civil society and mainstream CSOs (civil society organizations) into IDB development projects." A recent publication states:

> Although the term "civil society" is relatively new to the Bank, the institution has pioneered in making loans, grants and technical assistance to the citizens' organizations which constitute civil or service institutions. Small projects, micro-enterprise activities, and more recently the Multilateral Investment Fund have provided grants and seed money directly to civil society organizations (CSOs). To fulfill the 1994 Eighth Replenishment's mandate to reduce poverty, improve the accountability and effectiveness of governments, and preserve the natural environment, the Bank will find civil society to be an able partner.[3]

Two primary purposes appear to underlie this strategy. First, by soliciting citizens' and organizations' investment in policies, the programs reduce protest against structural adjustment policies. Verónica Schild (1998, 104–5) has indicated that the purpose of social investment funds like Chile's FOSIS (Solidarity and Social Investment Fund) is to

> soften the extreme social effects of structural adjustment policies, and of the neoliberal development model more generally. The goal of these projects is to help the poor and marginalized access the market by financing small social and economic infrastructure programs. Hence they represent a sort of "social adjustment" strategy that, as the World Bank readily admits, are politically motivated because they seek to guarantee political support for neoliberal economic reforms.

Such projects make the poor into entrepreneurs and thus invest them in the capitalist system by engaging them in microenterprises and other small business ventures.[4]

Coordinators of some civil society groups have themselves said that their organizations should lend support to transnational agencies and governmental policies. The head of Corporación PARTICIPA, a Chilean organization that promotes civic education about democracy, reflected on how civil society organizations could contribute to the international Summit of the Americas scheduled for April 1998. She suggested that "civil society can make constructive contributions to the governments participating in the…Summit *so that the agreements made will have the backing of the citizenry and therefore guarantee social order* and the maintenance of democracy [emphasis added]."[5] Although the term *civil society* is conventionally used to indicate that groups are outside the power of the state, the kinds of relationships generated when national governments and international lending agencies make community groups part of their strategies mean that organizations are more likely to facilitate than critique donors' and governments' practices.

Civil society organizations serve as more than legitimating and demobilizing mechanisms for international lending institutions and governments; they are also used to deliver services that, before structural adjustment policies, the welfare state used to provide. In a thoughtful essay exploring why international aid organizations have recently focused so much attention on civil society, authors from the North-South Institute note that "the role of the state is being revised through the dismantling of state-provided services."

They quote Bruce Schearer as saying: "'As government budgets, staff and foreign aid resources have shrunk or, in many cases, failed to materialize, NGOs have sprung up to fill the gap in supply of services, materials, technology, training, credit and communication with rural villagers and urban slum dwellers.'" The authors continue: "Civil society organizations are seen not only as more effective, credible and *equitable* agents, they are also to become replacement agents, filling in the ranks left by states and by donors alike. Indeed, in certain countries, the explicit installation of an 'autonomous civil society' has been part of the donors' exit strategies."[6]

This is borne out in the United States Agency for International Development's description of its New Partnerships Initiative of 1995, which it calls "an integrated approach to sustainable development that uses strategic partnering and the *active engagement of civil society,* the business community, and institutions of democratic local governance to bolster the *ability of local communities to play a lead role in their own development* [emphasis added]."[7] The agency defines "local empowerment"—what in 1991 Chile was often called "participation"—as "citizens working together to solve their own problems and build their own future." In this process, "there is growing interest in the 'privatization' of public functions at the local level in which a *reoriented public sector facilitates* business and *civil society provision of local services* [emphasis added]." The state, that is, coordinates local efforts by the private sector, nongovernmental organizations, and grassroots community groups to provide social services. From USAID's perspective, these projects of "local community involvement" are aimed at "breaking the cycle of dependence on development assistance" and allowing donor agencies to create "exit strategies."

In his introduction to *The Foucault Effect*, Colin Gordon (1991, 45) considers the idea that the state might have a new role of redistributing tasks once performed by the welfare state. Drawing on Foucault's concept of governmentality, he describes the state as "distributing the disciplines of the competitive world market throughout the interstices of the social body."[8] The pressure of the global economy, which in neoliberal economics has privatized formerly public services, puts the onus on individuals and citizens' groups to fill the gap. Retreating from the provision of public services, the state has not ceased all involvement. Rather, in its reinvented role, the state assigns the tasks and mediates disputes over expenditure. In Colin Gordon's words, "The state presents itself as the referee in an ongoing transaction in which one partner strives to enhance the value of his or her life, while another endeavors to economize on the cost of that life."

Another role of the state is in producing the motivating discourses for citizen activity. This chapter describes how the Chilean government creates health education material that implores citizens to use good hygiene, augmenting the appeal of these proposals by linking them to a sense of national identity, and offering the opportunity to participate in democracy. Participation in neighborhood activities has an immediate appeal. It creates a sense of meaning and gratification to know that one is actively helping one's community through difficult times. After years of living under an authoritarian regime that repressed neighborhood groups, many residents of La Bandera were pleased that the elected government was encouraging citizens to help out. Through these discourses and activities, self-regulating subjects are created—subjects who will volunteer their time and energy in the name of democracy and citizenship.

When the state delegates formerly public sector functions to citizens' groups, the supposedly neat division between state and civil society breaks down (see also Alvarez, Dagnino, and Escobar 1998, 18). The contracting out of services to community groups raises the question of the degree to which organizations can make claims on a purportedly separate state. If the responsibility for removing garbage rests on civic groups themselves, then to whom might social movements direct demands?[9] Under the guise of supporting civil society, the government may actually stifle a civil society that thrived more powerfully under authoritarian rule.

It is the fact that participation offered a sense of meaning to citizens at the same time as it limited avenues through which citizens could act that leads me to speak of the "paradox of participation." The double nature of participation obliges us to examine the discourse with a critical eye. For Llareta, the way participation was framed in the 1990s raised a series of questions. How could leaders hold the government accountable if they were providing services under its auspices? Why should people who for the most part lacked secure jobs offer their labor for free? And, finally, what would happen to urban social movements if they were organized not around local interests but instead around the needs of the state? In addition to these questions, we might also ask: How might participation simultaneously operate both as a motivating force and a mode of control—a form of governmentality—that is characteristic of democracy amid neoliberal economics in Chile? And what, if any, forms of resistance have developed to respond to this form of power?

In this chapter I examine two kinds of participation that emerged in the field of health care in the early 1990s. The first is *auto-cuidado*—self-care, or prevention based on personal responsibility. The Ministry of Health's campaign to prevent the spread of cholera is a pertinent example. As part of this campaign, citizens were encouraged to take hygienic measures to protect themselves and their families from disease. In so doing, they would simultaneously be reducing public health expenditures and protecting the health of the nation.

In the second kind of participation considered in this chapter, the government encouraged grassroots organizations to deliver services to improve their community. For example, health promoters could assist local health clinics by providing child care, and community groups could clear littered fields of trash. If *auto-cuidado* reduced the financial burden on health clinics by reducing the number of people who got sick, community groups' "participation" in providing services could cut labor costs for the state.

As it explores new forms of power, this chapter also examines emerging forms of strategic resistance to the discourse and practice of participation. Llareta and other organizations in La Bandera sought to reclaim the word *participation* for their own purposes, insisting that participation meant being involved in decision making as well as implementing programs, and that it meant holding the government accountable for public services more than providing them for themselves. They sometimes met resistance from neighbors who agreed with officials that citizens should take direct action in cleaning up the *población*. Few issues could exemplify the tensions and confusion among the many actors involved better than the struggles over garbage dumps and disease.

PARTICIPATION AS INDIVIDUAL RESPONSIBILITY: THE CHOLERA CAMPAIGN

"Cebollas, cien pesos el lote!" "Acelga a cien!" (Onions for a hundred *pesos* the lot! Swiss chard for a hundred!) The merchants' voices called out and intermingled in the morning air. At the end of the *feria* (market) vendors displayed their household wares on pieces of plastic on the ground. Digna, leaning over to show some fabric to a customer, appeared too busy to talk as I walked by, but I greeted an older couple who lived on my block. On the ground they had arranged a collection of well-worn shoes—old work boots frayed along the front and edges, ladies' shoes bent

outward at the sides. At the post next to them was an assortment of hardware, including rusty faucets, miscellaneous bolts and screws, and pieces of plumbing pipe. A little farther along I spotted a collection of reading materials displayed on the ground. Sometimes warped with water or tattered from use, they were an odd assortment—dated news magazines, educational pamphlets for schoolchildren, booklets containing lyrics and guitar chords for popular songs, paperback books missing their front covers. I stopped to take a look, then headed farther along to get my shopping done.

At one of the stands, I stopped to buy a kilo of oranges. As the brightly colored fruit dropped into my white burlap bag, the stiff handles cut harsh red ridges into my fingers. The bag was already heavy with produce—potatoes, a cauliflower, and a thick wedge of squash. These hearty vegetables were best eaten cooked. They could be flavored with lemon or vinegar as a side dish, added to soup, or mixed with other vegetables in a stew. At the top of the bag I added a bunch of fragrant cilantro and a head of lettuce. I thought I would use the cilantro in a classic Chilean salad of tomatoes, onions, and garlic, and I expected to serve the lettuce the way most local residents did, dressed with oil and salt. But I reminded myself that I had run out of disinfectant. Produce was routinely irrigated in untreated human waste, and raw vegetables were often contaminated by typhoid and hepatitis. So, I added to my shopping bag a plastic bottle of chlorine in which the greens could later soak.

A bit farther along, I squeezed between the carts to exit the market, hoping to find a less congested road on which to walk. As I emerged, I found myself facing the cluster of public buildings that served this sector of La Bandera. Situated among them was a store, and I entered it to buy a few goods unavailable at the market. It was at this shop that families on the surrounding blocks made their daily purchases. In the afternoons just before tea time (which for many households in La Bandera was the only evening meal),[10] a member of each family would join the jostling crowd gathered at the counter to purchase a kilo or so of bread and something to accompany it—jam, margarine, a small amount of deli meat or paté. The store also sold liquor, household goods such as floor wax and detergent, packaged dairy products, and a meager assortment of vegetables that became increasingly wilted as the week wore on. Stores like this were the only local alternative for produce on the days no open-air market took place. The owner and his family did a robust business thanks to a captive audience: few residents could afford the transportation to travel out of the *población*, and it was a rare family that had sufficient cash to justify large purchases at supermarkets along Santiago's major roads. Instead, *pobladores* sent their children down the street to buy eggs, tea bags, or matchboxes one at a time. They paid higher prices, but it was the most they could manage with the few coins they had obtained during the day.

I bought half a kilo of bread and some cheese and then walked outside. Just next to the store lay an open field. Blueprints from the 1960s that I had obtained from the housing ministry indicated that this area had initially been planned as a park. But no recreational facilities had ever taken shape, and instead the land had become littered with garbage. Rats, old clothing, disintegrating mattresses, and food remains could all be found amid the debris. Some of this material was local. Garbage was picked up from residences twice weekly, and old food sitting for days attracted insects and rodents into the house. Since there were no public garbage cans or dumpsters in the *población*, residents sometimes dumped their trash outside. Moreover, not all materials would be accepted by the garbage trucks, leaving people on their own to dispose of large items. But not all the waste was of local origin. It was said that vehicles came to leave garbage there from other parts of the city. The public area had become a dumping ground because it was space abandoned—owned by government and maintained by nobody, it continued to accumulate trash.

Beyond its symbolic significance, the dirty field harbored disease. Like the produce grown in sewage water, the garbage was fertile ground for spreading typhoid and hepatitis. Children had trampled a diagonal path through the rubbish on their way to school, and their trail provided tangible evidence that this place was used by residents daily, and thus daily put people at risk. Holding my breath to avert the foul smell, I took one last glance at the dirty field and saw a skinny dog scavenging among the food remains. Then I turned and headed home to put my groceries away.

On the next scheduled *feria* day, April 18, the market was nearly empty. Barely a soul walked through the street. Vendors called out their prices for a while, then gave up in exasperation. That afternoon they threw out great quantities of vegetables— nearly all of the lettuce, carrots, potatoes, beets, and cauliflower they had intended to sell. What had happened to provoke such a change in market conditions? On April 17, news came over the radio that cholera had arrived in Santiago.[11]

The coming of cholera to Chile caught many people by surprise; the disease had not existed in Latin America for a century. Recent news stories had confirmed that the illness was having devastating effects in Peru, but many Chileans considered their country more advanced than other parts of Latin America.[12] The international press claimed that as a result of its economic success, Chile was leaving the Third World and entering the First. Although cholera might infect populations elsewhere, people thought, Chile would somehow be immune. By April 1991, however, it was clear that there were cases of cholera in Chile.[13]

The infected Santiago man appeared to have contracted cholera by eating raw vegetables. In the early 1990s, human waste was pumped into rivers and then used to irrigate farmland to the west of the city. The dirty water returned to human consumption through vegetables grown in the ground. Given the prevalence of typhoid and hepatitis, passed on in the same way, it seemed possible that cholera would spread rapidly. But cholera was also different from typhoid and hepatitis. Cholera could be prevented, but not by simply soaking vegetables in chlorine. And cholera was curable, but only if a person received immediate medical attention. If left untreated, the disease quickly killed. Given the likelihood of contamination and the severity of the disease, the health group Llareta expected the spread of ill-ness and a spate of deaths.[14]

In contrast to the outbreak of meningitis experienced in the *poblaciones* a year earlier, the Chilean government took the threat of cholera seriously. Given the death rates in other Latin American countries, officials knew they needed to take action to avert an epidemic. So as the first signs of the disease appeared in Chile, the government launched a public health campaign.

The Ministry of Health focused its attention on simple procedures through which individuals could prevent the spread of the disease (Rebolledo 1993, 153). These included washing one's hands before eating and after using the bathroom; covering the garbage; thoroughly cooking fish and shellfish; cooking any vegetables, like onions or cabbage, that grew on the surface of the earth; heating unpasteurized milk; boiling unclean water; and sanitizing bathrooms with chlorine. People could implement these measures by modifying their own and their family's behavior.

Using this information, the ministry set about developing a set of public service messages that instructed people on how to avoid contracting cholera. Tapping into skills similar to those used during the NO campaign in the 1988 plebiscite, the designers of the cholera campaign decided to use communications media for public service announcements.

In the subsequent weeks and months, the government's messages could be seen everywhere. In La Bandera, we heard warnings about cholera on radio and viewed instructional spots on television. Pamphlets were left in public places to explain the necessary precautions. Posters explaining preventive measures could be found hanging on the walls of corner stores, in the health clinics, and in municipal offices. In the municipal high school, students' drawings, illustrating the preventive techniques, were displayed on the bulletin board near the school's entrance. In a variety of ways, the Ministry of Health's publicity campaign reached nearly every corner of the *población*.

Embedded in the Ministry of Health's publicity materials was a philosophy toward public health and a specific notion of the role citizens and the state should each play. In one poster, with the headline "Let's Protect Ourselves from Cholera," individuals are shown taking precautions in their homes and workplaces. Two women wash their hands, another boils water, three more clean and cook their food. In illustrating the practices necessary to prevent cholera, the art zooms in on the characters' immediate actions. The tools they use are simple, everyday items—a sink, a garbage pail, a pot. Sometimes two figures appear—one woman is seen washing in a sink while another uses a pitcher and bowl. This juxtaposition conveys the message that the preventive measures can be put into effect regardless of a person's economic background. Indeed, these characters could be in homes, kitchens, and workplaces anywhere. The sense of placelessness is conveyed visually, for around the figures the black background fades out at the edges. The social context in which they live is literally out of the picture.

...HIRVIENDO EL AGUA NO POTABLE Y LA LECHE NO ENVASADA

...COMIENDO COCIDAS LAS FRUTAS Y VERDURAS QUE CRECEN A RAS DEL SUELO. EL RESTO DEBE LAVARSE Y PELARSE CUANDO CORRESPONDA.

Figure 12. Details from a Ministry of Health poster headed "Let's Protect Ourselves from Cholera." The illustrations shown here give instructions about (a) "boiling nonpotable water and unpackaged milk" and (b) "cooking fruits and vegetables that grow in or near the ground. The rest should be washed and peeled when appropriate."

Because cholera is conceptualized as primarily a biological problem, the social and economic location is immaterial to understanding its causes and unnecessary to implementing solutions. The materials communicated the idea that cholera was caused by bacteria. Because biological contamination was at the root of the pending epidemic, people could prevent the disease from spreading by improving their hygienic practices.

Within the paradigm of disease as biology, the Ministry of Health focused its campaign on getting individuals to change their sanitary practices. In the words of César Rebolledo (1993), adviser on communications to the Ministry of Health, "It appeared to us...that [controlling cholera] implied provoking a change in habits of the household and individuals." The Ministry of Health intended to communicate the idea that "you are the responsible one...and you have to...demand that the norms are followed for not contracting cholera." With their focus on individual activity, the posters sent the message that everyone was responsible for their own and their family's health.

The interest in having individuals prevent the spread of disease fit into a public health strategy called *auto-cuidado* (self-care), which was predominant in Chile in the early 1990s. "We felt that the responsibility...was not only governmental but rather of each one of us," wrote Rebolledo (1993, 154). If individuals could prevent themselves from contracting disease, fewer public resources would need to be expended on treatment. By placing the practical and financial burden for preventing an outbreak of cholera on individuals and their families, the campaign was alleviating a potential financial burden from the state (e.g., the cost of building a water treatment system for the Santiago region). But the government was not merely absent. Rather than make major expenditures on public health measures, the government would create the educational and communicational materials through which to coordinate this sum of private efforts for public health.

The posters themselves were framed not around cost cutting but in terms of national identity. By washing their hands and covering their trash, the materials implied, all citizens were involved in the larger project of safeguarding the health of the nation. Posters and leaflets sported the phrase "All of Us Are in Action in Chile. We Can Control Cholera," which conjured up a united Chile, a nation that had pulled together to prevent the spread of disease. Subsequent public health themes reinforced that idea. The stage of the cholera campaign launched in February 1992, for example, used the slogan "Remember, the Health of All Begins with You." Although they implemented the measures at an individual level, citizens were to consider themselves as joining in a collective effort to protect the health of Chile.

By protecting its health, they were also protecting its image, and—given the marketing of Chile as an economic and political model—its economy. Cholera was considered a disease of the Third World, and a disease of the nineteenth century. In the 1990s, when Chile was spoken of as First World and modern, a cholera outbreak threatened to defy this internationally marketed image and put foreign investment at risk.[15] Government health posters asked citizens to protect the nation, because it was the nation that was at stake in both international images and internal legitimacy. More than just an economic or a public health strategy, *auto-cuidado* required the self-regulating habits and active engagement of citizens.

To a degree, the Ministry of Health's information campaign was empowering and effective because it gave families in popular sectors a sense of control. Everyone knew exactly what to do to protect themselves and their children from cholera. And the fact that the images on the posters were decontextualized meant that a standard set of materials could be distributed quickly and efficiently throughout the country.[16]

But members of Llareta, in cooperation with both the Metropolitan Coordination of *Poblacional* Health (or Metro for short) and EPES, began to develop an analysis that held that there were conditions specific to the *poblaciones* that were not remediable by changes in personal behavior. It was the impact of the *población*'s environment on the spread of cholera that most worried the health group. The raw sewage escaping broken pipes where children played; open garbage dumps that children walked through on their way to school; shutoffs of potable water for those who could not afford to pay their utility bills; the high cost of cooking gas; cesspools *(pozos negros)* rather than sewage systems on people's property; rats in the houses and fields—all these environmental and infrastructure problems characteristic of poor neighborhoods contributed to the spread of cholera and other diseases. No matter how many times an individual in these neighborhoods washed his or her hands or covered the household trash, health group members asserted, the environmental and infrastructure problems would still spread the disease.

Health group members also noted that facilities to treat people once they had contracted cholera were inadequate in their part of Santiago. La Bandera's health clinic had far too few staff members to serve the thousands of people in its area of service. Residents routinely waited on line at five in the morning to get one of the scarce numbers for an appointment, and once all the numbers were gone, the rest were turned away. The hospital zoned for this area had not been built—the Ministry of Health owned the property, but the land on which it was to be constructed was, in 1991, a field of trash.[17] La Bandera residents traveled to either of two hospitals located in other parts of the city.

The need to leave the *población* for hospital care made access to transportation crucial. There were few cars in the *población*, and most people could not afford a taxi. That left buses, which were often overcrowded, did not run frequently at night, and sometimes required long waits. The fact that no ambulance served La Bandera had always been a problem, but now it became an urgent issue. Cholera killed through dehydration. If a sick person received immediate medical attention, his or her life could be saved. Without transportation to a hospital, however, an otherwise nonfatal disease could rapidly take a life. The health group held that inadequacies in medical facilities and transportation, like environmental and infrastructure problems, could not be overcome by changes in personal behavior.

The individual prevention measures seemed not only insufficient but also impracticable, and health group members had doubts that *pobladores* would follow them. Although the practices were for the most part simple, many of the preventive measures required resources poor people did not have. Boiling drinking water was often impractical, for example, given that families could not always afford even enough fuel to cook a meal. The instructions to heat fish and milk seemed distant from *población* reality. Vendors in the market sold vegetables, fish, and milk every week, and those who consumed these items would benefit from the Ministry of Health's warnings to cook their food. Yet families I knew survived mainly on rice, noodles, potatoes, and bread, sometimes supplemented by beans, vegetables, or a small bit of the most inexpensive meat.

The unavailability of nutrients was poignantly expressed by children. Identifying me as a potential source of food, Valeria's five-year-old daughter explained to me that she absolutely needed milk to grow. "Tea does not nourish a child," she stated emphatically.[18] When a nurse told one six-year-old that her health problems derived from not eating enough iron-rich foods like spinach, the girl told the nurse that her father worked as an organ grinder, and that they could not afford to buy vegetables. Adults were also well aware of their nutritional deficiencies. In the words of one man, "We don't live, we merely survive." Referring to a diet that consisted mainly of broth, potatoes, bread, and tea, he said "We are only half-eating." For these families, illustrations on the government publicity posters showing women cooking fish and heating milk only reinforced their sense of deprivation. These families could not comply with the government's instructions because it was impossible to sterilize food that you did not have. Because of these inconsistencies between the precautionary measures advocated in the Ministry of Health's posters and the key sources of disease in the *población,* health promoters expressed skepticism that the government's campaign would prevent the spread of cholera and other diseases in La Bandera.

Despite the fact that the precautions did not exactly fit the circumstances, *pobladores* took the Ministry of Health's warnings seriously. Residents of La Bandera became so cautious, in fact, that they stopped buying fresh food altogether. It was for that reason that on April 18, the day after we heard news that cholera had arrived, the usually crowded outdoor market was virtually abandoned.

The lack of customers had a potentially devastating impact on the small business people who sold food in the market. The merchants at La Bandera's market, many of whom lived in the *población,* survived on the proceeds of what they had sold that day. With the precipitous fall in sales, their already precarious income was threatened. On April 18, they had spent their capital on goods in the morning, only to lose their investment in the afternoon. As they disposed of their perishable merchandise, the workers talked among themselves, many expressing anger that they had lost money and worrying about how they would feed their families. Lili, a former member of Llareta who sold vegetables in the market, had an additional concern. She feared that by selling produce to a few people that day, she had transmitted cholera to her neighbors. Her logic was a stunning display of the government's premise that every citizen was responsible for preventing a cholera epidemic. This individual blamed herself, not her circumstances, for spreading the disease.

The absence of customers in the market had other serious consequences. It meant that people who already had a poor intake of nutrients would consume fewer vegetables. It also meant that residents of La Bandera who worked as vendors would be unemployed. These problems compounded the environmental hazards for contracting cholera that existed in the *población*. Dissatisfied with the steps the Ministry of Health was taking to prevent an epidemic, Llareta, in conjunction with EPES and other health groups in Santiago, decided to organize a campaign.

On May 1, Llareta held a public act in the outdoor market. By this time customers had returned to the *feria*, although many were still cautious about buying vegetables and fish. Llareta chose to hold the activity on May Day, an international holiday commemorating workers' struggles. Members of the health group stood out in the *feria* that morning handing shoppers an open letter; their supply of one thousand sheets was gone in about an hour and a half. The immediate goal was to support the merchants in the *feria* by explaining to residents that they could continue to purchase and eat vegetables as long as they cooked them thoroughly. But beyond expressing solidarity with the vendors, the health group had a broader agenda. It hoped to change how the problem of cholera was being handled by the government. Its efforts over the next months would include identifying houses without indoor plumbing, or without running water, and pressuring to have garbage dumps in the *población* cleaned.

The letter the health promoters handed out was written by Llareta in cooperation with the Metro. The letter contrasted with, and responded to, the publicity produced by the Ministry of Health. The Metro's materials framed cholera as not simply a biological phenomenon spread by bacteria but a problem with political roots, and a subset of the broader problem of poverty. They situated cholera within the failure of government in Latin America to install adequate public sanitation systems and the failure of the neoliberal economic model to meet basic human needs.

In this line of analysis, the open letter addressed to "the *Pobladores* and Workers of *Poblaciones* and Squatters' Settlements" began by situating cholera within a global political and economic perspective. It read:

Cholera is in Chile as in Peru, Columbia, Ecuador, Argentina, Brazil, Bangladesh, etc. Countries where misery and marginalization affect millions of human beings.

Why does cholera attack principally the most poor?

Because malnutrition and poor nutrition lower our biological defenses. The problem with cholera is POVERTY...our situation of garbage dumps and "black holes" [cesspools] in our *poblaciones*, of bad sewage networks and insufficient health attention, of lack of stable work and a dignified salary; all conditions that for years have injured our health; affecting our children with diarrhea, malnutrition, scabies, impetigo, pediculosis[; and] provoking sicknesses like typhoid, hepatitis, intestinal parasites, and so on.

The letter did not deny a biological element to the disease. But neither did it limit the understanding of cholera to an issue of bacteria and personal hygiene. Instead, it focused on how poverty and the long-term conditions of life endured by the poor—malnutrition, faulty sewage systems, inadequate income—contributed to the conditions that allowed many diseases to spread. The health groups considered these conditions political outcomes with political causes and saw the lack of adequate sanitation systems as the result of a political system and an economic model that distributed resources unevenly, with the result that cholera and other diseases had a disproportionate impact on the poor. For this reason, the letter asserted, "thousands of posters and warnings on television will not resolve" the more fundamental problems, nor prevent the spread of disease. The statement was in direct response to the Ministry of Health's campaigns.

In critiquing the ministry's publicity campaign, the Metro was not negating the idea that preventive measures like hand washing were necessary. As was evident from the meningitis campaign described in chapter 4, Llareta regularly distributed information on concrete measures that families could take to avoid contracting a disease. Instead, it was the ministry's narrow focus on individual responsibility and self-care and its limiting of the state's role to providing information without making infrastructure improvements that provoked the critique. Without denying the value of preventive measures, the health groups were asserting that the government publicity campaigns were insufficient. "We are not against the informative campaign to prevent cholera," the open letter stated, "but we want to make it clear that [one] must not only think about sickness."[19] Rather than construct the issue as one of hygiene and disease, the Metro advocated taking into account the political decisions and power relations that framed biological issues.

The letter linked the idea that the causes and effects of disease were political to the situation of workers who were harmed economically during the cholera scare. The open letter drew readers' attention to "the thousands of workers who remain unemployed, small peasants, fishermen, craftsmen, and small business people who have lost their work capital and that in contradiction with previous situations have not received any state support." The letter challenged the state's assertion that the lack of economic support for small business people was the result simply of a lack of public funds. Rather, the letter argued, lack of financial backing occurred because the wealthy and the poor—agricultural owners and workers—were treated unequally. It compared the situation during the cholera scare to events in 1989 when cyanide was found in two Chilean grapes imported into Philadelphia. The Chilean government eventually compensated the large agricultural companies that lost their export sales at a total of two hundred million dollars. Meanwhile, the letter stated that thousands of fruit workers who picked and packed the grapes were fired. The state gave "a response to the powerful" while letting the less powerful suffer the economic consequences. The letter compared this to the case of cholera. The government did not compensate those workers who, like Lili, lost out financially as a result of the scare. Instead, the state "rapidly asserted the lack of resources."

The government's claim that there were no available public resources to deal with the epidemic was significant because, in the health groups' view, spending money to curb cholera at its source could stem the spread of the disease. The letter proposed that public money be used for "decontaminating the waters of Santiago, which would guarantee the population the consumption of vegetables and sea products free of contamination." Rather than place the burden on the population to cook every vegetable and piece of seafood, the health groups argued, the government could ensure that vegetables were irrigated and fish were raised in uninfected water. The government's decision to place the burden and expense of preventive health measures on citizens rather than on the state was, in their view, a logical component of the neoliberal economic model. By neglecting infrastructure improvements for years, the health groups argued, this economic model enabled a disease once eliminated from Latin America to reappear. But, their discourse implied, the model was not a fixed and static entity: political choices could be made about where to invest public funds.

If the open letter distributed in the *feria* made the health group's analysis explicit, a poster jointly designed by the Metro and EPES made it popularly accessible. Using a homemade paste made of flour and water, health group members hung the posters on walls around the *población*. To understand the differences in ideologies, it is useful to compare their poster with the one produced by the Ministry of Health.

Entitled "Cholera, One More Effect of Misery," this poster, like the Metro's open letter, situated cholera within the larger problems of poverty, politics, and the economy. The top of the poster states, "Hepatitis, typhoid and now cholera make us sick because we have a social system that harms the interests of the majority, causing unemployment and low salaries, destruction of the environment, lack of dignified housing, and an insufficient health system." The words reframed the question from an exclusive focus on cholera to a consideration of the array of diseases affecting the poor. They tied those diseases to an unequal social system and harsh living conditions in poor neighborhoods.

The poster's illustration situated the people most affected by cholera in their own environment. A woman stands in front of her house, a small structure made of wood. She obtains water from the only source available to her—a community tap—and carries it in a pail. Around her lies a much broader explanation of the spread of disease: a rat lies by the side of the river, an old tire and other garbage float by, and crops grow alongside the contaminated water. The houses are surrounded by dirt, and one can see an outhouse off to the side. The place pictured here is a *población* or squatters' settlement, and the living conditions depicted differ sharply from the environment in middle-class and wealthy parts of the city. In

Figure 13. EPES and Metro cholera poster.

contrast to the Ministry of Health poster, which acquired its effectiveness through decontextualization, this poster made people's environment and life circumstances central to the understanding of the disease.

Clearly, each of the posters was related to a larger political agenda aimed at consolidating identities and staking out particular kinds of political action that extended beyond the immediate case of cholera. In saying "Let's [all] protect ourselves against cholera," the Ministry of Health's poster highlighted the commonality and mutual responsibility of Chileans. It implicitly advanced a collective identity for Chileans as citizens of the nation. In contrast, the Metro and EPES poster created a sense of interests organized around class. By saying that the existing "social system…hurts the interests of the majority," it distinguished winners and losers of the economic and political model.

The posters converged on the question of who did the work related to cholera. Both the government poster and the Metro and EPES poster portrayed women as central actors. In the Ministry of Health poster, women do the cooking and cleaning that prevent cholera—only the garbage is taken out by a man. While the term *auto-cuidado* (self-care) or the phrase "We are all in action in Chile" implied that responsibility was shared equally among Chileans, both in actuality and in the image, preventing cholera was work done by women fulfilling their domestic responsibilities. In the Metro and EPES poster it is a woman who bears the burden of sustaining her household under harsh conditions. Potentially, she is also an actor who, by organizing, can reclaim her rights.

The different analyses implicit in the two posters corresponded to support for different forms of political action. The Ministry of Health asserted personal hygiene as the key and took the government's responsibility to be creating a preventive publicity campaign. It oriented public policy toward educating the public, so that it could act through the behavior of individuals. In so doing, it put the burden of controlling the disease on citizens. The state would take on an educational role, without making major expenditures in public services and infrastructure.

The analysis expressed in the Metro's poster implied a different role for the state. "Hepatitis, typhoid, and now cholera make us sick because we have a social system that harms the interests of the majority," the poster read. The Metro held that the state had a responsibility for public health that went beyond disseminating educational materials. The government needed to spend public money on improving infrastructure, redistributing resources, and improving nutrition and housing. The implied proposal, that the social system be transformed so that the majority would benefit, contrasted with the government's interest in relocating responsibility onto citizens.

Health groups participating in the Metro knew that the state was unlikely to respond to their demands in a time of reduced government and an era of neoliberal economics. Therefore, the umbrella organization of health groups asserted that the poor would have to organize to demand accountability from the government on public health. Their open letter ended with a "call on all the *pobladores* and workers to organize in order to confront this epidemic in a dignified way and demand our rights."

The government had constructed individuals as responsible for controlling cholera through behavioral changes. In this sense, citizens would be implementing an agenda set by the Ministry of Health. The open letter addressed to *pobladores*, in contrast, maintained that popular sector organizations needed to denounce bad circumstances, claim rights, make demands, and hold officials accountable to an agenda set by popular organizations. The task of the urban poor was to use collective pressure to obtain responses from public officials.

The types of action suggested by the Ministry of Health's and the Metro's publicity materials were not mutually exclusive. Both personal hygiene and infrastructure improvements would contribute to halting the spread of disease. Nor did either party claim that the other had complete responsibility for preventing the spread of cholera. But the philosophies embedded in the posters and letters conveyed very different worldviews and strategies. In 1991, one could see on the bulletin boards of schools and health clinics in La Bandera, on the stone and brick walls bordering houses, and on flyers distributed at the outdoor market, competing interpretations and courses of action. Both popular organizations and the government were battling to frame the issue in the minds of neighborhood residents. And, for both, the question went beyond cholera. It was a fight about the type of political action appropriate to the kind of democracy emerging in a neoliberal age.

But how could the health groups hold the government accountable, given the politics of the new Chilean political system that operated through agreements between elites? How might they demand more public expenditures when the state had strictly curtailed the use of public resources? And how could they achieve mobilization to impact policy in a time of generalized demobilization?

The opportunity for confronting public officials directly came sooner than expected. For in July 1991, the Unión Comunal de Juntas de Vecinos de San Ramón (the coordinating body of local neighborhood councils) scheduled the first public assemblies *(cabildos)* to take place in La Bandera under the newly elected government. At the assemblies, community groups would engage in direct dialogue with politicians about improving conditions in the *población*. The subtext of this dialogue would be discussions about the kind of political action appropriate to, and the meaning of "participation" in, Chile's new political democracy.

PARTICIPATION AS CARRYING OUT PROJECTS:
THE FIRST PUBLIC ASSEMBLIES IN DEMOCRACY

Until the winter of 1991, the Concertación government had made its presence felt in La Bandera primarily in indirect ways. News of national events and interviews with politicians arrived in La Bandera through the media, particularly television shows. Public service announcements on the radio, as in the cholera campaign, communicated the Ministry of Health's messages to a wide population. And the

Figure 14. Poster for the *cabildo*. The poster reads: "First Democratic Public Assembly for San Ramón: Participate, Denounce, July 28 [1991], La Bandera. Convoked by the Coordinating Body of Neighborhood Councils."

new government's ideology reached popular sectors through institutions such as the Catholic Church, which joined efforts to promote national reconciliation. But amid this indirect contact, few events brought elected representatives into direct dialogue with members of the *población* itself.

It was this fact that made the *cabildo* a potentially important event. It was to be the first occasion on which elected officials would interact publicly and face-to-face with La Bandera's community organizations. At the meeting, residents could voice their concerns to elected officials. In turn, the Concertación would present its ideology and practice directly within the *población*. Organizers, primarily the heads of the *juntas de vecinos* (neighborhood councils) in the *población*, designed the event to take place in two stages: first a preliminary assembly—a *precabildo*—on July 20, then the *cabildo* itself a week later on July 28.

To make the meetings as comprehensive as possible, a broad array of public officials were invited to attend. Among them were the minister of health, the minister of education, and the minister of housing and urbanization. The regional intendant for the Santiago metropolitan region was invited, as were congressional representatives. From the municipality, the mayor and local council were asked to attend. Organizers also extended an invitation to clergy and other "religious authorities." The governmental invitees represented a mixture of politicians from the elected national government and the military-appointed local municipality.[20]

Organizers also invited a wide variety of community groups. According to a flyer announcing the event, local organizations asked to participate included neighborhood councils, committees of those living overcrowded, unions, youth centers, cultural centers, health groups, women's groups, senior citizen organizations, ecological committees, committees for street paving, human rights committees, sports clubs, firefighters, Christian base communities, the scout troops, small business people, midsize businesses, unions of the open-air markets, and common kitchens. It was an ambitious and arguably out-of-date list, given the decline in local organizations in recent years.

For social organizations in La Bandera, the *cabildos* provided an opportunity not only to hear what government officials had to say but also to directly address representatives of the municipal and national governments. In this, there was a double significance. On the most immediate level, the community groups would raise specific problems they encountered in the *población* in the hopes that public officials would address the issues. But the assemblies had a more profound significance. They were a space in which the community organizations and politicians would negotiate the kinds of relationships to develop between them in the post-dictatorship period. In this sense, the *cabildos* were about the meaning and practice of democracy.

While the stated goals for the assemblies were straightforward, the events were unlikely to be simple and cordial encounters. From their inception, the *cabildos* were contested among different political parties, ideologies, and factions, and thus they carried a set of conflicting agendas.

The flyer distributed by the Unión Comunal said, "The *cabildo* will leave us with a diagnosis of the district, a platform of struggle, and the disposition to push forward the solutions to the most serious problems of San Ramón." The flyer promoted a scenario in which popular organizations could reanimate organization and put pressure on the state. It represented the perspective of leftist leaders in the *población* who did not support the government's policies and who considered the *cabildo* to be "a form of participation of the people so that the *poblaciones* could denounce and initiate the solution of the immense gamut of problems that affect it."

In contrast, members of the Christian Democrat Party and elements of the Socialist parties within the *población* opposed the staging of a *cabildo* that would criticize governing officials. The Concertación had consistently called on the population to support its actions. As shown in the 1990 meningitis campaign discussed in chapter 4, politicians expected loyalty from citizens and discouraged demands or critique. Those who opposed the *cabildo* as a criticism of the government acknowledged that living conditions were not perfect, but they asserted that the Concertación was doing its best to overcome the obstacles left by the military regime. The fact that the social organizations that called the *cabildo* were interested in voicing a critical analysis of the current government's practice, and the fact that they hoped to use the event to pressure the state into solving local problems, meant that competing agendas were at work. The public assemblies were politicized and contested events from the start.

Anticipating some of this conflict, leaders from organizations in one of La Bandera's four sectors held a planning meeting on Thursday night, two days before the *precabildo*. Although they did not share a common perspective on the Concertación or the purpose of the *cabildo*, they did share a common interest in using the *cabildo* as a vehicle to improve conditions in the *población*. That evening they gathered around a table in the *junta de vecinos* building to plan their approach for the public assembly.

A quick survey of the people gathered at that meeting offered an initial diagnosis of the current state of organizing in the *población*. Representatives had come from some of the *población*'s youth organizations. Members of the neighborhood council were there, as were health promoters from Llareta. Leaders from a few more groups brought the total number to twelve. Those in attendance did not begin to cover the long list of organizations mentioned in the Unión Comunal's flyer. Moreover, a number of those present represented organizations that were nearly defunct. While the groups had robust histories, in recent years their membership had dwindled. The people at the meeting were without a base, leaders searching for a way to revitalize their organizations.[21]

The discussion that evening reflected a concern with that organizational reality. Many of the people expressed preoccupation about the state of social organizations in the sector. As part of their critique, they directed sharp criticism at the political parties. The leaders accused the parties of trying to manipulate events and people, of not knowing the reality in the *población*, and of not having the right to speak for *pobladores*. The bulk of the discussion focused on questions of how to reactivate collective action. The words *representatividad, participación*, and *organización* surfaced repeatedly as people searched for ways to explain the fragmentation of organizations and come up with ways of reanimating community groups.

The attendees had more to discuss than the general state of organizations in the *población*, however, and the conversation soon turned to devising a strategy for the upcoming event. This was no simple task because at that moment in the political transition two forms of government overlapped. At the national level there had been elections, and Concertación or opposition politicians filled most ministry and congressional posts. But at the local level, elections would not be held until August 1992, still a year away.[22] Therefore the mayor and other municipal officials appointed by the former dictator remained in office.[23] Given these circumstances, the question of how to approach a public assembly in which both forms of government would attend was complex. Social organizations faced the challenge of dealing at once with two different political logics: an elected national government and an authoritarian-appointed municipality.

It could be argued that the appropriate politicians to address at the public assemblies were representatives of the national government. After all, these politicians were elected, giving them at least formal responsibility to respond to constituents' needs. Moreover, the authoritarian system was nearly obsolete. Because municipal elections would be occurring in a year, it made little sense, in this line of reasoning, to focus on getting concessions from the current mayor.

But, as a result of the privatization and decentralization of public services during the dictatorship, the municipality played too central a role in local politics to ignore. When the national health service and national education system were dismantled, for example, the bulk of these services were turned over to competitive private enterprises like insurance companies and for-profit schools. For those unable to purchase insurance or education on the private market, public facilities existed, but these were to be administered by municipal governments. So, for example, the municipality of San Ramón, where La Bandera was located, ran elementary and high schools and managed the local health clinic. Garbage collection and maintenance of public areas was the responsibility of the municipality as well. This had obvious implications for resource distribution. Given residential segregation in Santiago, poor districts did not have sufficient money to address the many problems in their jurisdiction, yet that is where the responsibility for public services lay. Municipalization was retained after the transition to democracy, with effects for political activity. In the new period, even after municipal elections were held, the municipal government served as a de facto buffer shielding elected national politicians from public demands. After all, all problems had to be routed through local authorities first.

When the community leaders met that Thursday night, they deliberated about what would be the best approach to take at the *precabildo*. After some discussion, they made a decisive move. They oriented their style of action toward the political structure of the still authoritarian municipality. Based on this choice, they agreed to use the *cabildos* to denounce—that is, identify and criticize—problems affecting the *población*. Denouncing had been used during the dictatorship as a way of voicing concerns and discrediting the regime. Along with choosing to denounce, community leaders decided not to bring forth concrete proposals at the *precabildo*. Their concern, based on prior experience with the municipality, was that the mayor would appropriate their ideas as his own.

This tactical decision to orient their approach toward the municipal government would have consequences for the outcome of the *precabildo*. At one level it avoided conflict among community leaders over whether the *cabildo* would be a direct attack on the Concertación and, with it, the transition. However, the fact that most of the officials who attended the *precabildo* were not municipal officials but rather members of Concertación parties from the national government— and, indeed the fact that the municipal mayor did not even show up—would generate tension and provoke conflict at the assembly itself. It would also clarify the forms of power and kinds of organizational alternatives operating during political democracy.

Precabildo

The *precabildo* was scheduled to take place at the site of the neighborhood council *(junta de vecinos)*, a sizable brick building situated among the public buildings of the sector. The building's entrance opened into a large, undivided room ideal for a major assembly, and when I arrived that Saturday morning, the room was already crowded. People had been entering the building for some time, arriving individually and in groups. Some stood outside chatting, waiting for the program to begin. Others milled about inside talking to neighbors, while many more sat on the seats that filled the room. There was an air of anticipation as people meandered in, and eyes kept turning toward the door where political officials and members of the press were entering. Through the window, we could see that Senator Eduardo Frei had arrived, accompanied by police.[24] A newspaper reporter entered and stood by the door.

The dignitaries had arrived, but the president of the neighborhood council was nervous, afraid that too few residents would show up. Saturday mornings were busy times for nearly everybody—one of the few times when working people could clean, cook, shop, sleep, or repair the house. In retrospect, it seemed poor planning to have scheduled the *precabildo* at 9:30 A.M. instead of in the afternoon, when people customarily attended meetings. And although many seats were filled, the council president kept postponing the meeting in the hopes that more *pobladores* would arrive.

Finally, at about 11:30 A.M., the event began. A representative of the Unión Comunal announced that it would receive as many "denunciations and proposals" as possible until July 28. On that date the *cabildo* proper would take place "before all the authorities." The process, he said, would advance the community toward achieving "our local government in democracy." In that spirit, various community organizations and committees were to present their critiques of the current situation and voice their demands.

After the introductory remarks, representatives from a series of organizations stood up to delineate the problems they faced. A woman from the *unidad vecinal* spoke of poorly constructed *casetas sanitarias*, small brick kitchen-bathroom units built as part of "progressive" housing construction (i.e., built in stages), the need for a garbage truck, and the necessity of paving the streets. A person who worked with youth talked about drug addiction and lack of interest among teenagers. Another made note of the low salaries paid for available work, the enormous number of young couples living overcrowded with relatives, and the inadequate education system, all of which added up to an absence of opportunities for youth.

In addition to identifying collective problems, individuals described their own specific dilemmas. One woman described her living conditions. For lack of better housing, she lived in a *caseta sanitaria*. Because the *caseta* had no glass in the windows, the mattress she had placed across the narrow floor remained soaking wet, and as a result she and her children were continually sick. Valeria's niece Carolina had other problems with housing. The municipality had assigned her a site that had been abandoned for eleven years and had become a public eyesore. After paying to have seven truckloads of garbage hauled away from the site, she built a wooden house. Only after she had begun living there did the owner come to throw her and her family out. Now she had nowhere to go. In another case, an advocate described the story of a woman whose baby had died in the hospital. After raising 3,500 pesos for burial costs, the woman had gone to the municipality to request 2,500 pesos (US$7.50) more for cemetery and transportation expenses to bury her child. Instead of helping her acquire the money, a municipal social worker told her to put the child's body in a sack and take a public bus to the cemetery. These and other people had come to the *precabildo* to try to obtain solutions to their immediate problems and to illustrate broader issues of lack of resources or callousness of the municipality.

Members of Llareta focused their presentation on environmental and infrastructure problems in the *población*. Among other concerns, they highlighted the garbage dumps covering the *población*'s open fields. Speaking publicly, Iván acknowledged that the government had taken steps toward preventing a cholera epidemic by creating media campaigns that encouraged residents to take hygienic measures to halt the spread of the disease. But he articulated the health group's position that such publicity campaigns were insufficient. To prevent disease from spreading, he asserted, the garbage dumps scattered around the *población* should be cleared. Cleaning them was the responsibility of the municipal government.

Following the speeches by *pobladores*, governmental officials replied. When Hernán Rojo, the Christian Democrat congressional representative from the district, spoke, his anger was palpable. He said that he did not accept the criticism that the elected government had done nothing to improve people's lives. The government had made immense progress in its year and a half in office, he said. It was beginning to reconstruct health, education, and housing systems left in shambles by the military regime.

Having outlined the government's successes, he proceeded to speak about the meaning of political participation. "What is lacking here is knowledge of how to operate in democracy," Rojo told the audience. His statement was important because it represented one of the clearest public articulations by an official in the *población* of what it meant to live and take action within the new political system. Speaking to community groups in what had been one of the most politically active *poblaciones* in Santiago, he outlined the kinds of political action they should be using in democracy.

The first part of his lesson had to do with the role of the state. "It is not the state" that is responsible for solving these problems, he said. In saying this, he was stating that the government could no longer be expected to make major public expenditures and could not be called upon to address local needs.

The corollary to the reduced responsibility of the state was the expanded obligation of citizens and community organizations. Rojo went on to say, "Everyone should participate. When it comes to garbage, and pavement, you are the ones who are going to propose the solutions and establish the projects. It is the very *poblador* organizations that are going to execute them." Other officials on the panel echoed his words. A representative from the Ministry of Housing said, "We are not going to advance without participation. It is not [that] the government gives us [solutions]. It is a problem of organization, not just of money." In contrast to the practice of making demands and stating grievances, these politicians were saying, residents grouped into social organizations should be developing and implementing solutions.

Ironically, Rojo's speech came remarkably close to employing the same language that had been used by community leaders at the planning meeting two nights earlier. Like the community leaders, Rojo problematized the small number of people involved in *población* organizations. He criticized what was perceived as a low level of attendance at the *precabildo*. Using the same vocabulary as community leaders did, he called for "participation," "organization," and "mobilization."

Also like community leaders, Rojo defined democracy as hinging on widespread participation. In particular, he urged *pobladores* to be involved in all aspects of improving living conditions. He asked them to propose solutions, define projects, and implement them. He warned organizations not to be dependent on the state. And, echoing the leaders' criticism of political parties, he emphasized that the work needed to involve everyone and should not allow itself to be divided by political parties. As he said a few minutes later, "Health, education, housing— these things have no colors" (i.e., they are not exclusive to any particular political party but are common to all). The language of the Concertación officials and the community groups seemed to converge.

While the language of the speeches was similar, the discourses drew upon very different philosophical and political sources. When Rojo told those gathered at the *precabildo* that in democracy everyone needed to participate to solve common problems, he was referring to a very different concept of participation than that advanced by community leaders. What was different was the sort of organization advocated by each.

The type of organization Rojo advocated was rooted in the preoccupations of the Concertación government in the early 1990s. From one perspective, it was ironic that the Concertación supported the maintenance of social organizations at all. Grassroots organizations had been central in the mobilization that ushered in Allende and had been key players in the protests launched against the military regime. For the sake of stated interests in stability, governability, and consensus, the government stood to benefit from the decline of militant social organizations in the first years of democracy.

Nonetheless, during the Aylwin years, government officials also tried to convert grassroots community groups into permanent fixtures of the economy. In their new incarnation, popular organizations would play two primary roles. The first role was as profit-generating enterprises. This was key to an economic development strategy that sought to reduce poverty by generating small businesses in poor neighborhoods. The plan was for families to increase their income by producing and selling goods. Popular craft workshops could put their art up for sale, social organizations could start microenterprises, and collective kitchens could become for-profit restaurants. In an age of limited income transfers to poor families, the cultivation of local businesses, it was hoped, would begin to cut the levels of poverty.

The conversion of social organizations into microenterprises had political implications. Now grassroots groups would be dedicated to generating income rather than expressing protest. Training was oriented toward developing technical skills, not building consciousness or extending political *formación*. The changes in organizational purpose also had cultural ramifications that further diminished local organizing. Microenterprises would inculcate an entrepreneurial spirit appropriate to a neoliberal economy. While some saw this as a positive outcome, others worried that an individualist and competitive culture would replace the ethic of solidarity cultivated during the anti-dictatorship struggle (Leiva 1998). People would now be working to increase their own income rather than to benefit the community at large. Their neighbors would be seen not as a support network with a common identity and interests but as competition in the marketplace. Finally, running businesses also made sustaining local organizations logistically difficult. Women and men who put long hours into their businesses could, as a result, well be unavailable to attend community meetings. As grassroots organizations became microenterprises in a free market system, their capacity to level pressure on the state would decline.

The second role that Concertación politicians envisioned for community organizations was as extensions of government services. In a time of limited government, this was an important cost-cutting measure for the state. If volunteers and community organizations became auxiliaries of the health clinics, the state could maintain or even expand service without raising payrolls. When the health clinics were short on staff, health groups could fulfill functions like providing child care, distributing subsidized milk, or reminding residents to go for preventive health checkups. Whereas during the dictatorship, money from foreign aid organizations had gone directly to nongovernmental organizations, now much of it was channeled through FOSIS, a branch of the government. Local organizations were to compete in the FOSIS funding cycles for financing of community development projects. Groups that had been created for survival amid the poverty generated by neoliberalism and organizations that had been networked in a struggle against the dictatorship could become permanent vehicles for delivering social services at a time when the state could do "only so much" because of limited public resources.

In the post-dictatorship and postwelfare period, local organizations would provide services that a downsized welfare state could no longer afford.

It was this second role for social organizations that Rojo referred to when he suggested that neighborhood organizations coordinate paving the roads and cleaning the garbage dumps. Rather than call upon the state to solve problems, he was saying, community groups should do it themselves. What was most notable about his talk was that his focus was not on economics. Although it was mainly to cut costs that the organizations would be encouraged to operate, Rojo framed the issue in the much more meaningful and attractive terms of "democracy" and "participation." He told those assembled at the *precabildo* that the government could not be expected to solve the problems of the people *in democracy*. The reduced role of the state was framed as integral to the democratic political system itself. And democracy, of course, was something residents of La Bandera would want to support.

Instead of relying on the state, Rojo continued, community residents would need to *participate* in solving community problems. The use of this word was crucial, for it referenced an idea dear to those who considered the deepening of democracy to involve an increase in citizens' participation, a revitalization of civil society. Implied in Rojo's talk was the idea that, by participating, residents could take pride in helping improve their community. After a decade and a half in which social organizations had been repressed in Chile, the prospect of a government official welcoming citizens to participate sounded, to some, like a very appealing idea.

The meaning Rojo gave to the term *participation* presented community groups with a dilemma. Because survival issues such as hunger and inadequate housing were still prominent in La Bandera in the 1990s, community leaders wanted to preserve and reactivate popular organizations. Yet the government's welcoming attitude toward certain kinds of organizations created new dangers. Rather than repression, the groups risked absorption by a state that was asking them to conform to its own objectives and organizational structure. The use of social organizations by the state became a key way in which power was exercised, and one that Llareta dedicated itself to analyzing and resisting in the new political period.

Rojo's speech was not the health group's first encounter with these principles. In the past, health promoters in other *poblaciones* had been invited to participate in a child nutrition program. They were asked to reconstitute powdered milk supplied by the government, weigh babies to determine which were malnourished, and distribute the milk to those babies deemed most in need. At another time, Llareta was asked to take part in an antidrug campaign. And a newly formed health group in La Bandera received a request from the health clinic to go door to door reminding neighborhood women to keep their appointments for checkups. Those who accepted these invitations found the opportunities to help provide public services enticing—they saw them as a chance to make concrete contributions to the health of residents in the *población*.

But members of Llareta, other health groups, and the staff of EPES saw these invitations to "participate" as an attempt by the government to appropriate popular organizations for its own ends. They became acutely aware that in delivering health services, they would be providing free labor, thereby enabling the state to continue refusing to meet its obligations for financing health care. They held that in a time when many residents were unemployed, the state should hire paid workers at the clinics rather than rely on volunteers. The role of social organizations, in the view of Llareta, should be to hold the government accountable for assuring their rights to health were met. For this reason, action needed to be directed not only toward daily survival but also toward keeping social organizations autonomous and independent and toward pressuring the state to meet social demands.

One health promoter from another *población* contrasted her own concept with the idea of participation expressed by the health officials when they tried to get her group to participate in a campaign promoting Pap smears by inviting women to get the Pap smear done, looking for a place to do it, and making lunch for the workers that do the exam. "This is not the participation we want," she said. "What we want is to participate in all aspects of the campaign: in developing the campaign, the evaluation, and not only be[ing] the implementers of the campaign. That is not community participation. It doesn't have anything to do with it."

For her and for the health groups, participation meant not just executing decisions made by professionals but setting priorities, outlining strategies, and evaluating outcomes. It was this kind of relationship they wanted to forge with the municipal health clinic and the Ministry of Health.

On the surface, this health promoter's definition of participation sounded similar to Rojo's agenda at the *precabildo*. Rojo had called on popular organizations to be involved in all aspects of the campaign. "You are the ones who are going to propose the solutions and establish the projects," he said, implying that community groups would do the thought work involved in designing campaigns. "It is the very *poblador* organizations that are going to execute them." But community leaders, reflecting on their own experience with government-initiated campaigns in the 1990s, held that the roles they were asked to play were much more constrained in practice. They were asked only to implement—that is, do the daily labor of—projects designed by experts and officials.

In Valeria's words,

> They [the Concertación] have a concept of participation that is very different from ours. The government has a concept in which participation is "to use." To use the other for my benefit. So that they end up doing very well. Nonetheless, we understand participation from a much broader point of view. *We want participation from the beginning of the work until it ends, with some analysis or synthesis of the work....* [What] they request of us, as a health group, [is] to "participate" in the health clinics. The promoters are for nothing but holding the arm [i.e., when a child is given a shot]. So this type of participation, no.

A community leader in another *población* agreed. The current use of social organizations does not constitute participation, he said, but rather "nonparticipation." He explained,

> Today there is less participation, less organization, less mobilization.... The system functions precisely by way of this. They offer us work on issues defined from outside. From the state, from the municipality, from the health clinics. Already designed. Therefore, we are...executors of the policy made on our backs. But this clearly is not participation. If we want to be subjects [i.e., have agency], that implies having participation in the elaboration of these policies and not only in executing them, and making the cost of labor cheaper.

The concept of participation that these leaders laid out situated themselves as decision makers and intellectuals. Engaging in analysis and synthesis of the work meant that they would be the people who designed, rather than just implemented, policy. This was consistent with their many years of engaging in political analysis, setting agendas in their communities, and providing and receiving education.

The kind of participation social organizations were demanding grated against the cultural climate of Santiago. *Pobladores* were envisioned by officials less as the initiators of proposals than as the source of the *población's* problems. The poor needed to be educated and disciplined more than listened to.

This attitude was revealed as Rojo continued his speech at the *precabildo*. During his talk he reacted to Llareta's demand that the municipality clean the garbage dumps. It quickly became clear that he wanted *pobladores* to resolve the garbage issue themselves because he held them responsible for generating the litter in the first place. "What will we get out of planting trees if it is the same neighbors who ...destroy them?" he asked the group. "Why should we clean up the fields, when it is the people of this *población* that dump garbage in them? The minute that field is cleared, you will just fill it with garbage again." This was not a construction of *pobladores* as intellectuals and social actors who might set agendas. It was a portrayal of La Bandera residents as dirty and as the source of pollution. He told the people assembled that he would not support any efforts to get the municipality to clear the garbage from the fields.

Rojo's passionate speech about the garbage dumps revealed much about his vision of posttransition political action. Most of the Concertación politicians present at the *precabildo* made a distinction between the elected national government, which they expected citizens to support, and the still authoritarian municipality, which they agreed that citizens needed to confront. They noted in their talks that the municipality, which had been appointed by Pinochet, had neglected the needs of residents for nearly two decades.

Representative Escalona argued that the former dictator had left a time bomb by keeping the municipalities undemocratic after the transition to an elected national government. He feared that this failure to bring democracy to the local level would create widespread disenchantment and frustration with the new political system—undermining not only the Concertación government coalition but also the entire system of democracy.

One public official, unique in his congenial, sympathetic, and respectful manner, expressed his support to *pobladores* in making demands on the authoritarian local government. And Senator Eduardo Frei drew a clear distinction between approaches to the different kinds of government. He supported *pobladores* in mobilizing against an authoritarian municipality. But, he told them, it is the duty of everyone to support the new elected government, for "it is our government."

Rojo went farther than others on the panel by rejecting confrontation of any kind, including toward the municipal government. He declined to endorse any type of social action in which *pobladores* asserted rights, claimed services, or made demands on the state or local governments. Rather, he held residents responsible for cleaning their environment because he held them responsible for dirtying it.

By rejecting all forms of popular mobilization that might hold public officials accountable for enforcing laws and protecting people's rights, Rojo was advancing a notion of participation that fit a limited and "pacted" democracy in a neoliberal era. Rather than make claims against the government, the role of citizens was to support it and provide their own services. While other politicians exempted the municipality from this logic, they, too, advocated this role for citizens in relation to the national government. And the principles would apply to the local government as well, once there were elections the following year. Because they conceptualized the Concertación government as a popular victory over authoritarianism, politicians considered themselves by definition to be representing the Chilean people. And because they had been elected, they considered their actions by definition to be democratic. Not unlike during the 1990 meningitis campaign described in chapter 4, the role of community groups and residents was to support this government—*their* government—lest in resisting it they destabilize democracy.

Rojo's position on the garbage dumps resonated for some residents of La Bandera. At the *precabildo* one member of a neighborhood council backed up Rojo, saying to the audience, "Come on, now, we all know that we are the ones who dump that garbage there." Actions of self-sufficiency that followed from this logic were put into practice by community groups in the following weeks. For example, on weekends scout troops could be seen picking up garbage piece by piece from the field next to an elementary school.

Because of the attractiveness of Rojo's assertions to some residents, what was at stake for community leaders who were critical of government policy was the meaning of participation that would remain in public discourse. They sought to advance a meaning of participation that allowed organizations to pressure the state, that had *pobladores* setting agendas and designing programs rather than just implementing campaigns. The use of the term *participation* in two very different political ideologies constituted one of the most slippery discursive struggles in the early 1990s.

When community leaders entered the *precabildo*, they had oriented their strategy toward confronting the municipal government, the most relevant power in local politics. To an extent their decision made sense, given that the municipality was the governmental body in charge of most public services. However, the *precabildo* ended up revealing conflicts with the Concertación and generating insights into the power issues in political democracy. It revealed that the Concertación's concept of participation was one of the prime issues they needed to confront. In the *cabildo* that followed, Llareta focused its attention on responding directly to the Concertación.

In the week following the *precabildo*, leaders discussed what it had revealed about the nature and limitations of the elected government and generated discussions on where to go in relations with it. One of the key observations was the degree to which elected officials did not take *pobladores'* demands seriously. Rojo's denigrating remarks were a galvanizing force in the *población* and the central topic of conversation among community leaders during the following week.

Llareta critiqued its own performance at the event as well. Health group members concluded that it had been a tactical mistake to criticize without bringing forth proposals. Their original decision to denounce was based on an assessment of the most effective way to address the municipality. But it was Concertación politicians, not the mayor, who actually attended the assembly. The group decided to develop concrete proposals with corresponding deadlines to present at the *cabildo* itself.

In preparing its presentation, Llareta changed its approach in a second way. It decided not to direct its comments toward government officials. After all, they might not attend the assembly. And, judging from their performance at the *precabildo*, even if they did attend, chances were they would not listen to what community organizations had to say. Instead, the health group framed its document as an open letter to "the *pobladores* of San Ramón." The letter was to be part of a strategy of raising consciousness and reviving community organizations. Embedded in their decision to address *pobladores* was the idea that the most important relationships they had were those forged with other residents of their own neighborhood.

Cabildo

The morning of the *cabildo*, the lights were out at the school where the assembly would be held. As we walked across a soccer field toward the building, we could see two buses of policemen parked nearby. They had been there since seven in the morning and would stay for the duration of the event. Inside the school yard, a stage had been set up toward the left. A crowd of people, eventually numbering two hundred, milled about, searching for acquaintances and talking. We recognized many familiar faces—the faces of people active in local organizations. But more striking were a significant number of unknown individuals, whom the health promoters I was with quickly identified as plainclothes police. Combined with the uniformed police outside, these repressive and surveillance elements of the state immediately gave the *cabildo* an atmosphere of danger and mistrust.

Meanwhile, members of the press circulated amid the crowd. Television cameras focused on public officials, around whom reporters clustered closely. Speaking into the cameras, the officials dropped hints of future candidacies. Rarely, if ever, did reporters interview the La Bandera residents and community leaders who had gathered for the event.

At last the *cabildo* began. During the five-hour session, most of the community leaders attending gave long, disconnected speeches denouncing human rights violations and miserable living conditions. When it came time for officials to talk, three representatives gave nearly identical speeches. Almost all of the talks were theoretical, speaking of hardship and injustice (community leaders) or the benefits of democracy (politicians). During the lengthy session, no engagement took place at a policy level between government officials and *pobladores*, and neither *poblador* speakers nor politicians took up specific issues. In all, few governmental figures attended, perhaps due to their experience being criticized at the *precabildo*.

Llareta sought to change the tone of the proceedings by identifying concrete proposals for improvements in the *población*. But first the health group aimed to refute the denigrating image of the urban poor expressed in Rojo's remarks at the *precabildo*.

To this end, the health group had prepared a photographic exhibit, displayed on folding panels. Large and colorful, the majority of photographs showed scenes of garbage in the *población*—half the body of a rotting dog with its innards spilled over the ground; a dead rat crushed into the grass; old workers' gloves saturated with mud; children peering out through a school fence, their feet blocked by garbage heaped just feet away from their school dining room.

In the photo exhibit, the health group noted that *pobladores* dumped some of the garbage. The display included a photo of a woman tossing the remains of a meal onto the ground. The snapshot caught the food in midair. "Neighbor, you too are responsible," the caption read.

But Llareta was advancing a different analysis of why the creation of garbage dumps occurred. In the next panel, the group displayed a photo of a woman sweeping the dirt in front of her house. The caption said, "We clean and build our *población* with pride. Just walk its streets to see." This assertion fit with my own observation that most residents of La Bandera kept their own property clean. Every morning, women could be seen watering their front yards with garden hoses to restrain the dust and sweeping the debris from the sidewalk area. Some even swept the dirt street in front of their houses. As a result, the roads and adjacent property were nearly always free of trash. In fact, the only places in the *población* where garbage accumulated were large public spaces, like open fields and the areas around school yards. These places had once been designated by city planners for public services like parks and community centers, but the facilities had never been built.

Littered with corpses during the early years of the dictatorship, they became filled with garbage toward the end. These places were space abandoned. Belonging to the government and maintained by nobody, their filling with litter symbolized dashed expectations of residents toward the state.

The health group asserted that since the open areas were public property, government offices were required to clean them. Their claim was supported by the law. Alongside the photos, health group members pinned a photocopy of the legislation regarding public spaces. The law specified that municipal governments were responsible for keeping public areas clean. If municipalities failed to do this, the law said, responsibility shifted to the Ministry of Health to enforce sanitary codes. The law holding government responsible for the upkeep of public space directly contradicted Rojo's assertion that *pobladores* should remove the garbage themselves.

But the main point of the display was summarized by one caption. "The little or nothing we have, we made through our own efforts," the comment read. It was a claim that the years of joining housing committees, building homes, laying bricks for schools, paving roads in minimum wage programs, pooling resources for common kitchens, and sharing health education information were what ultimately built the *población*. Rojo had constructed *pobladores* as those who created problems. The health group countered with the idea that *pobladores* had spent years overcoming an overwhelming number of problems, including hunger, inadequate housing, and poor health. According to Llareta, La Bandera's history was a story of hard work by residents enduring harsh conditions with little governmental aid.

The open letter that the health group read at the *cabildo* reinforced these ideas. "The *pobladores* of San Ramón know very well what it is to be poor because we know unemployment, hunger, and lack of dignified housing," Valeria said publicly. "For that reason, we do not accept the deprecating and insolent tone that some media of the press and authorities have used to refer to us, the *pobladores*. . . . We *work, clean* and *build* our *población* with effort and dignity." Having asserted the dignity and hard work of La Bandera's residents, the open letter then returned to the relationship social organizations would have with the Concertación government. Here it spoke about the particular dilemmas raised during democracy: Today the party members of the Aylwin government "intend to make us believe that it is the poor ourselves who have to resolve our own problems. What is more, the Christian Democrat representative, Señor Rojo (who earns more than two million pesos monthly for our votes), intends to make us the causes of our misery." "To demand our rights *does not* endanger this political transition," the health group argued. "On the contrary, it calls things by their name and makes demands from those of us who have paid the greatest costs in these years." As they had done in the meningitis campaign when they insisted on holding a march despite accusations of being disloyal to democracy, the health group was staking out a definition of politics in which making demands was an integral part of what democracy should be.

The letter repositioned *pobladores* from being the source of problems to being people who were able to speak and create proposals. Under the headline "We Recuperate Our Voice," it paved the way for concrete steps through which to hold the government accountable: "For this reason before this District *Cabildo* we put forth our *demands* ('complaints' or 'laments' in the insolent manner that they incriminate us), but also we make concrete proposals, to which we believe it is necessary to attach deadlines and concrete responsibilities." In contrast to the tactic of merely denouncing problems at the *precabildo*, and unlike other groups at the *cabildo*, the health group then raised specific policy issues, proposed solutions, and set target dates. The bulk of its issues were environmental: cleaning garbage dumps, creating parks, paving streets, addressing air pollution, and improving health services. The health group also made a political demand: that space be created for democratic participation in the district. By setting forth these proposals, the group's members were asserting themselves as the ones setting priorities for what government action should be.

Like the Metro letter about cholera, the open letter at the *cabildo* recognized that government officials were unlikely to meet these demands without sustained pressure from the population. Valeria's presentation ended by calling for ongoing organization. She said,

> *Unity, organization, and mobilization* are a just and necessary path. We call on all the *pobladores* to unite before these statements and raise their own voice. Organization and mobilization have always been our path to dignity as a people, and this is not the hour to abandon it. Because we believe that a *Cabildo* Does Not in itself resolve our problems, we will work together, organized, and mobilized. *Health is a right and not a privilege!! Responses now!!*

The health group's statement ended by calling for unity and organization. It demanded renewed mobilization under the Aylwin government.

The health group evaluated the *cabildo* as largely a failure in which no real proposals were agreed upon, to which many important authorities did not attend, and at which few *pobladores* were present. Yet the aftermath was dramatic. The municipality, spurred by the denouncing that went on at the meetings, responded with hostility. As stated in Valeria and Iván's written analysis,

> Things got worse in the weeks following the *Cabildo*.... the mayor—who did not attend the *Cabildo* of July 28—felt injured at the public denouncing his poor leadership in the municipality and the use he made of the resources that belong to the neighbors. So, he took a series of persecutory measures against the leaders of the Unión Comunal:
>
> In the first place, he cut off by an hour the schedule of use of the locale in which we had meetings, obligating us to leave at 5:30 P.M. and not at 6:30 P.M. as we did before. In the second place, he prohibited us from making use of the photocopy machine, even if we paid. In the third place, he broke all type of dialogue, in such a way

that he repeatedly refused to see us. In the fourth place, he took away the telephone and later took away the office from us, threatening to throw us into the street if we didn't go voluntarily.

The members of the Unión Comunal and the *juntas de vecinos* held a strategy meeting in which they agreed to forcibly occupy the meeting room. The seizure lasted twelve days, with people standing guard to make sure the leaders were not injured. According to Iván and Valeria, "There was fear that the armed groups of the right could make a physical attempt against the leaders. In fact, during the first day of the seizure, there was an intimidating *balacera*. On the fifth day, the chief of the guards closed the bathrooms on us, shut off the water and electricity, and left us locked in a room of three by three meters." Despite, or perhaps because of, the repression and the resistance against it, there were results.

> With the seizure we achieved about 75% of what the Unión Comunal requested: a subsidy of $600,000 [pesos] with which to buy a prefabricated house. It was put together [and] . . . functions currently. We also got an agreement that the mayor meet [with] the Unión Comunal on a weekly basis, and created the conditions [for meetings] with the *juntas de vecinos* as well.
>
> In this way, the seizure that followed the *cabildo* accomplished something. Because before this, we did not have anything. Now the leaders feel as if in their own home, because before, in the office that we occupied in the municipality, we felt repressed.

This particular fight with the municipality bore fruit, for it resulted in space for leaders to organize. This was one of the demands made in the open letter at the *cabildo*. In the next few weeks, the pressure brought to bear on the municipality would also succeed in getting the littered field cleaned up.

PARTICIPACIÓN VECINAL:
THE CAMPAIGN TO CLEAN UP GARBAGE DUMPS

In the weeks that followed the *cabildo*, leaders of organizations in La Bandera who had attended the planning meeting for the *precabildo* decided to continue functioning as a working group. The main objective of what they called Participación Vecinal (Neighborhood Participation), was to rejuvenate community organizations. The leaders who organized Participación Vecinal hoped to get more and more people "out of their houses" and to accumulate political strength. In the course of their actions, they hoped to redefine what the term *participation* might mean.

As mentioned earlier, by 1991 many of the organizations that had previously been active (youth centers, cultural centers, clubs) had closed down, leaving still committed leaders without organizations. To reactivate groups, the members of Participación Vecinal decided to choose one issue around which to organize. They chose one that had been left unresolved at the *cabildo:* getting the municipality to remove garbage dumps.

The effort coincided with the ongoing campaign by Llareta. Health promoters and their children had painted in enormous letters along the wall lining a field of garbage: "Enough with Epidemics and Garbage." The large lettering tied the question of garbage dumps directly to the issue of cholera. Llareta painted the mural on the wall above the garbage, as if to make the wall writing a caption that turned the dirty field into an image to contemplate. The health group had turned the landscape into illustration and added commentary to interpret that reality.

For its part, Participación Vecinal prepared a petition and ran a signature campaign in the vegetable market demanding that the field be cleaned. On that day, members set up tables at both ends of the market to collect signatures. Alongside the tables, the health group's photography panels illustrated the garbage problems in the *población*. A number of people gathered at the ends of the market to direct shoppers' attention to the panels and to hand out information sheets. At the conclusion of the activities, Participación Vecinal submitted the petitions to the municipality.

Following the pressure brought to bear on it, the municipality cleaned up the trash. Where there had once been a littered field of garbage, suddenly there was only dirt. As with the case of the occupation of the municipal building, during the weeks that followed the *precabildo* and *cabildo*, it appeared that the conflictual relationship with the municipality had borne fruit.

The *precabildo* and *cabildo*, two public assemblies to which officials from both the holdover municipal government and the newly elected national government were invited, crystallized the double face of power in 1991 and revealed the complex situation faced by social organizations at that time. Ironically, although community leaders had some success with the municipality, the question remained of how to challenge the Concertación's discourse of participation. The local government would be elected in a year, and that government was likely to be led by Concertación politicians. At that point, community leaders were unlikely to have the same kind of conflictual relationship they had with the appointed municipal mayor. Preparing for that time involved a continued struggle over the meaning of participation.

Because the main purpose of Participación Vecinal was to involve more people in organizations, getting the field clean was only half the battle. The task still at hand involved interpreting the event and staking out the meaning of "participation." The now empty patch of ground became a playing field on which to make this larger symbolic point. Participación Vecinal made it a priority to win the *symbolic* battle over the meaning of participation at the same time as it won the concrete demand of cleaning up the garbage dump.

Above the trash-free field of dirt, members of Participación Vecinal created a mural. Like Llareta's wall writing, which they painted over, it was stationed as if to comment on the transformed condition of the landscape below.

Creating a narrative that read like a story from left to right, the mural consisted of three panels. The first panel showed a field strewn with garbage: apple cores, soda cans, a box of wine, a bone. These images jutted into each other and over-lapped, as if to represent the randomness with which the items had been thrown and the abandon with which they had been allowed to remain.

A second panel depicted a group of people marching. A man in simple cloth-ing led the way, holding a Chilean flag. Close behind him a woman carried a bag of bread. Next came a long line of other people, portrayed indistinguishably, as silhouettes. Beside them, bright letters read, "With your signature, with partic-ipation, organization, we will achieve our goals."

The third panel showed an ideal, and clean, *población*. The painting depicted a cultural center with the words "freedom for political prisoners" marked on its side, and next to it a white church and a school. In the foreground stood trees and flow-ers, swings and slides for children, and a wide swath of grass with not a bit of gar-bage anywhere to be seen.

With the three panels in sequence, the story line was clear. The *población* had been littered with garbage. Then, through organization, including a signature campaign, *pobladores* had pressured the municipality to clean it up. With ongoing organization, this would lead to an improved *población*.

The central message of this mural was agency. At the *precabildo* planning meet-ing, community leaders had decided not to announce proposals because they were afraid the mayor would appropriate their ideas as his own. Therefore, the issue of credit for cleaning the field was crucial to its interpretation. Although the munici-pality had sent workers and equipment to empty the field of trash, in the mural the municipality was not acknowledged as an actor. In pictures, in slogans, and in public space, members of the coalition interpreted the event not as the product of an obliging municipality that had responded to people's needs but as the result of organization by *pobladores* who had made demands. If they had not organized, the mural suggested, the field would still be brimming with trash.

By highlighting the agency of *pobladores*, the mural paralleled accounts made by local history workshops throughout Santiago. Local history publications em-phasized the importance of collective action in creating the *poblaciones*. Here, members of Participación Vecinal applied the narrative to a current event. They redefined the sequence of events that led to the cleaning of the dirty field as one of protagonism.

Having established the importance of agency, they sought to equate this pro-tagonism with "participation." Therefore, a second important lesson of the mural was about the type of organization that could impel change. Rather than showing people bending over to pick up garbage, the mural portrayed them marching and creating a petition campaign ("with your signatures"). It was an assertion that mo-bilization, organization, and conflictual action remained necessary tactics for achieving local goals.

It was this mural, this creation of a narrative in which *pobladores* took subject po-sitions as agents of change, this emphasis on the utility of organization, and this definition of participation as demanding rights and pressuring the government that constituted the main import of the campaign. The fact that an empty section of bare ground now stood where garbage had once been was significant because it illustrated the potential for achieving change by rejuvenating organizations in the *población*. How the cleaning of the field was interpreted, who was given credit, and the lasting impact on organizations were as important as the fact that the task had been done.[25]

The community organizations won a fight with the municipality to get the garbage cleaned up. But it is not clear they won the fight with the Concertación to redefine the meaning of participation. The definition of participation advanced by Rojo—in which all neighbors could pitch in and solve problems rather than wait for solutions from the state—had broad currency in the early 1990s. It appealed to people's desire to make concrete contributions to improving their neighborhood. And there were many in the early post-dictatorship years who wanted to support the elected government in both word and deed.

More important, the Concertación government had far more power than local organizations, which were weak in the post-dictatorship period. The Participación Vecinal group, for example, soon fell apart as a result of infighting among leaders. Community groups that did not fit into the state's agenda for participation were isolated and marginalized, finding themselves excluded from broader roles in local politics. Their isolation was exacerbated by the fact that most funding from international organizations had dried up or was being channeled through the state. As a consequence, both grassroots groups and nongovernmental organizations saw benefits—financial and otherwise—in conforming to the role for organizations designated by the state. These processes would intensify in 1992, when municipal elections created space for the Concertación at every level of government.

CONCLUSION

"Participation" was a symbolic discourse well suited to the kind of political democracy to emerge in Chile. Like "empowerment" and the "active engagement of civil society" advocated by USAID, "participation" enabled the government to count on the support of citizens to provide social services no longer considered the responsibility of the state. It curtailed protest by investing residents in the system in which they lived.

Community organizations faced a difficult situation. The state expected them to provide services formerly delivered by government itself and did this under the appealing rubric of "participation." While there was disagreement within the *población* about how to respond to this new political situation, Llareta and other social organizations in La Bandera actively contested the meaning of participation and attempted to reclaim it in the service of revitalized mobilization. With uneven success, they insisted on the necessity of maintaining organizational autonomy and experimented with the kinds of resistance effective in confronting new and changing political forms.

The paradox facing Llareta illustrates broader issues at work in the literature on civil society. The idea of active citizen engagement has been lauded both in academic literature and in development policy. But the more relevant question is not whether citizens participate more or less, but rather how participation functions as a form of power—as a kind of governmentality—within the context of political democracy.

CHAPTER SIX

Legitimation of Knowledge

August 13, 1996
Philadelphia

I pull my car up alongside the Greyhound bus station in Philadelphia. Taxis on all sides of me are picking up passengers, and drivers swing the heavy luggage into trunks. Vicente is standing on the steps when I arrive. It takes me just a second to pick him out—the tall figure with the shoulder-length hair. We have not seen each other since my last trip to Chile. Since we met in 1991, we had spent many hours talking about Chilean politics, history, and social movements. He suggests we get a cup of coffee, and so I find a parking place a bit farther south, and we walk to a café.

Vicente is in New York this week for a sociology conference. It's a short visit—in just a day or two he will return to Santiago to teach a university class and then fly off again to Honduras, where he is consulting for a project on malnutrition. But knowing that I had a lot of questions remaining from our last conversation, he has carved out some time to come to Philadelphia. I want to ask him about political processes in Chile, especially what has happened with sociologists and other intellectuals. After we settle down at a table and order, our conversation leads to a discussion of the differences between anthropology and sociology.

Vicente: The basic difference... [between anthropologists and sociologists] is that we [the sociologists] don't believe what people say.

Julia: [In anthropology] it doesn't matter if they're right or wrong. What's important is what it means to them.

Vicente: That's the whole point of your epistemology.... You say the knowledge people have is valid.... We sociologists, at least in Chile, usually say that approach is populism.

...

Julia: ... Explain populism to me.

Vicente: Populism is easy to explain. It's a movement [where] you go to the people, and then, as you anthropologists say, you...go native. You believe everything people say....Our generation of sociologists...in Chile, we [were] denied society. We were students...[at] the time of the coup d'état....For our experience as social scientists, [it] looked like the whole society had become a political system. The society was the government and the government was society. So, in the 1980s, we began to try to find society. So we went to where the people [were]. We went to the unions, we went to the *poblaciones,* we went to the soccer [fields], we went to everywhere...the people [were]....And our intellectual production of that time is mostly trying to show that there is a society alive behind, under this political system. Following Gramsci, we called ourselves organic intellectuals. And we wrote pamphlets, we wrote newspapers, and we wrote plays, even...songs,...to express what was underlying in the popular culture of the people....Well, at some point, and for very different reasons, we began to think that we were wrong. That that was part of the story but wasn't the whole story. That if we wanted to speak seriously about what was going on in the country, we should take a more theoretical viewpoint....For different reasons we began to think that there was no such thing as a popular subject. Or at least that this so-called popular subject was always falling apart. Was always breaking down....

In 1986, there was a national congress of the *pobladores* movement where I expected them to unite, finally, and become only one movement. At that point there [were] I don't recall—four or five associations....And I made a mistake in my calculations because I thought the division in that congress [would go] along party lines. And it didn't. There was a division between what they called the...*cúpulas* and the grass roots....We represent the bases, we are the grass roots of this movement, and then they have the leaderships....And I said, well I don't understand anything. So I better go...someplace to try to understand what is going on with this movement [this is when I went to Canada to do a Ph.D. in sociology]. So. That's the way I broke with populism. And even though I am still sympathetic to *pobladores* and to unions and to [those] kind[s] of organizations, I wouldn't say that...right now I would act in the same way I did ten or fifteen years ago. Because I think that I have [a] legitimate viewpoint as a sociologist. As a person with status...[who] knows theories...and does research. And I can speak from that viewpoint. With deep respect for the viewpoint of other people, but I wouldn't believe that a *poblador* is correct because he is a *poblador* as I believed fifteen years ago.

Julia: ...I'm...interested in this...conversation because I was seeing it from the other point of view. I was seeing...[that] what [community leaders in the *población*] were grappling with was the effect of your and others' transformations....It was about them not being taken seriously. Now maybe from your perspective, it was about not overestimating how correct they were. But from their perspective, you...(sociologists in general, not you particularly) ended up being...the only people who could talk or be listened to.

...

Julia: The question of what's actually going on among *pobladores* is still open because...what you're describing is that you collectively were going through transformations based on theories that you were dealing with....But all of that ...leaves it...disconnected from what was actually happening with people in *poblaciones.*

Vicente: No, we were speaking with them.... [The NGOs] were...going to *poblaciones* [all the time]. I told you,...this is a movement of going to the people. ...We wanted to promote collective action. We thought that repression was causing all this apathy of the people, and we thought that we could move them. So I spent five days a week in *poblaciones* speaking with people and watching what was going on in there and organizing meetings and printing pamphlets and doing things like that. So we knew what was going on with the poor. Moreover, I was regularly a member of different groups, human rights groups....And I went there as...a supportive professional. I was there to write the statements and do whatever I could to be a sort of secretary of these groups....And...I organized [a] workshop [Urban Analysis Workshop], and that was another place where I was listening to the leadership of *pobladores....* Other sociologists and I believed that there was a subject behind the *pobladores* or the working class, and that subject could emerge. And I would say in the mideighties... [we] realized that this theory...wasn't a good theory and we moved to different grounds. And then [one of us] moved into communications, and he said this [is the] business of the future. As early as '84, '85. And [another of us] moved into other kinds of social work and communication. And I moved to social networks. I was interested in the elements of continuity in the action of *pobladores.*

...

Julia: So what do you think that the impact of your change in theories was on *pobladores?*

Vicente: I don't know. I really don't know....I left Chile in '86 and came back in '91, so I don't know....I missed a whole period of our history that was crucial to understand what happened.

Julia: Yeah, '86 to '91, [those were] big years.

[both of us laugh]

...

Julia: But it sounds like...regardless of the theory...that kind of research that was going on in the eighties isn't happening now. Is that true?

Vicente: That's true absolutely.

Julia: And...all the research institutes where they were working are closing down.... [A] lot of people have started doing contract work for the government and evaluation of particular programs that the government runs.

Vicente: That's right.

Julia: So there isn't really research and theorizing.

Vicente: I'd say there are a couple of places, and mostly within the government.

Julia: ...When you read my dissertation, you said...Julia, you're saying there's been an abandonment of *pobladores* by sociologists or researchers, and that's just not true. That people have really strong connections with *poblaciones*....But it sounds like the ties were really from the eighties or the mideighties and maybe somewhat in the early nineties, but that there's actually not that much work going on now.

Vicente: ...No. Work as research, not much. But on the other side what you've got is the...program for the improvement of the quality of education, you've got the FOSIS working, you have, I don't know, [the] Ministry of Health has some participation programs, the Ministry of Housing, so there are contacts.

Julia: But they're all through the government.

Vicente: Most of them through the government. Yes.

...

Vicente: So then what is true is that most social scientists are working from the government or on the side of the government rather than on the side of the *pobladores*.

Julia: Right, so...people in the *poblaciones* were dealing with that....They would say stuff like, I had all of these friends who came and they worked in the *poblaciones*, and they said we're doing this work so that the history will be known or we're doing this work to improve [things] and now that they're working in the government, they say now we [the *pobladores*] can't participate or we can't be part of this process because we're not trained professionals. And that the kind of autonomous organizations that they were promoting in the eighties, we shouldn't be participating in now because it's a new era....And secondly that making decisions or participating in programs or whatever required credentials, and people in *poblaciones* didn't have those credentials, like training or degrees...and so that they couldn't be part of that process. Those were the two things that I was hearing.

Vicente: Well, probably that's the experience for the people you were speaking with.

Julia: Right.

Vicente: Well, how can I tell if that's true or not true. The point is that—what can I say. Well, first of all, the whole thing of intellectuals working with the working class or with the *pobladores*...was part of the...organization of the people to...[end] the dictatorship....

. . .

Julia: So, okay, the relationship between the intellectuals and the *pobladores* was specifically part of the anti-dictatorship movement. And so it had its boundaries around that moment. And probably previous to that there weren't such strong ties except maybe in the late sixties...or the early seventies.

Vicente: Right.

Julia: Which was in a different context. So now that there's no anti-dictatorship movement, there's no need for those kinds of studies and for those kinds of relationships.

Vicente: Mmmmm. I mean there are always studies, and there is always need for studies. I was working all '95 doing studies in *poblaciones*. I mean I was doing this impact analysis of FOSIS programs....We did [an] evaluation of...230 projects all over the country. We [ran] about 2,500 interviews. So that's...research. We wrote a report. The problem is that the report is a secret. I mean we made nine copies for—

Julia: Why is the report a secret if it's for the government?

Vicente: Well, that's the way things work.

Julia: Shouldn't it be a public document?

Vicente: Nope. No, no, no, no, that's not the status of consulting in Chile. And that's one of the reasons why there is no debate. Because most of [the] good researchers are doing research for the government, and once you have your research done, you can't publish it.

. . .

Julia: So [given the fact that sociologists were not doing much publishing], the other thing we were seeing...[community leaders] experiencing [was] how do we theorize this...[when] this interesting...tension-filled but nonetheless existing alliance with intellectuals in the eighties now isn't there.

Vicente: What kind of alliances do you mean?

Julia: Well...for example...people who were critiquing [the economic] model in the eighties aren't critiquing it in the nineties.... *[Pobladores']* economic experience...[is] quite dire in the nineties....But the people who are producing the knowledge about it and publishing about it and speaking about it, who criticized it in the eighties are saying it's successful in the nineties, which in part has to do maybe with an economic turn in '86, but it also has to do with where they're positioned relative to the government. So that the people in the shanty-town who are living a really difficult economic situation...[are] not backed up by a critique at a national level, published, a critique of the economic system. So the people I was with were trying to diagnose and theorize and voice and were being undermined in what they were saying by all the other sources of information. But they had to do that intellectual production.

Vicente: Right, yes. Yeah, I see your point. If these people have experience that ...goes against all the information they are getting,...so they try to create their own knowledge in order to take it out of their experience....

...

Vicente: The main part of your argument is, well, *pobladores* are saying one thing, and they've been abandoned again. And that's what they're saying when they say we're still hungry, we're still jobless, we...still [have] bad pay....They say, well, they made us a lot of promises and none of this comes true. And then in the beginning you put some responsibility on the intellectuals who left the *pobladores,* and I reacted to that assumption, saying that it's not that we are not worried about the social situation, in Chile.... [It's that] we are working from a different position now. And the story I am telling you from the position I am [in] now...confirms that there was a process of separation.

Julia: Yeah. Now it falls into place. What you're saying is confirming what I'm saying.

Vicente: ...What's more interesting for me is...when you ask where can we theorize what has happened. And I guess that's the most scary question you can ask...any Chilean because there are no places to theorize...what happened. There's nobody...[no] groups, nobody writing articles, there are no journals that [publish this kind of analysis]....I got an interview on TV, and they put thirty seconds of [people] who are speaking forty-five minutes.

...

Vicente: You say the *pobladores* are trying to build their own theory. Now I understand...your point with that. And [right now] I wouldn't say...[that that's a] [p]opulistic approach.

...

Julia: What I was saying is that there's a particular situation in the 1990s that the social organizations that I knew were confronting. And...knowledge was part of the power dynamic that framed their situation. And the changed relationship with the intellectuals was also a part of that power situation. And so they had to...theorize in order to understand the situation they were in and be able to do something about it....So to the degree that I wanted to privilege that or listen to what they were saying or coauthor with a community leader...was precisely because I saw that at this moment that was a particularly important situation given the different trajectories of intellectuals....

Vicente: Okay.... At first I didn't understand why were you trying to give ... epistemological status to the discourse of the *pobladores,* and now I see ... your point in doing that. However, what strikes me when I read your dissertation is that I didn't hear [anything] new. There are few things that were new in the arguments or the discourse of the *pobladores.* I mean, all things they were saying about intellectuals and professionals going there and then leaving them ... I've heard many times.... The first time I went to work [in a *población*] I was a student in high school ... They [said], well you come once, twice, and then the third time you don't want to come and so we don't really rely on you. So ... you may be right [that] they are trying to theorize their experience, but they were theorizing with old frameworks ... using old theories.

But I do not think it is fair to say that Llareta and other organizations that survived the transition are locked in old frameworks. It seems more accurate to me to see them as developing analyses geared to making sense of the new conditions of the post-dictatorship era.

HEALTH SEMINAR

It was a rainy winter day in Santiago. A day when dirt roads melted into puddles and mud, and paved avenues flooded so severely one had to walk blocks to find a shallow place to cross the street. A day when clothing worn outside stayed eternally damp, and when pants or shirts hung out on the line to dry became immediately wet again. It was a day, in short, on which it was best to stay at home, put some water up to boil in the teakettle, place pots under newly sprung leaks, and climb onto the roof when the rain let up to patch the places where the water was dripping in.

Despite the inauspicious weather conditions, I found myself walking along muddy streets with members of Llareta toward an elementary school a few blocks away. The occasion was a health seminar, the first ever to occur in San Ramón.

This seminar was designed to bring together a wide range of organizations in the district of San Ramón. Invited groups included members of the neighborhood councils *(juntas de vecinos)*, grassroots organizations, nongovernmental organizations, workers from the local health clinic, officials of the municipal government, and representatives who had been elected to the district's council during the first municipal elections just weeks before. These diverse organizations would come together for a two-day conference to identify problems and outline possibilities for improving living conditions in the area. Organizers hoped that the seminar would provide a forum in which the groups could "share their visions" and advance "proposals for improving the situation of health in the *comuna* [district]" (Programa Primer Seminario Comunal de Salud 1992, 1).

This seminar could not have taken place during the dictatorship. During those years, the disparate groups were in too great a tension to cooperate. Popular organizations had a difficult relationship with a municipal health clinic that provided insufficient services and treated them with disrespect. Even the *unidades vecinales* had a strained relationship with other community organizations, for rather than being popularly elected, the representatives had been handpicked by the authoritarian regime, creating widespread mistrust. And officials who worked for the municipality constituted a local branch of a military regime against which community groups were in open opposition.

Because such conflicts would have made cooperation unthinkable during the dictatorship, the health seminar reveals a unique kind of local politics beginning to emerge within democracy. The last chapter described how the health group Llareta had used conflict to gain concessions from the municipality in 1991. But the health group and EPES were also trying their hand at cooperation. In 1991, about the same time that the *precabildo* and *cabildo* were happening, they had co-sponsored a training program for new health promoters with the health clinic. Through this joint effort, EPES and Llareta sought to gain access to the internal workings of the clinic, to have some influence over its functioning, and to increase their power over decision making in the locale.

Now, a year later, in August 1992, the health group tried this kind of intersectoral cooperation again. This time, although the mayor appointed by Pinochet was still in office, municipal elections had just taken place, and a Christian Democrat mayor had been voted in. In this context, the seminar represented a new form of post-dictatorship community politics.

Choosing to cosponsor the health seminar represented a strategic decision—still experimental—for Llareta and EPES. In other districts, health groups had chosen not to cooperate with the municipality. They believed that they could retain more leverage by maintaining an oppositional relationship. By deciding to collaborate with its local clinic, Llareta hoped to expand the arena in which *pobladores* and popular organizations could influence local health policy and build stronger connections to municipal health care workers. It wanted to move beyond the kind of impasse reflected in the failed *precabildo* and *cabildo* to come up with workable agreements and processes for implementing them to improve health in the *población*. More than just a conference about health, the seminar signified an effort to forge new relationships between popular organizations and municipal institutions.

The seminar also marked changes in the relationship between EPES and Llareta. In large part, the role of EPES had been to train and support the local health group in its work in the *población*. By the 1990s, when Llareta had built up years of experience and strong internal leadership, EPES's role was shifting. The health group now met regularly without an EPES adviser present and planned its own activities. EPES came to see itself as a social actor with a clear public profile in the *población*, working alongside the health group and not only through it.

In order to make strategic gains through the health seminar, Llareta and EPES needed to influence the content and procedures of the event itself. In the weeks before the seminar, they attended a series of tense meetings in which they battled out the characteristics the seminar would have.

At the top of EPES and Llareta's agenda was to make *pobladores* and their organizations important players in determining health policy. They wanted to avoid having popular sectors be subject to the decisions of a narrow group of experts and health clinic staff. They wanted, in short, what community leaders defined as real participation. In the words of María Eugenia, an EPES staff member, "It was the moment for proposals. It was the moment in which supposedly there was going to be participation. Therefore, there was a need to generate the conditions so that the [popular] organizations had a place in creating the proposals." Creating such a role for *pobladores* would have ramifications after the two-day conference had concluded, for "the idea was to generate an intersectoral

Figure 15.   Valeria makes a presentation at a workshop cosponsored with the municipal health clinic. Photo: Gordon Whitman.

working space after the seminar"—an ongoing role of dialogue and input. Such a goal defied actual practices in the district, where popular organizations and *pobladores* had little say in health policy. For EPES and Llareta, a priority in the planning meetings was to ensure that in designing the seminar, at the event itself, and in the months and years that followed, *pobladores* would be active and leading players in decision making about health.

A second point of contention revolved around the seminar's content. At the planning meetings, a vocal set of attendees insisted that the seminar focus on issues of health narrowly defined. They wanted to exclude environmental issues from the agenda. It is not that the environment is unimportant, they said. It is just that this seminar is about health. We can hold a seminar about the environment at a later date.

This question became a pivotal point for EPES and Llareta, whose definition of health included a broad array of factors. They insisted on looking not just at respiratory disease but at the pollution that caused it; not just at typhoid but at the garbage dumps that spread it; and not just at alcoholism but at the unemployment that provoked it. On the second day of the conference, Valeria found the perfect example to make her point. Walking to the school where the conference was held, she took off her shoes to cross a muddy river running down the street. With her feet drenched in the winter cold, she turned to the woman who had asked her what the connection was between environment and health. "See?" Valeria said. She was saying that the lack of pavement and drainage, as well as her inability to afford a decent pair of boots, had a direct impact on her ability to protect herself from getting sick. The health group's priority was to put environment at the center of the seminar's agenda and to broaden the concept of health to extend beyond narrow questions of medicine and disease.

When we crossed the road and entered the school gate on the first morning of the seminar, members of EPES were already signing people in. Next to the registration table, the EPES staff had stationed a poster explaining the organization's role in preventive health. In the tradition of popular education, the poster used both words and cartoons to convey the ideas. Members of Llareta hung their photographic exhibit about garbage—the same one they had used at the *cabildo* a year earlier—on a large wall by the entrance, where participants could see it as they walked in.

After registering, we entered the large room where the seminar would be held. Benches had been assembled in neat rows, facing a long table at the front of the room. In a kitchen, visible through a window along the left wall, women dressed in white uniforms served breakfast: sweetened tea, bread spread with margarine, and a slice of ham. These women would spend the morning cooking lunch to serve after the initial sessions. Attendees milled around the room, drinking tea, finding seats, and talking to the others present. At last a master of ceremonies opened the seminar by outlining the sequence of fifteen-minute talks.

The speaker explained the schedule of events. On the first day, the various grassroots and nongovernmental organizations, as well as health clinic representatives, would present their assessments of the health problems in the district. The afternoon would be devoted to small-group sessions in which individuals representing a range of organizations would develop proposals for improving health. On the second day these proposals would continue, and the small groups would present their conclusions before the entire assembly. Finally, the coordinators would use these diagnoses and proposals to draw up the final document: an agenda for the future that all would sign.

The seminar began, and the various groups gave talks on the issues most pertinent to them. Grassroots and nongovernmental organizations spoke about problems such as alcoholism and AIDS. Health clinic functionaries focused on clinic staffing, disease, and medical care. What most stood out for me during the proceedings was health clinic staff's public displays of professional knowledge. One functionary presented elaborate diagrams on flip charts to describe the floor plans of the clinic. Another health clinic worker used an overhead projector to present organizational flow charts, lists, and percentages about the doctor-to-patient ratio, the health clinic budget, and the various duties of the staff members. Substantive comments on health focused on disease, for example, the most common illnesses affecting children in the *población*. These technical accoutrements, quantitative data, and bureaucratic information made the session seem more like a profes-

Figure 16. Sonia presents health group survey results at district health seminar. Photo: Gordon Whitman.

sional seminar than the kind of popular education sessions I had been accustomed to seeing in the *población*.

Strikingly, EPES and Llareta used similar techniques of presentation. Before the seminar, Eladio had told me that he planned to use statistics, graphs, and sophisticated vocabulary in his talk because he knew that that was standard procedure at professional conferences. He spent many hours preparing quantitative data to be shown through visual aids. At one of Llareta's planning meetings, Sonia had suggested that the health group members perform a skit, a method they used at many of their activities to illustrate the health problems they faced. Her suggestion was quickly dismissed. The group came to an agreement that the only way to be taken seriously at a forum such as this was to use more sober—and more professional—means of presentation.

It was with this in mind that members of Llareta conformed to professional approaches for presenting knowledge. Valeria, the group's coordinator, gave a talk based on the analysis of quantitative information. She illustrated her points with a series of pie charts and bar graphs shown on an overhead projector. Valeria's data were based on the results of a study the health group had conducted in La Bandera two years earlier. Not unlike the pollsters who routinely arrived at shantytown houses to ask questions, members of the health group had designed and conducted a survey.[1] They chose a sample of houses on a number of blocks and asked questions about employment, overcrowding, income, housing, debt (water, electricity, and housing), plumbing, and environmental hygiene (parasites). They asked how many unemployed teenagers lived in the home, how many people there were per room, what kind of fuel was used for cooking, and whether the household had rats.

When I first saw the results of the survey, they were in the form of averages and were arranged in columns, which EPES staff had calculated and typed up. Gordon entered their data into a graphics program on our laptop computer and printed out charts. What had seemed distant and difficult to comprehend suddenly came alive, and health promoters gained new interest in the data they had collected. Llareta subsequently used the charts in various presentations and studied them to analyze conditions in the *población*.

The health professionals' presentations had centered on illnesses and disease, which were described and ranked in terms of their frequency. Valeria's talk addressed similar concerns but analyzed them along another track. To frame the health group's analysis, she organized her speech around three themes: poverty, housing, and environment. Each of these situated specific health problems like disease within a much broader framework that took into consideration the environment in which people lived. The study showed, for example, that 67 percent of families owed debt for electricity, water, and housing payments; 37 percent of families lived doubled up with relatives; 75 percent of houses had rats. Valeria emphasized the connection between environment and health when she concluded, "Our children...live in an environment that [does] not allow them to develop in a healthy way."

Valeria's comments built on a long-standing claim by Llareta that the idea of health needed to be reconceptualized. Health was not just the absence of disease, a technical issue managed by doctors and clinics, the group argued, but rather involved all the things that allow people to develop and live: education, housing, human rights, recreation, a clean environment. Valeria stated in her presentation the following definition: "Health is not only the absence of sickness, but rather also is housing, dignified work, nutrition, clothing, education that values and stimulates the capacities of our children, recreation, physical and mental development in an environment clean of pollution and free of repression; with equal access to health and a real participation in health policy decisions." In addition to connecting health to the environment, Valeria emphasized the political roots of miserable living conditions. "Why is this environment so unhealthy?" she asked those assembled. "Because those in charge of this area aren't doing their job. And because there is a lack of political will to do it."

She then connected the political situation to the lack of respect shown toward those who lived in the *población*, which she called "contempt for poor people." Her words emphasized the many times health promoters' knowledge and rights had been rejected—the times they had been kicked out of a school, looked down on in the health clinic, and disrespected at the *precabildo* the previous year. She was saying that it was precisely the lack of respect—and the construction of them as objects of knowledge and policy rather than as knowing subjects with rights—that ultimately subjected *pobladores* to dismal living conditions.

The conditions they endured were not just works of nature or manifestations of biology, she was further asserting, but reflected specific priorities and agendas that directed resources away from infrastructure and environmental improvements, as well as medical resources, in the *población*. Like the health group's open letter during the cholera campaign, this was a critique that, far from limiting health to a discussion of disease, germs, and medicine, directly implicated the broader political system and the ability of popular groups to hold officials accountable for public services.

By presenting quantitative data in a formal way, the health group had conformed to a dominant way of legitimating knowledge. Yet the group was simultaneously critiquing professionalized forms of knowledge. Llareta contended that narrow technical definitions of health constrained the thinking of professionals and made it impossible for them to see the real causes of the health problems in the *población*. Valeria's last words drove home this point: "What we are trying to tell you is that at bottom the problem is that today health professionals and the state are working with too limited a concept of health. If health is not related to housing, work, education, and environment, it is very difficult to achieve real solutions because *health is not a technical problem, but rather is a social, political, and economic problem.*" What is striking here is that Valeria, a *pobladora*, was publicly criticizing professional forms of knowledge. In fact, she was asserting that health professionals' and politicians' ways of organizing knowledge—their focus on germs and disease—was one of the key impediments to health in the *población*.[2]

This story raises two important questions. Why, at a seminar designed to diagnose health problems in the neighborhood, did members of Llareta state that the most significant problem affecting health was the ways in which professionals organized knowledge? And why, if they were critiquing technical thinking, did health group members use surveys, pie charts, and overhead projectors—all the trappings of professionalized knowledge—to make their points?

I will return to these questions and the health seminar in which they were raised at the end of the chapter. For now, it is necessary to look at the significance of expertise, credentials, and professionalization in post-dictatorship Chile.

HEALTH PROMOTERS' KNOWLEDGE

One of the most common issues health group members raised in the early 1990s was their frustration at having their knowledge dismissed because they lacked formal academic credentials. Valeria remembered vividly the time Llareta had been invited to conduct an educational workshop at a school. It was during the first campaign against meningitis in the mid-1980s, not long after seven children had died of the disease. Valeria emphasized that no other groups had taken action around that illness: "We [Llareta] were the only people working on this issue of meningitis. It was we who were handing out the...informational bulletins, the preventive measures about what to do, everything. We were the only ones working on this." In seeming recognition of its efforts, the group soon "received a notice from [the school] calling us to do a workshop for all the teachers."

Accepting the invitation, the health group prepared a presentation and arrived on the appointed day to talk to the faculty. When the health promoters had gathered near the front of the room and the teachers had assembled, the director introduced the speakers. As she described the incident years later, Valeria repeated the director's words slowly, in a high-pitched voice, to indicate the haughtiness with which he spoke. "'A lady—a nurse—from the University of Chile is coming,'" she reported the director as saying. In phrasing his introduction in this way, the director was credentialing the invited speaker as an educated, middle-class professional affiliated with a prestigious university. Karen, the coordinator of EPES who had accompanied Llareta to the event, and who did have a degree in nursing, realized that the director must have been referring to her. She corrected his mistake by indicating that she was not a nurse from the University of Chile.

At that moment, Valeria stepped in to clarify who they were. "I explained that we were a group of *pobladores*, that we had worked all this time and we saw that no one was doing a campaign, nor was anyone dealing with the problem [of meningitis]." Upon hearing her introduction of the health promoters as a group of *pobladores*, the director refused to let them proceed with their presentation. Valeria recalled, "The guy said, 'You know what? We thank you very much, but really we were expecting professionals. See you later. You can leave.'" Grasping the situation, Valeria confronted the director: "I said to him, 'Are you throwing us out because we are poor, or because we don't have the knowledge? Because you haven't even given us the opportunity.'" "How dare you say that," the director said, and Valeria replied, "That's what it is. You are throwing us out because you don't see us in white coats." Members of the health group concluded that they had been refused the opportunity to speak because they did not have professional affiliations and degrees. Without displaying credentials, they realized, they would not be given a platform on which to present their information and views.

What professionals in health clinics, public seminars, and schools did not take into account when they dismissed the health promoters' knowledge was that these *pobladores* had indeed been educated about health. Most had been through EPES's training program, which did not give them comprehensive medical knowledge but did make them aware of a wide array of health problems, preventive measures, and remedies. When their own knowledge did not suffice, the health promoters consulted printed material or tapped into networks of nongovernmental organizations like EPES whose professionally trained staff shared information.

The health promoters also drew on experience. Over a ten-year period, they had done everything from treating sporadic illness and chronic disease to healing injuries and organizing preventive activities. Members of Llareta were frequently asked by neighbors to identify a strange tumor or clean a wound. During my time in La Bandera, I saw health promoters administer injections, remove a bullet from a young man's arm, prevent the onset of shock when a woman had been electrocuted, save a child from choking on a candy, and give advice on healing a puncture wound caused by stepping on a nail. Valeria believed that it was because they treated other *pobladores* with respect that their neighbors came first to them rather than the health clinic.

In some cases, health promoters had knowledge available only to people who lived in *poblaciones*. Familiar with health conditions in their neighborhood, they were able to distinguish measures that would work in a poor area from those that would not. For example, when municipal health workers claimed that the way to halt the spread of meningitis was to quarantine the infected persons in separate quarters, health promoters explained that in La Bandera families lived overcrowded, sometimes with four or five people sleeping in a single room. Under these circumstances, isolating sick persons at home would be impossible.

Beyond taking advantage of available information, health promoters themselves created and disseminated knowledge. They researched issues of public health such as garbage dumps, diseases transmitted by animals, domestic violence, sexual abuse, and household accidents. As described in the accounts of the meningitis and cholera campaigns in previous chapters, they analyzed public health situations, produced and distributed instructional material on health issues, and led workshops for their neighbors. Well informed about local health problems, members of Llareta were themselves educating others in the *población*.

The fact that health promoters' knowledge was not taken seriously by professionals had potentially life-threatening consequences. In a context in which public health services were inadequate, and treatment often unavailable, the health group's educational efforts were sometimes the only source of information in the *población*. When the director threw members of Llareta out of the school, he prevented them from disseminating information that might impede the spread of meningitis and prevent additional deaths. For health promoters, lack of respect for their knowledge was itself a threat to public health.

Having their knowledge taken seriously was, to them, also a key ingredient for collective action. A premise of the training they had received through EPES, and critical to the social movements in which they were leaders, was that the urban poor could make intelligent and informed decisions about their own lives. Such education positioned them as thinkers, decision makers, and actors. Along these lines, the health promoters saw themselves as capable of identifying community needs and planning for the solution of problems. They believed that because public services were inadequate, they needed to make sure officials and professionals did their jobs. To them, having their knowledge respected and taking charge of their community tapped into the larger meanings of protagonism and agency at the heart of popular social movement strategy. It was a matter of being constructed and constituting themselves not as objects of medical knowledge and bureaucratic practice but as knowing subjects who collectively and intentionally transformed the world in which they lived.

How did professionalization come to be a key axis of power in post-dictatorship Chile? How and in what way did it become central to the operation of a particular kind of democracy? Answering these questions is tied to understanding the links between economic restructuring and expertise.

PROFESSIONALIZATION OF KNOWLEDGE

While health promoters in *poblaciones* like La Bandera were grappling with the lack of medicine in the hospitals, the lack of food to nourish their families, the lack of an ambulance to get immediate medical care, and the lack of telephones with which to make emergency phone calls, downtown Santiago was bustling with technological innovations. Health insurance had been privatized, giving families in wealthier parts of the city access to the most advanced medical treatments. In the business district of Santiago, cellular phones, fax machines, and laptops abounded, their widespread presence signaling that information transfer, rapid communication, and global financial transactions had facilitated Chile's foray into "modernity." Coming of age during the years of dictatorship, these innovations expanded after the end of military rule.

What was most striking to me was not the sophistication of the technology but its visibility. I was startled one day in 1991 to see a businessman grasping his laptop by its small gray handle as he walked along a crowded Santiago street. It was not the machine itself but the absence of a computer bag to conceal it that I found most remarkable. The computer, like the business suit and the cellular phone, signified expertise, power, and the ability to communicate internationally. Exposed for all passersby to see, the laptop radiated an aura of professionalism that reflected onto its owner.

Patricio Silva (1991) has put this observation in historical perspective. In his study of Chilean politics, Silva indicates that financial consulting and technical advice are not new to Chile. Indeed, financial experts assisted Chilean governments prior to and during the 1960s and early 1970s.[3] At that time, as now, institutions' staffs were giving detailed recommendations on dealing with inflation, minimum wages, exchange rates, and the money supply.

Despite the existence of expert consultants, however, during the late 1960s and early 1970s a different cultural premise framed the actions of Chilean politicians. Advancing the idea of "popular protagonism" in which the poor would be at the forefront of transforming Chilean society, politicians and academics of the Left asserted their credibility by showing their support for the poor. As mentioned in chapter 1, at the 26 de enero squatters' settlement in La Bandera, university students and professors demonstrated their commitment to popular struggles by teaching revolutionary history at a cultural center, and politicians gained fame as they interceded to protect squatters from the police. As one academic said in 1992,

"In the sixties, there weren't intellectuals. Due to the Marxism in use it was discredited, it was 'ugly' to be one. All of us were militants [political party activists] and the intellectuals painted walls. For the idea of the protagonistic role of class" (Elgueta 1992, 18). In the cultural current of the day, professors avoided advertising their formal credentials, lest they be derided as bourgeois (Silva 1991, 389). They would be publicly judged not by their university degrees but by their commitment to the class struggle. The change that occurred during the dictatorship was less about the existence or influence of experts than about the cultural value placed on expertise. It was not that experts did not advise the Chilean government before 1973, but that only after 1973 did they take their diplomas out of their desk drawers, dust them off, and hang them on their walls.

The cultural change in how knowledge was legitimated was intimately tied to economic restructuring. In the mid-1970s, General Pinochet justified military intervention by saying he was ridding Chile not just of communism but of politics in general. He ordered torture and killings to eliminate subversives; closed social science departments in universities in the name of depoliticizing education; and shut down Congress, political parties, and unions to excise political distortion from public life.

Just as he used the goal of freeing the country from politics to justify military activity, Pinochet held that he was freeing the economy from political influence. The general presented the market economy as a rational system and envisioned the "Chicago Boys" as neutral experts who could manage it scientifically. Their educational credentials and technical skills made them competent technicians who could run the economy efficiently, unsullied by political agendas.[4] The Chicago Boys themselves agreed. They argued that by reducing the state role in the economy, they were freeing market forces from the distorting effects of political intrusions. "'I don't understand what political power the economic team could have,' [one economist] said. 'We are making a policy in order to lose power, so how can we be concentrating it?'" (Constable and Valenzuela 1991, 188). They asserted their own authenticity by emphasizing their technical skills and denying any connection to politics.

Pinochet's economic program was in fact deeply political. Crackdowns on unions artificially reduced wages and redistributed income upward. Privatization did not eliminate human intervention from policy decisions; it merely relocated those decisions from elected bodies (over which, in theory, the population had some control) to private firms presided over by a narrow, privileged segment of the population.

In defending economic restructuring as politically neutral, Pinochet reshaped the way knowledge was legitimated. Prior to this era, the political Right had struggled for power over the political Left and vice versa. Now to have a political agenda at all was to distort the true workings of the free market. Chile was seeing a new cultural valorization of neutrality, technical ability, and expertise.

Changes in the legitimation of knowledge were so powerful in Chile that they structured not only the work of free market proponents but also the work of those who opposed neoliberal economics and military rule. Despite an environment of censorship and repression, social scientists of the opposition published an impressive quantity of literature during the military years. Think tanks that had been small before the coup expanded after it, becoming a refuge for academics who had lost their jobs in universities and government. Other research centers were founded during the 1970s and 1980s. The Christian Democrat research institute CIEPLAN, for example, became a major center for economic analysis where professional Chilean economists, some of whom had earned doctoral degrees while exiled in Europe and the United States, gathered to develop a sophisticated economic critique of the dictatorship.

Academic dissidents at these research institutes survived censorship and repression because they challenged regime policies in the same technical language used by the Chicago Boys (Silva 1991, 403). To cite just one example, a CIEPLAN article by Alejandro Foxley entitled "The Neoliberal Experiment in Chile" (1982) provides twenty statistical tables to detail the economic effects of adjustment and shock. The author establishes his authority by using quantitative measures that could rival the analyses done by Pinochet's economists. Although he opposed the economic program of the military government, he could criticize that program effectively only by conforming to its strategies for legitimating knowledge.

The fact that the opposition adopted the same model for legitimating knowledge as the military regime put poor communities in a difficult position. As highly educated people became positioned as experts, the poor had little role in knowledge production other than as the objects of studies. In investigations that measured the poverty rate, unemployment, and infant mortality, whether done by the regime or opposition researchers, the poor surfaced in public discourse as statistical constructs; aggregate objects of professional knowledge.

While *pobladores* were surfacing in public discourse as the objects of studies, because of increasing inequalities in education, they were also losing what little access they might have had to gaining credentials themselves. Under Allende, college education for many was free; under the military government, in contrast, universities became for-profit enterprises available only to those who could pay the price. The reduced access to higher education occurred precisely at the time when professionalization had become most highly esteemed. The effects of the neoliberal model combined with the new value on credentials gave many Chileans little access to any role in creating publicly respected knowledge.

The language of expertise was not the only legitimating mechanism used by opposition intellectuals during the 1980s, and researchers did not only position the poor as objects of studies. At that time, many professionals in nongovernmental organizations and research institutes were engaged in qualitative research in the *poblaciones*. To obtain grant money, jobs, and attention for their books and articles in international and domestic circles, these scholars emphasized their professional credentials. Yet they gained the trust, support, and cooperation of *pobladores* through a very different legitimating mechanism: the language of solidarity.

During the 1980s, a range of nongovernmental organizations functioned in Chile, most of them financed by foreign foundations. Many of these organizations considered intellectual and cultural work to be an integral part of a larger struggle to overthrow the dictatorship. Books about community organizations produced during the 1980s were often crucial in documenting living conditions and highlighting the struggles of survival organizations in the *poblaciones.* Both poor people and their middle-class allies were involved in this effort to destabilize the military regime by producing certain kinds of knowledge.

Professionals in nongovernmental organizations linked their studies to the work of grassroots groups by using participatory research techniques that involved *pobladores* directly in research not merely as the objects of knowledge but also as central to the process of generating data. Representation of them was different as well: in some books they were profiled not just as statistics but as individuals with unique life histories.[5] Despite tactical alliances between popular groups and nongovernmental organizations, and despite efforts to make the research participatory, however, the processes through which studies were produced and distributed often reinforced uneven relations of power and knowledge.

The power relationships involved in solidarity-justified social science during the 1980s were clarified for me in a conversation with Rosa, a health promoter at a different *población.* Women involved in the *ollas comunes* (cooking collectives) in her *población* had agreed to collaborate with the staff of a nongovernmental organization in a study of their organizations. The members of the *ollas* were to participate in many aspects of the research process. "The people worked so hard in that investigation," Rosa recalled. "The *ollas comunes* did surveys, asked questions...tons of things."

Although researchers intended for the process to be participatory, some of the *pobladoras* involved in the study ended the process feeling more resentful than satisfied. Rosa remembers what her friend Elena said after seeing the resulting book: "After I knocked myself out doing the work...they didn't even acknowledge us...they have the book, they have their curricula vitae, and we are left without anything."

Nor, she said, did the community organizations get copies. Rosa recalled that Elena "robbed ten books the day of the book launching." She said she was furious that after doing so much work, the social organizations would be excluded from access to the final product. Recognition of their work and access to the final product were only two of Elena's concerns. She was also disturbed by the way *poblador* women had been represented in the photos and the text. Rosa remembered Elena's reaction when she saw in the book a photograph of herself working in an *olla común:* "We serve for that—to show an old fat lady without teeth, the leader of an organization. *And they don't mention that we did the investigation, we conducted the survey,* that they brought it to us and didn't pay us a penny, that it was done in solidarity, it was done so that the history could be known." "Because that's the story they tell you," reiterated Rosa, " 'So that the history can be known.' "

The fact that the members of the *ollas* did decide to participate in the study despite the time commitment and risk suggests that the women saw the production and dissemination of knowledge as integral to the mission of their group. The argument that the "history must be known" resonated with the framework of popular education and social movements in Chile. It meant that grassroots efforts toward survival and resistance should be documented and shared in order to advance ongoing organizing and elicit support for social movements. Like local history studies of the *poblaciones*, accounts of popular organizations functioned to establish *pobladores* as social actors and protagonists who had taken initiative to improve their communities' lives.

Despite the importance of historical and intellectual work to community groups, the book on the *ollas comunes* included no photos of the women conducting interviews, filling out forms, planning the research, tapping into their organizing networks to find interviewees, or evaluating their work. All of the photos showed them working in the common kitchen. To a reader this might seem reasonable, given that the book was about common kitchens, and preparing food was ostensibly the *ollas'* primary purpose. But in the eyes of Rosa and Elena, the omission was of crucial importance. By congealing *pobladores* into the image of fat old ladies without teeth who spooned beans out of a pot, the book froze them out of the roles of author, investigator, and thinker that they fulfilled. By displaying them as manual workers, not investigators, it affirmed that they would always be the objects, not the authors, of knowledge.

If the language of solidarity secured cooperation of *pobladores*, it also masked the power differentials implicit in the control and acquisition of knowledge. Research on the *ollas comunes* was ostensibly done to empower *población* residents, to involve them in participatory research, and to emphasize the dignity of their organizations. Yet in Rosa's view, because it attributed knowledge production only to professionals, the book simultaneously had the opposite effect. While lauding the popular organizations, it constructed the researcher as knowledge creator and *pobladores* as manual workers.

Clearly not all nongovernmental organizations had this kind of relationship with popular organizations. Some, like those supporting popular history workshops, were specifically dedicated to cultivating *pobladores* as authors. And EPES gave priority to developing the intellectual capacity of *pobladores* and preparing them for doing their own political analysis. The staff opened opportunities for health promoters to give talks at international conferences, to speak to the press, and to get formal educations. Yet if it was not universal, the story told here is nonetheless important, for it speaks to the ambiguous role of social science research in the 1980s and the way in which the legitimation of knowledge was central to power relations at that time.

As the stories here indicate, two legitimating mechanisms intertwined during military rule. The claim that intellectual production counted when it was based on apolitical expertise became the military government's official mechanism for legitimating knowledge. Under repressive conditions, technocratic language also became the legitimizing mechanism for professionals and academics opposed to the military regime and its economic policies. The professionalizing strategies of both the regime and its opponents coincided with the stratification of formal education, thereby narrowing who had the credentials to participate in decision making.

For opponents of the military regime, a second legitimating mechanism operated in tandem with professionalization. Staff of nongovernmental organizations legitimated their work to *pobladores* through a language of solidarity. This approach was important for creating alliances between the organized urban poor and middle-class professionals in a common struggle against the dictatorship. Nonetheless, solidarity work also reinforced inequalities of knowledge by constructing professionals as thinkers and *pobladores* as workers. In the languages of both expertise and solidarity—in the sophisticated research institutes in middle-class neighborhoods and in the incursions of nongovernmental organizations into the *poblaciones*—the unequal valorization of knowledge was reinforced.

Power and knowledge inequalities arguably had only moderate significance during the 1980s, when the overriding goal was to overthrow the dictatorship and grassroots organizations were in a cross-class alliance with professional staff of nongovernmental organizations. But the unequal relationships forged during the years of national protest against the military regime, and articulated in the language of solidarity, would have new ramifications when many of the professional staff of NGOs moved into government positions or shifted the focus of their research in the first years of political democracy.

Upon taking office in 1990, President Aylwin maintained not only Pinochet's economic model but also the culture of expertise that had intensified during the dictatorship. For economic policy positions, he chose professionals accredited by their graduate degrees at U.S. and European universities. They included, for example, Alejandro Foxley, an economist with degrees from Harvard and the University of Wisconsin who became minister of finance, and Andrés Velasco, who had earned his graduate degrees at Columbia University and Yale and who became chief of staff at the Finance Ministry (Briggs 1992, 110).

In the elected government, however, experts took on a new role. Policies now had to be marketed to the nation at large, and support built among different political factions. To create political consensus, Aylwin filled his ministries with what Domínguez (1997) has called "technopols." Like technocrats, these professionals were hired for their expertise and expected to make key policy decisions. But they were also chosen for their political party affiliations, the political alliances they could build, and the support they could generate through persuasion. Whereas technocrats had imposed an economic model under an authoritarian regime, technopols could maintain that model within political democracy by generating agreement across political parties, assuaging both the business community and labor, and creating a sense of national backing for Chile's insertion into the international economy.

Included in the Aylwin government were not only economists but also sociologists and political scientists, many of whom had been leading figures in opposition

to the dictatorship. Some of them had formerly been employed by nongovernmental organizations, where they had worked with popular sectors. In their new
government positions, they performed a different role: they were now responsible
for making policy decisions regarding the same issues they had previously researched. As they shifted from critiquing the model to administrating it in the
context of limited change, they moved apart from and at times into tension with
leaders in popular sectors who had been allies in the struggle against the dictatorship. Resentment voiced by *poblador* leaders was intensified by the general expec-
tation that policy makers be formally credentialed. This practice resulted in the
continued exclusion of the urban poor from decision-making positions (see also
Schild 1998).

The new climate affected not only those professionals who took government
jobs but also those who remained in nongovernmental organizations. Many international organizations had decided that after transitions to democracy, Latin
America was not a priority region for funding. Money that did continue to enter
Chile from abroad no longer went directly to nongovernmental organizations but
was channeled through the government's "Solidarity and Social Investment
Fund," FOSIS. FOSIS, in turn, directed money to local communities by holding
competitions to which community organizations could apply. Since the priority
areas were microenterprises and community development, grassroots organizations needed to submit proposals that met those goals. Although FOSIS requested
applications for locally organized initiatives, receiving a grant meant working
within the guidelines, conforming to the formal application procedure, and developing a technically competent proposal, often in consultation with professionals.
Although the idea was to fund locally defined initiatives, the new funding arrangement meant that recipients of the money no longer had independence from
official agendas. The new financial arrangements had a powerful impact on
Chile's nongovernmental organizations, many of which closed down as they lost
funding or found that their staff members had taken jobs within the government.
Those that survived saw their organizations transform. One main difference was
that studies were now funded through government contracts.

Not surprisingly, the use of government contracts for funding social science had
implications for intellectual work in Chile. As independent funding for nongovernmental organizations dried up or was channeled through the state, and as
many social scientists who had worked in these organizations or research institutes
in opposition to the military regime became absorbed into the government, there
arose a significant vacuum of critical thinkers outside the state. Those employed
in the government were expected to maintain a climate of consensus and support
for the Concertación government. It was a strategy appropriate to a coalition that
had come to power through negotiation and that hinged on multiparty cooperation. Under these circumstances, politicians needed to agree on a common vision
for the nation and put forward a common plan of action. This commitment to po-

litical consensus limited the possibilities for intellectuals to express dissent or develop a critical analysis of the Aylwin program and the new Chilean democracy.

Significantly, it was not until 1997 that Chile would see a highly public intellectual critique of the political transition. In that year, Tomás Moulian published *Chile Actual,* which went into numerous printings and sold more copies than any other book that year. Many people would comment that the basic argument of Moulian's book was not new. What made it exceptional was that it had taken so long for this critique to be presented by a leading intellectual. It demonstrated how limited intellectual criticism was during and after the transition.

The weakening of alliances between popular movements and professional intellectuals and the decline of critical writing about the state and economy made intellectual work by *pobladores* themselves an urgent task. Community leaders needed to be able to perceive the ways in which power had shifted in the post-dictatorship period and to ascertain the directions popular social movement strategy might take.

Intellectual work among the poor has a long trajectory in Chile. Labor unions, political parties, nongovernmental organizations, religious communities, and grassroots groups themselves all provided *formación*—training in political analysis—to a wide segment of the population. The contention that poor people could create the basis for knowledge by analyzing their own experience in a systematic way was expressed in the popular education approach common to nongovernmental organizations in Santiago during the 1980s and 1990s.[6] The organization PIRET, for example, sponsored a workshop called "Why Are the People Hungry?" in which participating residents from La Bandera pooled their knowledge based on life experiences with hunger, then analyzed the causes of that hunger in political and economic terms. In the post-dictatorship period, members of Llareta were hearing lectures on Chile's possible entrance into NAFTA, attending seminars on international politics, and using board games to identify health problems in their own community.

By the early 1990s, health promoters were also coming to the conclusion that popular education was not enough. They decided they needed formal degrees that would give them both standard educational skills and the credentials they needed to get jobs and speak at public forums. When I first worked in Santiago in 1991, only one or two health promoters were working toward formal degrees; by 1999, many more had gone back to school. Deeply aware of the importance of developing their own capacities, they saw their educations as not only advancing their personal growth but also strengthening the social organizations and popular movements of which they were a part.

Of the health promoters going to school, Valeria became the most advanced. Having initially left school in grade 11 for lack of money to purchase supplies and shoes, she completed her high school degree with honors at the age of thirty-five. As of this writing, she has finished her fifth and final year at the university, with a specialization in psychology, and is writing a thesis and doing an internship. Getting to this point was not easy. Valeria had barely enough food to keep herself and her children fed, much less pay for carfare and school supplies. Often during her education her husband was unemployed. She persisted, with her tuition covered through an education solidarity fund established by EPES and later a scholarship.

Health promoters were also engaged, in the 1990s, in disseminating their analysis beyond the *población*. To this end, they increasingly traveled abroad to give talks or help lead international workshops. Valeria spoke at a health conference in Tanzania, Sonia attended a conference on politics and economy in Brazil, and Iván led a popular education workshop about health in Argentina and participated in the Proceso São Paulo, an international ecumenical forum in Latin America that tried to shift the balance of power with the countries of the North. These arenas allowed the health promoters to improve their own political analysis by putting it in international perspective, forge ties of solidarity and build international alliances, and state their messages publicly in locations where the audience would take seriously what they had to say.

At the same time as they were speaking internationally, community leaders began to publish their analyses. A number had already voiced their views in interviews published by others. Rosa wrote a book based on the life histories of five *pobladora* women leaders. Valeria and Iván wrote an analysis of the political situation. Although their piece was never printed because the journal never came out, they had prepared their essay for a publication of a local research institute. Some residents of La Bandera who were not themselves health promoters were doing similar things. One woman—who had taught herself English to communicate with North American medical specialists about her son's disability—asked for copies of my interviews with her so that she could incorporate them into an autobiography she said she planned to write. Cristina's son, who had been a leader while in prison, was writing a novel. Another woman I interviewed belonged to a poetry workshop. Her poems appeared in the group's literary journal. Intellectual work was an important activity in the *población*.

Health promoters' emphasis on their intellectual development, educational credentials, and ability to speak for themselves reflected a unique situation in the post-dictatorship period. The professionalization of knowledge that took place during the dictatorship was maintained in the new political era. Now, as before, the urban poor were excluded from decision-making roles and found their knowledge dismissed. But the implications of professionalization also transformed during the transition to democracy. Once professionals in nongovernmental organizations who had been allies of popular organizations during the military years took roles in the new government, their interests changed. The resistance some of them had toward popular organizing, and the decline in critical scholarly production about the state and economy, posed new challenges but also opened opportunities for popular movements. It led community leaders to develop their own capacities in political analysis, their own voice in public spaces, and their own formal educational credentials.

Llareta confronted the challenges posed by the professionalization of knowledge in a variety of ways. While improving formal educational credentials, members also critiqued the assumptions implicit in technocratic approaches to knowledge. And just as they appropriated professionals' skills, they developed their own kind of innovative political analysis. Few incidents expressed these intertwined and sometimes contradictory strategies better than the health group's decisions about how to participate in the 1992 district health seminar.

HEALTH SEMINAR REVISITED

The first part of this chapter raised two questions about the health seminar: Why did Llareta hold that the way professionals organized knowledge was the key problem affecting health in the *población?* And why, given their critique, did they choose to use professional forms of knowledge in their own presentation? In her presentation at the health seminar, Valeria made visible the processes that a technocratic legitimation of knowledge discussed in this chapter had made difficult to see. For example, she showed results of survey research that described the presence of rodents in people's homes, high levels of malnutrition, and inadequate housing. The force of her argument lay in the reasons she cited for those conditions: the neoliberal economic model, the 1980 constitution, which designated housing to be private property rather than a right, and politicians' contempt for the poor. These causes of bad living conditions had been made imperceptible within a technocratic language that focused almost exclusively on biological aspects of disease and cures. They were hidden in statistics that described the situation without identifying causes. Valeria reframed the issue to bring the political and economic determinants to light.

Members of Llareta not only tried to make economic and political processes visible; they also worked to bring visible and concrete problems in the *población* to the attention of residents. The photo exhibit that Llareta hung up outside the entrance to the health seminar—the one the group had prepared for the *cabildo* a year before—illustrated the problems of pollution and environment in the neighborhood. What was striking about the photos of dead animals and piles of trash was how they isolated and highlighted a reality people saw everyday in the fields around the *población*. Other exhibits during the early 1990s—one on household accidents, one on the work of housewives, another on animal pests—brought into relief aspects of the environment in which people lived on a day-to-day basis as well. It was as if these daily realities had to be set apart for view in order to be acknowledged and made perceptible.

In public forums like the health seminar, survey data collected by the health promoters allowed the health group to legitimate its knowledge publicly, just as similar quantitative research did for professionals. But for Llareta, the use of surveys also raised all the ambiguities about legitimizing knowledge in a professional atmosphere. When I asked the group's members about the kind of presentation they had chosen to do at the health seminar, Iván reflected on the techniques of presentation the health group used:

> I think that...we used this method because it's always as if the [grassroots community] groups serve for certain things in the *población*. And that we don't have other capacities. [That our] capacities are limited to doing a skit, for example, because we can't do it any other way. We can't present ourselves more technically. So I believe it was implicitly to demonstrate that we are capable of doing it technically as they do.

Here Iván was stating that the health group needed to refute assumptions that *pobladores* were incapable of professionalized forms of knowledge by demonstrating their own capabilities. Iván acknowledged both the health group's skills and its limitations, noting that María Eugenia from EPES had helped analyze the data and Gordon had turned them into graphs. But in the end, he said, the research and the presentation were work that the health group had done.

Llareta also used sophisticated methods of presentation to capture the attention and respect of professionals in order to persuade them of larger issues. As María Eugenia said,

> the idea was...to...generate a space of interlocution of distinct actors, to be able to generate modifications in the health programs in the district. And that the *pobladores* be present....
>
> I think that they decided to use these methods of exposition to ensure a level of alliance or the possibility of dialogue afterward with the professional people. Because undoubtedly there is no resolution to this problem of attention in health if there is not an alliance with the professionals.

The professional presentation was needed, she went on, "in order to win [professionals] over to this analysis of health as a social, economic, and political problem. Because from their training, the health professionals see it as a technical problem. Of more germs or less germs. They don't see it as a social problem. That is their orientation." The professionalized presentation was but a means by which to level a far more profound and substantive critique of professional knowledge and to build the relationships within which that critique could be made.

Beyond legitimating their knowledge, the surveys and graphs were concretely helpful to the health group. They provided information on which the group could evaluate its priorities and analyze its situation. Health group members appreciated the usefulness of quantitative techniques at the same time as they used their power to credential themselves.

But although the information was useful, the health group members also believed strongly that some aspects of life were impossible to summarize in quantitative form. Implied in this idea is that while nutritional status can be measured, hunger and demoralization cannot. Valeria expressed this when she presented statistical information at the *cabildo*. She asked, "But why continue, if the cold data doesn't demonstrate all the frustration and impotence and the humiliations that the economic and human disaster that we inherit from the dictatorship have meant" (Grupo de Salud Llareta 1991a). In saying this, she was voicing her frustration at having to use the language of statistics to authorize her knowledge, when that language systematically excluded her experience.

Members of the health group did not need statistics to know that many children and adults in their *población* were malnourished, nor that the vast majority were poor. Yet as *pobladores* they were unlikely to be taken seriously by professionals in describing the experience of hunger that everyone they know had lived. It was as if they had to translate their reality into professional language in order to be audible to public authorities. To be persuasive in the public forum of the district health seminar, they at times opted to use the language of expertise.

In using statistics, health group members did something more than legitimate their knowledge. They also constituted themselves as subjects. As noted earlier, in opinion polls and databases, the poor were represented in statistical form as a collectivity. For example, when reports stated that the population living in poverty was reduced in the post-dictatorship period from five to four million people, the only individual to emerge was an "average" individual. There was little in that construct to conjure up a human being with a personality, a family, an intellect, and a life. Nor was there a way for one of the four million poor people to locate her experience in the statistics.

For people in the professional classes, the constitution of the poor in abstract statistical constructions was complemented by daily interactions with them as servants. In the lives of professionals, the poor appeared less as statistical constructs than as the people who brought them tea, cleaned their floors, and washed their laundry.

Given these arenas of disrespect and dehumanization, a major effect of the health promoters' public talks was to constitute themselves, *pobladores,* as both human beings and intellectuals. Their use of statistics differed from a professional's use of data because by using technocratic language, they undermined it. The survey data collected and presented by the health group put the poor at the center of the statistics—not only as its objects of study but as its researchers, its interpreters, its authors, and its audience. By using statistical data in this way, the health promoters subverted the main power effects of professionalization—the assertion that only professionals can manage information.

CONCLUSION

The importance to health promoters of *pobladores* constituting themselves as intellectuals became clear to me in one statement Valeria made at the health seminar. After stating that 70 percent of people in La Bandera do not achieve even minimal nutrition, she asked the audience, "What does this mean for our children?" Her answer followed: "It means that they will not be able to develop their intellectual capabilities, and others will continue to speak for us, the *pobladores.*" This statement clarified the issues the health promoters had grappled with all that year. For them, the purpose of getting adequate nutrition was not merely to ensure physical survival. Rather, the purpose of being adequately nourished was to develop one's intellectual capacity, voice critiques about injustice, work for social change, and speak for one's self and community.

Professionals working for the government intended health group workers to assist—to "participate"—in providing what had formerly been public services. For example, they asked health groups to distribute subsidized milk to undernourished children. In that scenario, professionals would determine national budgets, ascertain the subsidies available for children living in poverty, and set up programs in poor neighborhoods. The poor themselves would provide the labor for and be the recipients of those decisions.

In contrast, health group members said that "democracy" and "real participation" meant full involvement in the decisions about their communities and lives. Valeria's comment highlights this distinction. She was not arguing that decisions needed to be made in the most efficient way possible by experts so that poor children could receive milk. Rather, she was suggesting, poor children need to receive milk so that they can develop intellectually and thereby be able to make decisions about their own and their communities' lives. *Who* made the decisions, set the agendas, and did the speaking mattered deeply.

In Llareta's participation in the health seminar, one can see the outline of a strategic resistance to the government's discourse of participation and the professionalization of knowledge. Members of the health group made visible the political, social, and economic processes that had been rendered invisible by the language of technocracy. They refused to become appendages in a system of "participation" that would reinforce a neoliberal economic model and a decentralized state. They asserted a different meaning to the term *participation*—a meaning that entailed a real contribution to decision making. And they constituted themselves as intellectuals and decision makers rather than as conduits for a predetermined policy. Their work entailed knowledge production and contestation of technocratic forms of legitimating knowledge. At the same time, through surveys, photography, and other forms, they selectively appropriated modes of information that could contribute to their own critical analysis.

Epilogue

We are gathering in Sonia's living room, in the remaining daylight hours before the sun will set in glorious color behind the Andes. The windows are open, leaving the thin curtains to flutter in the early evening breeze. Buses roaring by momentarily drown out the music playing inside the house—first dance melodies on the radio, then a cassette of Víctor Jara songs that seem eerily calming in the warm summer night. The weather has been unbearably hot all week long, leading the children to spend endless afternoons splashing in inflatable pools and running through the rushing water of fire hydrants. In the city center earlier in the week I laughed to see Santa Clauses sweating in their red and white suits. Outfitted for the North Pole, they looked comical in the warm Southern Hemisphere. Here in the *población*, we spent Christmas Day in sundresses and anticipated the New Year's celebration with its fireworks and barbecues.

Sonia uses the spare moments before the others arrive to continue working. She has set up her sewing machine on the dining room table. The lace tablecloth is barely visible beneath the clutter of work materials surrounding the machine. Large and small cones of bright-colored thread, fabric of many textures and sizes, scissors, straight pins, buttons, zippers, and wrinkled tissue-paper patterns rest on each other and occasionally fall to the floor. On a nearby shelf lies a stack of fashion magazines that show the current designs—hip-hugging pants, bell-bottom trousers, fitted tops, and sleeveless summer dresses—revivals of 1970s fashions that are circulating internationally in the late 1990s. Sonia has worked every day for weeks from early morning until 3:00 the next morning, completing shirts, suits, and dresses for clients who wanted to give the clothing as Christmas gifts. Now she is working to fill orders due before New Year's, in the hopes that these buyers, unlike the last ones, will pay her when she delivers the clothes.

Just a few minutes after 7:00 P.M., our scheduled meeting time, Valeria arrives, full of energy and talking excitedly about her school day. She is in her third year at the university, where she is completing a degree in psychology. She has been practicing interviewing techniques, learning how to administer psychological tests, and reading about the social context of psychological problems. I am struck by the social science concepts and vocabulary that have infiltrated her speech and become embedded in her thinking. Some of the terms I know from my own years of studying anthropology; others, unique to the field of psychology, I have to ask her to explain. Valeria has told me she wants to use her education to work with people in her community, especially women enduring domestic violence, and all those living in the harsh conditions of poverty.

Valeria's school schedule has kept her from spending much time with the health group this year, and even now she has three exams to study for in the following week. But we have scheduled our meeting in the evening to accommodate her and the other health promoters who work during the day. Valeria brings along with her two college classmates—a woman, Irene, who works with a church youth group in La Bandera; and Irene's boyfriend, Antonio, who spent years of his life exiled in Argentina but has now returned to Chile.

Mariela and Keka, the youngest members of the health group, walk over from their houses together. Mariela was a shy newcomer when I last visited three years ago, but in the interim she has become an active participant and is now the health group's coleader. Her responsibilities include going to coordinating meetings at the EPES office and organizing health group events. Under her leadership, the group's activities this year have included painting educational murals around the *población* and working on issues of sexual abuse and domestic violence. Now it is Mariela's friend Keka who is the newest member of the group. Of indigenous ancestry, she recently spent time in the south of Chile visiting her extended family. Now back from her trip, she arrives at Sonia's house pushing a baby carriage, for she is caring for her sister-in-law's child one day a week. The others coo at the infant and admire her as they take their seats on Sonia's couch.

Iván hops off a bus in front of the house and walks in, greeting everyone as he enters. He has just come from a reception for two North American missionaries who had decided to return to the United States after eighteen years in Latin America. Iván had worked as a clerk in their international church organization for ten years, but now that the office is closing due to their departure, he has lost his primary source of income. He is planning to make a living selling fried foods full-time in the open-air market. Meanwhile, he continues with his many organizational activities, as busy as ever in neighborhood groups.

The reason the health promoters have assembled today is to participate in a workshop on ethnographic methods. Three years ago, when I presented my dissertation research in La Bandera, was the first time it really became clear to health promoters what I had been doing all those months in their neighborhood—for what reason I had been taking notes incessantly, participating in activities, running workshops on social issues, and conducting interviews. I had explained the reason for my stay many times, but it was only upon seeing the results of the research that it all came together. "Oh," said Valeria at the time. "Now I understand. All that note taking was your methodology." The results of the study made her and others interested in learning how to do ethnographic research themselves.

There were two moments during that 1994 visit when the desire of health promoters to learn ethnographic methods crystallized. Both were occasions on which they could see the connection between ethnographic research and their own organizing. The first instance occurred when I presented my research to Llareta in the meeting at Valeria's house (see prologue). To focus their attention, I used the health seminar that Llareta had participated in as a window into issues of power and resistance in post-dictatorship Chile (see chapter 6). That day, I had divided my presentation into three parts. In the first part, I described the seminar, then I moved to my historical analysis of national politics, and in the third part I returned to analyze the health seminar in a new light. The three-part structure left room for feedback, and I asked for the health promoters' comments following each section.

I began my presentation by describing the health seminar. It was an event the people sitting around Valeria's table remembered well, since they had helped organize it just two years earlier. After reminding them of what I considered the most salient aspects, I concluded the first part of the presentation with the two questions I raised in this book: "Why did Llareta say a major health problem in the *población* was the way in which professionals organized knowledge? And why, given its critique of professionalized knowledge, did Llareta itself adopt technical forms of presenting information: survey data, graphs, illustrations on the overhead projector?" Before going on to the second part of the presentation, I stopped for commentary. It soon became clear that the health promoters had interpreted my questions as a critique of their strategy. They immediately became defensive. "You should not criticize our approach," said Valeria, as she delineated the health group's reasons for using survey data and graphs. Iván, too, defended the strategy by explaining the quandary the health group had been in and the advantages of doing a sophisticated presentation. Sonia said nothing but later told Valeria that she had been worried, thinking that this was yet another instance in which the group's intelligence had been disrespected and their efforts at analysis dismissed.

Rather than respond immediately to the health promoters' concerns, I went on with my presentation. This second part of the talk shifted to a historical view of national politics. I explained my reading of the transition to democracy; the way political structures, the economic model, and forms of legitimating knowledge had been maintained in the current political period; and the new forms of power embedded in the government's discourse of participation. I opened the floor to the health promoters' comments on these ideas.

Finally, after hearing their opinions about the national-level analysis, I returned in the third and concluding part of the presentation to the health seminar. Here I restated my questions and gave my own reading of why the health group had used professionalized forms to present their knowledge. I reminded the group of the notions of legitimation of knowledge in my larger political analysis and discussed issues of invisibility and their own strategy of creating popular intellectuals at a time when the critical discourse by professional academics had declined. I suggested that they were both appropriating professional forms and critiquing them to respond to the changed landscape for decision making.

As it turned out, my analysis closely paralleled the health promoters' own commentary an hour earlier. Valeria pointed to the last page of my handout, which laid out the ideas. "Here we were getting all defensive and explaining our motives," she said, "and you had the same thing written down here all along." During a year of research, they had given me an understanding of their way of thinking, and now I was returning it to them in a different form. The idea that ethnographic method could be used to capture someone's worldview and advance political analysis got the health group members interested in using ethnography in their own work.

The second moment at which the health group articulated a desire to learn how to do ethnographic research was at my presentation to a broader cross section of La Bandera residents at the Lutheran church (see the prelude to chapter 5). Cristina had stood up and publicly criticized the health group for organizing campaigns but not directly providing health services in the *población*. Her sister Valeria defended the health group's work, saying that the group did treat illnesses and educate about preventive measures but that it also had a different vision of what the role of social organizations should be.

That was Valeria's response at the time. A few weeks later, at my farewell party, she made another comment. "If our own sister thinks this way about the health group and health, how many others in the *población* must think like she does?" Valeria asked. Drawing on the vocabulary I had introduced in my dissertation presentation, she said, "What we need to do is to understand Cristina's worldview. If we can grasp the way she and others see the world, we can better communicate with our neighbors and create activities they will take part in." For that reason, she suggested, the health group could use ethnographic methodology as part of its organizing process. This was the second moment at which health group members thought that ethnographic methods might be useful in accomplishing Llareta's goal of involving their neighbors in health campaigns. I was on my way back to the United States, but I promised to return in the future to teach ethnographic methods in La Bandera.

Now, three years later, I was finally fulfilling that promise. When I returned to La Bandera, this time for a short visit, I suggested to the health group that we spend some time planning the workshop on ethnographic methods and gave them the option of implementing it at a future date. But the group members insisted that we hold the workshop immediately, since it was uncertain when we would have the opportunity again. They chose the five evenings between Christmas and New Year's for us to meet and selected Sonia's house as the location.

Figure 17. Health group members analyze field notes in the workshop on ethnographic methods. The author is seated on the right. Photo: Gordon Whitman.

In the days before the workshop began, I compressed my fourteen-week undergraduate curriculum on urban ethnography into five intensive sessions. Their themes were anthropological concepts, field notes, interviews, analysis, and writing ethnography. Sonia helped me adapt the teaching techniques I used at the University of Pennsylvania to the needs of the health group. For example, at first she was concerned that *pobladores* would be too embarrassed about their penmanship to show each other their field notes, something I have students do in my university course. In the end, however, the exercise worked well, since all the participants had relatively good writing and reading skills.

We spent five intensive days learning ethnographic methodology. The work was divided into four-hour sessions every night, with homework assignments during the day. At the first meeting, I taught concepts such as the emic-etic distinction, "the native's point of view," ethnographic fieldwork, participant-observation, and the four fields of anthropology. I had the health promoters practice taking field notes by describing what they saw in Sonia's living room, and then jotting down action and dialogue from a soap opera on television. We discussed the way their positioning in the room affected what they saw, and, using that experience, I explained the notion of reflexivity. At the next session I had them draw up ethnographic questions, open-ended enough to elicit the viewpoints of the people they were interviewing. They practiced interviewing each other and later transcribed the recorded speech into their notebooks. On the day after they conducted interviews with neighbors, I had them role-play their informants' responses to capture the interviewees' worldviews. We then went back to search the interview transcripts for local categories. At the fourth session, the group did its own analysis of the topic and identified questions for further research. Toward the end of the workshop, I handed out photocopied pages from Spanish-language ethnographies to illustrate the use of photos and captions, ethnographic description, and how to embed interview quotes in analytic text. Then the group paired off to complete different parts of their document. One pair drew from the field notes of all participants to write the ethnographic description of the field site. Two others wrote a section summarizing their methodology. And a third pair interspersed analytic text between the interview excerpts. As a group, we then taped the handwritten sections of the report into a long patchwork document, to be typed up the following week. At the end of the final session, we held an evaluation, in which the health promoters discussed how they would use ethnographic method, and the results of this first research project, in their ongoing work.

The topic the health group chose for its study had to do with a large piece of land in the middle of the *población*. This spot was part of the area that city planners had intended for public services when they designed the *población* in the late 1960s. From my fieldwork in the early 1990s and as late as 1994, I remembered the area as a soccer field where sports teams from La Bandera and around the city came to play. Since that time, however, the area had been transformed. No longer used for soccer, the land had become covered with trash. Because garbage dumps, and the environment more generally, had been central to the work of the health group for years, Llareta decided to take this newly littered area as the site for its ethnographic fieldwork. The group members wanted to understand the processes through which a soccer field became filled with garbage, how public officials could neglect to take care of the problem, and how the situation might be changed.

To link research to their own goals for improving the quality of life in their neighborhood, the health promoters organized their study around two questions. The first was an ethnographic question that could be answered through research: How did a field used for sports become a garbage dump? The second question was a strategic one that would be addressed in an action plan: How might a garbage dump be transformed into a place for recreation? The health group intended to apply insight gained through the ethnographic research to its forthcoming campaigns to get the garbage dump turned into a park.

That was the state of things in January 1998 when I left Chile. A while later, curious about the outcome of the group's study and the direction of its campaign, I wrote to ask what had happened. The reply came on March 26 in the form of an e-mail message from Valeria. This was the first time we had communicated electronically—when I had worked in La Bandera previously, there was only limited access to telephones, much less computers. But by this time Valeria often borrowed a laptop from EPES to do her homework or worked on a computer at the university. In her message, Valeria brought me up to date on the well-being of her family and described the courses she would be taking in her fourth year at the university. Then she filled me in on what had happened with the health group's ethnography.

> With respect to the garbage dumps, I can tell you that they are already gone. We found out that... the municipality showed up asking if people knew who the persons were who were taking photos. They thought that we were from a newspaper or something. Some of the people who had seen us told them we were a health group. [Evidently] they weren't convinced because they cleaned it up entirely, and they have maintained it that way [ever since].

An Ethnographic Study
by the Health Group Llareta
"From a Sports Field to a Garbage Dump"

INTRODUCTION

We find ourselves in the garbage dump, located between the fourth and second sectors of the *población* La Bandera. It is Saturday, at 11:20 A.M., it is hot out, and we can hear music. Supposedly this land was meant for soccer fields. We can tell because there are still three pairs of goalposts from the old sports fields on the land. We also know the area was used for soccer because it was our husbands and children who played on these fields. What we can now see is only dry grass, stones, and a lot of loose dirt, with hills of garbage, like old furniture, rags, mattresses, plastic items, and dead animals in a state of decomposition, where the air has become so unbreathable that some of us vomit.

In the midst of the garbage grow various plants, some with lavender-colored flowers and some with yellow flowers. It is incredible that in the middle of so much filth and garbage, flowers still grow. As we continue to enter, the odor is horrible. We jump, trying to advance without stepping into the garbage. Suddenly, one of us feels something very soft where her feet enter the ground. Upon looking at it, we see that is a rotting dog. She panics and pulls her feet out, thinking that it is lucky she is walking around in thick shoes and not sandals, for all of the worms of the dead dog would have touched her feet. Some birds pick at the garbage. It is very hot. Some of the people going to the market look as if they are walking comfortably. Others run, holding their noses, in order to cross quickly. Now we realize that the garbage is being burned systematically. As evidence, we can see pine trees from Christmas half burned, which makes the environment more unbreathable still.

The garbage covers about 40 percent of the land, leaving no room for sports. Only in the middle can you see a small area free of garbage. We should note that there is no lighting, which makes it dangerous for the people who pass through at night. This place is a natural walkway, and people cut diagonally across the field. We also notice that some inebriated persons occupy the place to sleep, which seems incredible to us. Upon taking the photo of a mountain of garbage where there is an enormous sofa, we see part of a body. We see a person's hair and we see his hands. Upon seeing his hands we know who it is. It is "El Piñiñento," an alcoholic who lives in this place. He is a kind person, a man very much liked by the people.

Looking panoramically around us, we realize that these garbage dumps are very close to the houses and the community centers, such as, for example, an open center for children and a gathering place of the Catholic church.

METHODOLOGY

How is it that we got this information? Why did it occur to us to walk amid this garbage, given that it is not pleasant for anybody to be in this kind of place? What sense does it make to have done it?

As the health group Llareta, we decided to carry out an ethnographic study because it would allow us to know, from within, the experience lived by the neighbors of this sector. On understanding the perspective of the people, it would allow us to approach the problem in a different way than we had been doing until now. We always see the problems from our perspective and not from others'. To know what they think with regard to the garbage dump will allow us to implement strategies that enable us to integrate the neighbors in confronting their own problems.

Before beginning the ethnographic study, we defined the problem we were investigating. At first we began with the idea of knowing the concept of health our neighbors had. Given that our concept of health is very broad, we focused specifically on the environment, and more concretely on the garbage dump.

You might think that the fact that we are *pobladores* could affect this investigation; that since we are from this place our objectivity would be nil. Nonetheless, we believe the opposite. By living in this place, we have come to understand it well. Also, our experience as a health group during fifteen years gives us the authority to speak about the problems that affect us. And in this moment one of the problems is the garbage dump. We did an ethnographic study to put distance between what we think and what the neighbors who live there think. In this way we can approach the problems in a more effective way, taking into account the points of view of the neighbors that as a health group we detect.

We did a theoretical/practical workshop on ethnography that we immediately put into action by way of different techniques. The ethnographic methodology that we used was done by way of participant observation, interviews, field notes, photos, conversations, and analysis. First, we structured an investigation in stages.

On Saturday, December 27, we gathered at 11:00 A.M. to observe the garbage dump that is located between the streets Almirante Latorre, Sargento Candelaria, Esperanza, and La Bandera. We began to take photos and notes on what we saw. Because it was participant observation, we felt many sensations such as nausea, the unbearable odor, and the heat of this place. Later, we tried to listen to what the neighbors were saying to us, and to listen as well to the people walking through. We spoke with them to see if the garbage dump is really a problem for them, and, if so, how they understand the problem.

On December 28, we requested interviews with neighbors whom we did not know, who live in the area. They were open-ended interviews so as to not impose our ideas on what they wanted to say. We tape-recorded the interviews and later transcribed the information. After that we read the information and extracted the local categories to understand the worldviews that the *pobladores* have about the garbage dumps.

On Monday, December 29, Llareta as a group analyzed the local categories and worldviews from the interviews. Afterward we put together a pasteup in order to later elaborate the document. We focused our analysis on two questions: How did a sports field turn into a garbage dump? And how can a garbage dump turn into a space for recreation?

HOW DID A SPORTS FIELD TURN INTO A GARBAGE DUMP?

The Views of the Neighbors

It emerged in the interviews that everyone was looking for who was responsible. There were various explanations.

For one part, the people who are foreign to the place tend to associate the garbage dump with the habits and customs of hygiene of the people who live in this sector. For example, neighbors who go walking in the middle of the garbage comment, "The people are very dirty. They are not accustomed to living decently." Curiously, the neighbors who live in the sector arrive at the same conclusion: "The people see a free space and think it is for throwing garbage.... It is the people from the very houses [who do it]. I have seen them leave their passageway. They go out to dump huge amounts of garbage." This opinion is the first version that emerges from the *pobladores* of the sector. But in the course of the interviews, other points of view emerge from the same interviewees. And the responsibility that in the beginning is attributed exclusively to the neighbors of the sector begins to open up like a fan to involve external factors such as the municipality, outside trucks that leave garbage, lack of control, and so on.

While some people think that it is the very neighbors from the place who dump garbage, others mention that there are people who do business with the dump and the garbage: "One time a kid came here. He took the garbage out of here and dumped it over there, across from the school. And the people around here paid him." One neighbor explains that she paid a kid. She lives four blocks from the garbage dumps. This is related to the municipal arrangement for garbage collection. They only take garbage that is light and from the household (kitchen garbage). The mattresses, building materials, and wood are not removed by the municipal garbage collection service. That is why the people have to pay for trucks to get rid of this type of garbage, which ultimately results in the "fields of garbage."

Others say that trucks bring in garbage from other areas. One man with whom we were speaking was, in the beginning of La Bandera's history, a leader in the neighborhood council. He said that the neighbors have already done everything possible to get the municipality to get rid of this garbage dump. And it was he who told us that this land belonged to the National Ministry of Sports and Recreation.

He mentioned: "We are already tired of guarding the area. The trucks arrive here at three and four in the morning to dump garbage. At times I have had to shoot into the air, and then they leave." This man feels impotence in facing the situation. But we can see that it is the very neighbors who are doing something to impede the dumping of garbage in the place.

We ask a woman, "What do you think of this garbage dump?" She responds, "Well, it's that the mayor is there and he doesn't remove it. [She laughs nervously.] It's the municipality that doesn't do anything. According to them, there aren't resources. It's always like that. There are never resources for anything." When we speak of the responsibility of eliminating the garbage dump, or the reason for its existence, she relates it directly to the mayor and the municipality. She laughs nervously because she doubts that the mayor will do anything, since he always has the same discourse.

This demonstrates a hopelessness about the possibility that the authorities have the will to create a solution, since the neighbors do not trust the political discourses that promise them a solution because they have seen year after year how the garbage dump is maintained. And it is they, facing this same impotence, who take some measures.

But as we have already seen, they are already tired of the fact that their own measures also fail. This impunity that maintains the garbage dump has closed the possibility that the neighbors of the sector see a way out. And so they opt for solutions of an individual nature: "And now if I had to leave, I would leave without hesitation. I have lost my affection for this place. Before because of the dirt, and now because of the horrendous smell." The degree of hopelessness we find in the neighbors does not permit them to see the problem from another perspective, nor to clarify those who are responsible. And all the less so to have the capacity for development and new initiatives.

Analysis

Regarding the sports clubs, we ask ourselves: Which came first? Did people stop playing because the space was becoming filled with garbage? Or was the garbage thrown there because this space had stopped being used as a sports field? Many factors can influence the fact that the sports clubs disappear and the fields fill with garbage. One could be the arrival of crack *(pasta base)* in the *población*, since the drugs leave the youth like zombies. They lose all interest in playing sports, even in dating. Another factor could be the growth of the Evangelical church, which the youth are entering in massive numbers. Most of their time in the church is absorbed in serving the Lord. Another factor was spoken about by an older leader who suggested that there is a loss of leadership. No one wants to serve others.

They prefer to go to the shopping mall rather than play a sport. It also may be that the youth who previously played soccer are now older. And because the men have to work a double shift, they are too tired to play a sport. The increase in work and consumerism means that the people make a double effort to have a better standard of living. Another reason for the loss of the sports clubs could be that in a period of our country's history, specifically in the dictatorship and with the onset of democracy, many social organizations disappeared. What is most curious is that the organizations that have historically existed—the mothers' centers, the sports clubs, and this might happen to the neighborhood councils as well—have disappeared, despite the fact that in precisely this moment the discourse is one of participation. This is quite a contradiction.

The result of all these things is that the field doesn't belong to anybody. Because the owners of the place were the sports clubs. And today, it's no-man's-land. Why do we say that today it is no-man's-land? Because we always clean in front of our houses, but if a place belongs to nobody, then it's as if it doesn't matter if we throw garbage. We don't identify with that place. The most curious thing is that we become accustomed to the garbage and it starts to feel like part of our landscape. And then we don't know who we are, whether we are part of this garbage. We get confused. It seems like someone took away from us that value that we had; that we lost dignity—our pride, our respect for the place where we live, our respect for ourselves. The most remarkable thing was to see the neighbors' surprise upon seeing the photos. They said: "Where is this dirty place?" And we said to them, "It's right there." "Ah, no, it can't believe it, I had never seen it." And it was right across the street. This shows how we accustom ourselves to this as if it's natural. In our *población,* we have lost identity. Before we had a sense of belonging, we identified with this place. Now we don't like the place where we live, and in our *población* each of us has so much anger that we throw our garbage outside, without caring whom it affects. Before, we didn't throw it out; today we're more individualist. Think about the woman who said in her interview that we no longer love this place. It took her so much effort to acquire this land. But now all she wants to do is leave, because of the garbage. It's hard to say which came first, the chicken or the egg.

And we don't know what to do with our garbage. Modernity came almost without us noticing it, and this modernity has broken down our own traditions. Now we don't go to the *feria* or to buy bread with our traditional canvas or cloth bags. Today, everything is sold in plastic bags. We don't know what to do with them, so we throw them away. Modernity also makes us feel guilty for not living well. We have plastic money, [credit] cards, and they tell us we can buy living room furniture, dining room furniture, refrigerators, and other things. So now we get rid of our old furniture. And because there are no garbage trucks [that pick up these kinds of items], we throw them in the fields. Today the cities are modern. We have discovered that the garbage of today is not the same as before. Before, there were bones, glass, rags, remains of vegetables, cans; there were also animals, old shoes (really, really old ones). Now, you see furniture and plastic (not cans). Before, people collected the bones, rags, and glass, and sold them. Because with bones, you can make hair combs. With the rags, they made pillows, and from the glass, they made bottles (recycling). The materials passed through a process in which they were ground down. Today finding something like that is very rare. You only find things of modernity, like disposable plastic bottles, aluminum foil, styrofoam containers, plastic spoons, and the furniture that we mentioned earlier—refrigerators, stoves. And one thinks to oneself when one sees the garbage: the people buy things, but the houses are falling down. Because there is no way of purchasing on credit materials for the house such as a roof or wooden boards. In the old days, people made do with their furniture; it was part of their history. Today the people have lost their history, their traditions, their culture. All because of modernity, this model.

This is our analysis after five days of research. But we have a series of questions to continue investigating. We want to find out what happened with the sports leagues, with the players. Are there too many fields, or are there too few players?

HOW COULD A GARBAGE DUMP BECOME A PLACE FOR RECREATION?

To turn the garbage dump into a place for recreation would require organizing the neighbors, the *pobladores*, and the social organizations of the *población*. It is the only way to move forward in this area. And we would do this by way of campaigns, by sending letters denouncing and generating pressure toward the various government agencies, such as the regional government (*intendencia*), the Ministry of Health, the Department of Sports, and the municipality. All the while keeping the population informed of what's happening with these lands, and reminding people that we cannot continue living in these conditions. Only then is it possible that the municipality will do something. Because it is unlikely that they will do it on their own initiative. They never have, and we think that they won't, because there isn't the political will to do it. Nor do they have the resources to do it. Or at least that is the discourse they use.

The task is not for just a few—not for Llareta alone—but rather for all the groups that have life in the *población*. Especially those that dedicate themselves to the theme of the environment.

To create a recreation area, we can write a proposal *(un proyecto)*. The problem is that once we have identified the government agency that is responsible for this area, the project has to fall within its functions, which in this case is sports. So we can propose creating a place where the kids can roller-skate. Because there aren't paved streets for skating, and this would be a safe place. We could recommend an Olympic-sized pool from the municipality. There could also be a space of three square meters where the youth could practice break dancing. We have heard that it should be made of shiny ceramic so that they can practice without difficulty.

And there could be a part that would serve as the lungs of the *población*. Because we see that within the *población* there is practically no significant green area, except small spaces, like plazas. A good way of producing a project proposal would be to go to a school of art and design at one of the universities so that they could offer us their services as part of their on-site work.

NOTES

PROLOGUE

1. Llareta is a flower that grows in the desert. At their request, I used the actual names of the health group, its current members, EPES and its staff, and the sociologist in the prelude to chapter 6. With the exception of public officials, all other names are pseudonyms.

INTRODUCTION

1. Petras and Leiva (1994, 64–67) hold that Chilean president Patricio Aylwin's policies were not neostructuralism proper but were profoundly influenced by it.

2. La Bandera spans an area of 2.5 million square meters and has a population of ninety to one hundred thousand people.

3. Demographic characteristics of the health groups trained by EPES in Santiago and Concepción, as well as information on their process of organizing, can be found in EPES's book *Monitoras de Salud: Trayectorias de Participación* (Calvin 1995). According to a summary of the "most important demographic characteristics of the members of the health groups" based on a survey conducted in 1992, 97.4 percent of the health promoters were women, 94.8 percent had families of their own, 73.7 percent were between twenty and forty years of age, 56.8 percent had children who were between seven and eighteen years old, and 55.2 percent had some years of high school (61). Other characteristics include the following: 91.2 percent were poor (including 47 percent classified as indigent, or living in extreme poverty), 62.5 percent worked outside the home, while 90 percent had a spouse who worked (83). Sixty-one percent of the health promoters were homeowners or property owners (80). At the same time, 47.4 percent shared a housing site with other nuclear families, 38.9 percent did not have their own housing, and 22.7 percent had housing debt (83).

4. This link between power and knowledge has been greatly developed in the social sciences, particularly through the work of Michel Foucault (1980), whose writings show how techniques of surveillance, the disciplines, and data collection operate to control and produce subjects. The Subaltern Studies Group (Guha and Spivak 1988) goes beyond explaining the operation of power; having identified inequities in the production of historical documents, its authors aim to reveal a subaltern consciousness—unarticulated in existing archives—by "reading against the grain" of colonial texts. See also work by Jennifer Terry (1991).

5. For a thoughtful essay about the positioning of the researcher in social science, see Fine 1992, which presents three "stances" through which researchers "situate ourselves within the texts we produce" (205). "Ventriloquy" is a position in which "researchers pronounce truths while whiting out their own authority, so as to be unlocatable and irresponsible" (214). "Voices" is a position in which scholars "appear to let the Other speak," yet "just under the covers of those marginal—if now 'liberated' voices—we hide, unproblematical" (215). "Activism" is "committed to positioning researchers as self-conscious, critical, and participatory analysts, engaged with but still distinct from our informants. Such research commits to the study of change, the move toward change, and/or is provocative of change" (220). Fine concludes by proposing a fourth strategy, "participatory, activist research," which assumes that "knowledge is best gathered in the midst of social change projects" (227).

6. Not being a Chilean, I had no relevant party affiliation. Nonetheless, the habit of identifying someone by his or her party was deeply ingrained.

7. As Lila Abu-Lughod (1990a) describes the purpose for writing about the Bedouin to her host, the Haj, he tells her, " 'Yes, knowledge is power. The Americans and the British know everything. They want to know everything about people, about us. Then if they come to a country, or come to rule it, they know what people need and they know how to rule' " (81).

8. For another example of an anthropologist initiating a history workshop in a South American shantytown, see Dubois 1993.

9. A partial listing includes Grupo Salud Poblacional and Paiva 1989; Díaz, Galván, and Taller de Historia La Alborada 1991; Lemunir 1990; and Morales 1989.

10. Theses written about La Bandera include Bello et al. 1973; Concha 1979; Farías, Gómez, and Ruiz 1977; Illanes and Gutiérrez 1980; Pinto 1986; Toledo 1991; and Universidad de Chile 1977.

11. "La Toma '26 de enero,' " in Espinoza 1988, 302–28.

12. Servicio de Viviendas y Urbanización (SERVIU).

13. Census data (Instituto Nacional de Estadísticas); CASEN (MIDEPLAN); employment survey (Universidad de Chile); Ficha CAS (Municipalidad de San Ramón).

14. Articles from newspapers *El Mercurio, La Epoca, La Nación, El Siglo,* and *Punto Final* and the magazines *Desfile* and *Ercilla.*

15. *Hechos Urbanos* (Santiago: SUR Ediciones); publications of the Vicaria de la Solidaridad.

16. A history of La Bandera, broadcast on Radio Umbral.

LA BANDERA IN THE SOCIAL IMAGINARY

1. An ad for Chilean wine reads, "Sensual. Full-bodied. Refined. It's not just a wine. It's a country."

CHAPTER 1

1. The house was "built between 1910 and 1912" (Illanes and Gutiérrez 1980, 10).

2. "Entregarán sólo 700 sitios para La Cisterna, La Granja y San Miguel," *El Siglo,* January 9, 1967, 5; reprinted in Toledo 1991.

3. According to one article, the basic diet of the poor consisted mainly of flour, potatoes, sugar, and rice. Moreover, 82 percent of families in poor communities consumed less than the minimal diet outlined by the National Health Service (SNS). "Una familia rica de Las Condes consume 23 veces más que una familia pobre de La Granja," *El Siglo,* March 29, 1967, 7; reprinted in Toledo 1991.

4. "Municipalidad granjina encara los más serios problemas que aquejan a sus vecinos," *El Siglo,* April 30, 1967, 49; reprinted in Toledo 1991.

5. César Godoy Urrutia, "Evolución del déficit habitacional entre los años 1952–1965," *El Siglo,* February 14, 1967, 7; reprinted in Toledo 1991.

6. "Proceso a la ciudad," *El Siglo,* February 27, 1967, 7; reprinted in Toledo 1991.

7. Interview with Cristina, October 1, 1991. I thank Josephine Greenwood for transcribing this interview.

8. " 'La Bandera' puede albergar a 7 mil familias sin casa," *El Siglo,* January 13, 1967, 8; reprinted in Toledo 1991.

9. The children's parents were in their twenties and early thirties, accounting for another 30 percent of the population. Few older adults sought housing in the new *población*. Data from the Instituto Nacional de Estadísticas, Chile; Censo Nacional 1970; data from the original La Bandera area.

10. "Carabineros impidió ocupación ilegal de sitios en 'La Bandera,' " *El Siglo,* January 27, 1970, 1, 6; reprinted in Toledo 1991.

11. Fernando Reyes Matta, " '26 de Enero': Matraz [*sic*] del extremismo," *Ercilla,* April 1970, 15.

12. F.C., "Escuadrón de la muerte secuestró a dirigente popular," *Punto Final,* March 31, 1970, 6–7.

13. "Acción directa de los 'sin casa,' " *Punto Final,* February 17, 1970, 30; reprinted in Toledo 1991; cited in Espinoza 1988.

14. F.C., "Escuadrón de la muerte secuestró a dirigente popular," 6–7.

15. Reyes Matta, " '26 de Enero': Matraz del extremismo," 15.

16. F.C., "Escuadrón de la muerte secuestró a dirigente popular," 6–7; Toledo 1991, 112–14.

17. F.C., "Escuadrón de la muerte secuestró a dirigente popular," 6–7; see also Toledo 1991, 110.

18. Reyes Matta, " '26 de Enero': Matraz del extremismo," 16.

19. *Punto Final,* March 17, 1970, 8; Toledo 1991, 117; "MIR entrega alimentos a pobladores sin casa," *La Tercera,* March 28, 1970, 5.

20. "MIR entrega alimentos a pobladores sin casa," 5; "Pobladores 'sin casa' iniciaron 1.er Congreso," *El Mercurio,* March 28, 1970, 21; *El Mercurio,* March 30, 1970, 23.

21. Manuel Castells (1983) researched Nueva Havana, a Santiago squatters' settlement that the MIR patterned after the 26 de enero. He argues that, unlike the MIR leaders, residents were less interested in revolution than in obtaining a house. In his words, they were "dreaming of a peaceful, quiet, well-equipped neighborhood, while MIR's leadership, conscious of the sharpening of the political conflict, desperately wanted to raise the level of militancy so that the entire *campamento* would become a revolutionary force. Their efforts in this direction proved unsuccessful" (204).

22. "Trasladan a la república '26 de Enero,' " *La Tercera,* May 6, 1970, 8.

23. Political scientist Cathy Schneider (1995) has argued that more than any other political party, the Communist Party created well-organized *poblaciones* that became combative

during the national protests many years later. Her analysis rings true—to a point—for La Bandera, where the Communist Party was a central player in later fights. But while the MIR may not have created the kind of tight organizational structure generated by the Communist Party, it contributed powerfully to a mobilized *población*. People who had participated in the *campamento* became active leaders in La Bandera's massive mobilizations, while some of the Communist Party–supported leaders withdrew from organized activity after the initial years of La Bandera's existence. Residents told me that the major fights during the protests occurred in the first sector of La Bandera precisely because that was where members of the 26 de enero ultimately settled.

24. "Chile: A Commune Called Paradise," *Time*, June 1, 1970, 28.

25. See notes in the introduction for titles of local history books.

26. For an account of the role of forgetting during the transition, see Moulian 1997, 31.

27. Newspapers from the time also indicated plans for a popular pool.

28. Prior to that time, the Chilean economic strategy had been based on the exports of raw materials, particularly nitrate and copper, a strategy that would be revisited in a different form under the military regime of the 1970s and 1980s (Bergquist 1986, 23–37; Pinto 1994, 42).

29. In addition to implementing Promoción Popular in the urban shantytowns, President Frei used other mechanisms to balance capitalist economic development with social reforms. While courting international investment, he also called for "Chileanization" of the U.S. copper mines, meaning that Chileans would control 51 percent of the ownership. He instituted agrarian reform, and health care and education received increased investment during his time in office. And for the urban shantytowns, Operación Sitio was created to respond to urgent housing needs.

30. Víctor Jara, *La población* (Santiago: Alerce, 1979).

31. In Chile, nationalizing copper was supported by the Christian Democrats and even some on the Right.

CHAPTER 2

1. "Proclamation No. 7 (Warning)"; reprinted in Meiselas 1990, 3.

2. She emphasized that to her knowledge no weapons were ever found because they did not exist.

3. For a more extended discussion of the training and influence of the "Chicago Boys," see Valdés 1995; Fontaine 1988.

4. Instituto Nacional de Estadísticas, Censo de Población y Vivienda, Comuna de La Granja 1970, Comuna de San Ramón 1982 and 1992.

5. There is a critique of the way employment figures are measured. If someone has worked one hour in the previous week, they are said to be employed.

6. Instituto Nacional de Estadísticas, Censo de Población y Vivienda, Comuna de La Granja 1970, Comuna de San Ramón 1982 and 1992.

7. For an overview of popular economic organizations, see Razeto et al. 1990; Valdés and Weinstein 1993, 141.

8. For accounts of the eradications, see Alvarez 1988; Morales and Rojas 1987; and Rojas 1984.

9. La Granja was later subdivided into three *comunas*, and La Bandera came under the municipality of San Ramón in 1984.

10. *Hechos Urbanos,* December 1985, 6.

11. Letter dated June 25, 1982, from Pedro Guzmán Alvarez, Alcalde, Municipalidad de la Granja, to Director del Servicio de la Vivienda y Urbanismo.

12. For an analysis of spatial segregation in urban Latin America, see Caldeira 1996.

13. Schneider (1995, 92) identifies it as "40 to 67 percent of the minimum wage."

14. See also De la Maza and Garcés 1985, 18; Oppenheim 1993, 185.

15. The left-wing (Almeyda) branch of the Socialist Party supported mass insurrection as a strategy for overthrowing the dictator. But the Socialist Party's history of popular mobilization and networks in the *poblaciones* was less extensive than the Communist Party's, leaving it less prepared to do the day-to-day grassroots organizing work. Moreover, the left wing of the Socialist Party was both ambivalent about violence and unprepared for it. In practice, therefore, the left wing of the Socialist Party put most of its energy into nonviolent community organizations (Roberts 1995, 504).

16. Interview, September 19, 1992.

CHAPTER 3

1. A survey of the participation of health promoters trained by EPES in a range of organizations indicates some of this decline (Calvin 1995, 117). The survey compares participation in various types of organizations in the periods 1982–86, 1987–89, and 1990–92. For Christian base communities, the percentage of health promoters participating was 36.4, 57.1, and 39.1 percent, respectively, showing an increase in the 1987–89 period over the mid-1980s but a subsequent decline in the first years of democracy. Other organizations showing this pattern were human rights groups (9.0, 14.3, and 8.7 percent), subsistence and income-generating organizations (45.5, 61.9, and 34.8 percent), and neighborhood councils (9.0, 19.0, and 17.4 percent). Participation in women's groups showed a sustained decline (45.5, 38.0, and 17.4 percent). Groups not fitting this pattern included cultural organizations (27.3, 19.0, and 30.4 percent) and housing groups (9.0, 9.5, and 21.7 percent). Citing Jaime del Pino (1993, 234), the book also indicates the overall existence of popular economic organizations in 1986, 1989, and 1991, independent of the health promoters' participation in them (108). These data show that community organizations such as *talleres laborales solidarios* (solidarity labor workshops), joint purchasing committees, collective kitchens, groups of people building their own houses, and health groups had declined between 1989 and 1991. An exception to this trend was committees of the homeless and those living overcrowded, which by 1991 had increased relative to 1989 (though not compared with 1986). At the same time that the number of other kinds of community organizations was diminishing between 1989 and 1991, the number of microenterprises was on the upswing.

2. There were marches on many of these occasions in the city center, with the customary repression (tear gas, water cannons, beatings by police, detentions).

3. For similar observations on the disenchantment of community leaders with the new democracy, see Schneider 1995, 201–2.

4. For a discussion of the lack of change in the distribution of income in Chile during the Aylwin government, see Fazio 1997, 89–98; Ruiz-Tagle 1996, 38–39.

5. For one perspective on the difference, see Arriagada 1988, 70.

6. The first public questioning of the mobilization strategy came in 1984. At the seminar "A Legal-Political Constitutional System for Chile," sponsored by the Chilean Institute of Humanistic Studies, the vice president of the Christian Democrat Party, Patricio Aylwin,

gave a speech. Swimming against the current of then-prevailing support for the protests, he suggested that there were only two possible exits from the military regime: civil war or a peaceful legal-political solution. The latter, which he advocated, would require coming to agreement with the military rulers. It would enable the coalition to avoid, "before it is too late, the danger of violence with its irreparable evils" (Otano 1995, 21).

7. *Vigésimo Tercer Congreso General Ordinario;* reproduced in Jobet 1987, 351; quoted in Silva 1992, 1.

8. "Por qué debemos anular," Princeton University Library Chile ephemera collection.

9. See also Hagopian 1990.

10. Interview in *El Mercurio,* February 2, 1992; quoted in Silva 1992, 1.

11. The idea of the "work of ants" derives from Gramsci.

12. For a different framework to account for changes in social movement action, see Espinoza 1994. Drawing on ideas of cycles of protest and repertoires of action, he looks at the cycles in the popular movement and forms of action. He sees 1970 as marking the end of one type of action, which raises the question for him about whether what the health group is doing now is a practice left over from the 1960s (personal communication).

For an account of different types of action, see Tironi et al. 1985; Tironi, Espinoza, and Echeverría 1985a, 1985b; Saball and Valenzuela 1985a, 1985b.

PART TWO

1. For a description of popular workshops on economic analysis, see Leiva 1990.

CHAPTER 4

1. For a discussion of the restructuring of health services in urban neighborhoods during the military regime, see Hardy 1989, 106–24.

2. Ultimately, the symbolic admonitions were backed up by use of force, for demonstrations during the 1990s were routinely dispersed through the use of tear gas and water cannons, as they had been during military rule.

3. I thank Laura Grindstaff for this point.

4. My thanks to John Kelly for pointing out the multiple levels of meaning in this ad.

5. For a similar argument, see Kandell 1991.

6. "The Democratic Consolidation and the Process of Socioeconomic Development in IberoAmerica: The Chilean Experience," conference at the First IberoAmerican Congress of Political Science, September 1993; quoted in Fazio 1996, 25.

7. South Africa later named its human rights commission "Truth and Reconciliation." However, the principle and procedure were different, with amnesty awarded to perpetrators only after confession.

8. For affirmation of this idea, see Flisfisch 1991.

9. The demobilization of social movements accompanying transitions to democracy has been commented upon elsewhere. Foweraker (1995, 108) writes, "In Chile the more moderate movements were rapidly drawn into political society as soon as a date had been set for the constitutional plebiscite, and grassroots mobilization only lasted as long as the plebisciary and electoral campaigns themselves. Participation rates dropped dramatically after March 1990, indicating that social movements were likely to be demobilized per-

manently by the return to democratic politics." Citing Escobar and Alvarez (1992), he goes on to say, however, that "in Latin America...it is not impossible that the entrenchment of electoral politics will finally favour the spread of social movements (and the character of social movements might change as a result)" (108). As an entry point into the large sociological literature on social movements, see Hunt, Benford, and Snow 1994; Snow and Benford 1992.

10. In the 1988 plebiscite, a vote for the YES meant that Pinochet would remain president for another eight years. A vote for the NO meant that there would be free elections for president.

11. The United States played a role in bringing political marketing skills to Chile. The congressionally funded National Democratic Institute for International Affairs (NDI) had initially worked toward a Chilean political transition in 1985 when it sponsored the conference "Democracy in South America." This meeting provided an impetus for Chile's National Accord, which temporarily brought together opposition groups. In 1987, the U.S. Congress dedicated one million dollars to be used by the National Endowment for Democracy (founded by Congress in 1983) to further democracy in Chile.

12. Estudio de Opinión Pública No. 46, June 1991, Gemines Ltda.

CHAPTER 5

1. For another account of garbage as a focus of organizing, see Gregory 1993.

2. For a perceptive analysis of the relationship among markets, citizenship, and the discourse of participation in Chile, see Schild 2000.

3. http://apu.rcp.net.pe/test/iadb/s-socciv.txt:1: "The IDB as Catalyst for Civil Society Participation."

4. For an analysis of social investment funds, see Stahl 1996. For an account of Chile's "Growth with Equity" strategy specifically, see Vergara 1996.

5. http://americas.fiu.edu/Chile/semminar/semminar.html.

6. http://www.nsi-ins.ca/civvil/csdpo1b.html.

7. USAID's New Partnerships Initiative (NPI) was launched by Vice President Albert Gore in March 1995 at the World Summit for Social Development. The quotations are from the document "NPI Resource Guide, New Partnerships Initiative: A Strategic Approach to Development Partnering, NPI Executive Summary," found in 1998 on the World Wide Web.

8. For other scholars who use the concept of governmentality as a springboard for analyzing power effects enacted through the discourse of civil society, see Cruikshank 1999; Hyatt 1997; Rose 1996; Yúdice 1998; and Slater 1998.

9. For an insightful reading of the dilemmas of nongovernmental organizations facing the "discourse of 'citizen participation'" (48), see Leiva 1995.

10. This was *onces*, or tea. In popular sectors, this had become the only evening meal. Families in wealthier neighborhoods often ate dinner around 11:00 P.M.

11. The first reported case of cholera in Chile was on April 12, 1991, according to the Pan American Health Organization (Tauxe, Mintz, and Equick 1995, 142).

12. For an anthropological treatment of cholera in Latin America, see the forthcoming book by Charles Briggs and Clara Mantini Briggs and their 1997 article. An account of the 1832 cholera epidemic in Paris can be found in Rabinow 1989, 30–47.

13. During 1991, there were 41 reported cases of cholera in Chile. During the same year, there were 322,562 reported cases in Peru (Tauxe, Mintz, and Equick 1995, 142).

14. For a discussion of the spread of cholera, typhoid, and hepatitis through the dumping of untreated sewage into the water system in Santiago, see World Resources: 1996–97, Costs and Benefits of Water and Air Pollution Controls in Santiago, chapter 5, box 3. http://www.wri.orgk/wri/wr-96–97.

15. I thank Fernando Armstrong for this point.

16. Additionally, some materials targeted specific sectors, such as people living in rural areas.

17. The hospital was finally built in 1997, three decades after the land had been allocated for this purpose.

18. Her list of material demands included a toothbrush (in support of which she gave a detailed explanation of the healthy formation of teeth and gums) and crayons, for she was a budding artist.

19. In various conversations with me, middle-class North Americans have been adamant about the importance of washing hands and avoiding contamination to prevent cholera. The Chilean Ministry of Health's approach to the disease resonates deeply and is defended strongly in these conversations. Next to the strength of these convictions, the health group's logic seems difficult to comprehend. It is for this reason that I have made a point of stating clearly that the health group did not reject actions such as hand washing or the government publicity campaign. As I explain in the text, health monitors and other *pobladores* did take measures to avoid contamination. The important point is that the health group was establishing a critique that situated the biological facts within political and economic context and was asserting the need for an alternative set of priorities.

20. Pamphlet, "Primer Cabildo Abierto San Ramón, 28-Julio."

21. Documents produced by SUR Profesionales (Saball and Valenzuela 1985a, 1985b; Tironi, Espinoza, and Echeverría 1985a, 1985b) have argued that leaders are a separate stratum, detached from their base. While the meeting before the *precabildo* supports the conclusion that these leaders were acting without a base or even members of their organizations, I would also argue that is the product of a very specific set of political processes that has generated demobilization in the 1990s. Furthermore, the strong grounding of health group members in their neighborhoods and their usually powerful ability of *convocatoria* (ability to get others to attend events) show their deep connections to the *población* in which they live. At the same time, they described themselves as "running against the current" ideologically and in terms of their actions, and they did seek to transform common sense, political culture, and political action in the *población*.

22. After municipal elections, the structure of the municipality—including a council with representation from social organizations—would change. Additionally, particular appointed officials would be replaced with elected ones. However, the municipality's staff largely remained in place, producing other mixtures of change, continuity, and tension.

23. Prior to municipal elections, a limited number of mayors were appointed by President Aylwin until elections could take place. The Comuna of San Ramón, where La Bandera is located, was not one of the places where this occurred.

24. In 1993, Senator Frei was elected president of Chile.

25. Subsequently, the field was turned into a park with swing sets and lights.

CHAPTER 6

1. "Encuesta Poblacional," a survey conducted by the health group Llareta.

2. For a discussion of the role of health professionals in social movements in a different ethnographic context, see Adams 1998. On the question of the "power inherent in expertise and…the deep dilemmas confronting social movements that seek to 'democratize' science," see Epstein 1996, 330.

3. Documents from the World Bank, Central Bank, and other organizations in the 1950s show this to be the case.

4. On the Chicago Boys, see Valdés 1995; Délano and Traslaviña 1989; Fontaine 1988; O'Brien 1981. For readings on technocracy and the role of economists, see Montecinos and Markoff 1993; Centeno 1994. James Ferguson (1993) uses the term *scientific capitalism* to describe similar processes in Africa.

5. See, for example, Raczynski and Serrano 1985; Valdés 1988.

6. For an excellent discussion of the various orientations of nongovernmental organizations in the post-dictatorship period, see Leiva 1995.

REFERENCES

Abu-Lughod, Lila. 1990a. "Anthropology's Orient: The Boundaries of Theory on the Arab World." In *Theory, Politics and the Arab World*. Edited by Hisham Sharibi. New York: Routledge.

——. 1990b. "The Romance of Resistance: Tracing Transformations of Power through Bedouin Women." *American Ethnologist* 17:41–55.

Adams, Vincanne. 1998. *Doctors for Democracy: Health Professionals in the Nepal Revolution*. Cambridge: Cambridge University Press.

Alvarez, Jorge, ed. 1988. *Los hijos de la erradicación*. Santiago: PREALC.

Alvarez, Sonia E., Evelina Dagnino, and Arturo Escobar, eds. 1998. *Cultures of Politics, Politics of Cultures: Re-visioning Latin American Social Movements*. Boulder, Colo.: Westview Press.

Apter, Andrew. 1987. "Things Fell Apart? Yoruba Responses to the 1983 Elections in Ondo State, Nigeria." *Journal of Modern African Studies* 25:489–503.

——. 1999. "IBB = 419: Nigerian Democracy and the Politics of Illusion." In *Civil Society and the Political Imagination in Africa: Critical Perspectives*. Edited by John Comaroff and Jean Comaroff. Chicago: University of Chicago Press.

Arrate, Jorge. 1991. "The Social Debt in the Chilean Development Process." In *From Dictatorship to Democracy: Rebuilding Political Consensus in Chile*. Edited by Joseph S. Tulchin and Augusto Varas. Boulder, Colo.: Lynne Rienner.

Arriagada, Genaro. 1988. *Pinochet: The Politics of Power*. Boston: Unwin Hyman.

Avello, David Jesús, et al. 1989. *Constructores de ciudad: Nueve historias del primer concurso "Historia de las poblaciones."* Santiago: SUR Ediciones.

Aylwin Azócar, Patricio. 1991. "Discurso de S.E. el presidente de la republica, Don Patricio Aylwin Azócar, al dar a conocer a la ciudadanía el Informe de la Comisión de Verdad y Reconciliación." Santiago: Secretaría de Comunicación y Cultura, March 4.

Baudrillard, Jean. 1983. *In the Shadow of the Silent Majorities Or, The End of the Social and Other Essays*. New York: Semiotext(e).

——. 1988. *Selected Writings*. Edited by Mark Poster. Stanford, Calif.: Stanford University Press.

Bello, Mirta, Eugenia Olguín, Cecilia Olcese, and Lucía Solanich. 1973. "Sistematización taller Población La Bandera." Tésis de Grado, Universidad Catolica de Chile, Escuela Servicio Social.

Bergquist, Charles. 1986. *Labor in Latin America: Comparative Essays on Chile, Argentina, Venezuela, and Colombia.* Stanford, Calif.: Stanford University Press.

Borneman, John. 1997. *Settling Accounts: Violence, Justice, and Accountability in Postsocialist Europe.* Princeton, N.J.: Princeton University Press.

Bourdieu, Pierre. 1977. *Outline of a Theory of Practice.* Cambridge: Cambridge University Press.

Briggs, Charles, and Clara Mantini Briggs. 1997. " 'The Indians Accept Death as a Normal, Natural Event': Institutional Authority, Cultural Reasoning, and Discourses of Genocide in a Venezuelan Cholera Epidemic." *Social Identities* 3:439–69.

Briggs, Jean A. 1992. "A Political Miracle." *Forbes,* May 11, 110.

Brunner, José Joaquín. 1990. "Chile: Claves de una transición." *Leviatán* 40(2):25–32.

Burdick, John. 1993. "Everyday Resistance Is Not Enough: Anthropology and the Study of Social Movements." Paper delivered at the annual meetings of the American Anthropological Association, Washington, D.C., November 17–21.

Caldeira, Teresa P. R. 1996. "Fortified Enclaves: The New Urban Segregation." *Public Culture* 8:303–28.

Calhoun, Craig. 1994. *Neither Gods Nor Emperors: Students and the Struggle for Democracy in China.* Berkeley and Los Angeles: University of California Press.

Calvin, María Eugenia. 1995. *Monitoras de salud: Trayectorias de participación.* Santiago: EPES.

Campbell, Howard. 1996. "Isthmus Zapotec Intellectuals: Cultural Production and Politics in Juchitan." In *The Politics of Ethnicity in Southern Mexico.* Edited by Howard Campbell. Vanderbilt University Publications in Anthropology. Nashville, Tenn.: Vanderbilt University.

Castells, Manuel. 1983. *The City and the Grassroots.* Berkeley and Los Angeles: University of California Press.

Centeno, Miguel Ángel. 1994. *Democracy within Reason: Technocratic Revolution in Mexico.* University Park: Pennsylvania State University Press.

Chikwendu, Eudora. 1996. "Authoritarianism vs. Popular Aspirations for Democracy in Nigerian Politics." *Dialectical Anthropology* 21:21–46.

Clifford, James, and George E. Marcus. 1986. *Writing Culture: The Poetics and Politics of Ethnography.* Berkeley and Los Angeles: University of California Press.

Collier, Simon, and William F. Sater. 1996. *A History of Chile, 1808–1994.* Cambridge: Cambridge University Press.

Collins, Joseph, and John Lear. 1995. *Chile's Free-Market Miracle: A Second Look.* Oakland, Calif.: Institute for Food and Development Policy.

Comaroff, John L., and Jean Comaroff. 1997. "Postcolonial Politics and Discourses of Democracy in Southern Africa: An Anthropological Reflection on African Political Modernities." *Journal of Anthropological Research* 53(2):123–46.

Concha D., D. 1979. "Un aporte de la labor del Diseñador Paisajista en el municipio." Santiago: Facultad de Arquitectura y Urbanismo, Departamento de Diseño, Universidad de Chile.

Constable, Pamela, and Arturo Valenzuela. 1991. *A Nation of Enemies: Chile under Pinochet.* New York: Norton.

Coombe, Rosemary. 1998. *The Cultural Life of Intellectual Properties: Authorship, Appropriation, and the Law.* Durham, N.C.: Duke University Press.

Coronil, Fernando. 1997. *The Magical State: Nature, Money, and Modernity in Venezuela.* Chicago: University of Chicago Press.

Cruikshank, Barbara. 1999. *The Will to Empower: Democratic Citizens and Other Subjects.* Ithaca, N.Y.: Cornell University Press.

de Certeau, Michel. 1984. *The Practice of Everyday Life.* Berkeley and Los Angeles: University of California Press.

de la Maza, Gonzalo, and Mario Garcés. 1985. *La explosión de las mayorías: Protesta nacional, 1983–1984.* Santiago: ECO.

Delano, Manuel, and Hugo Traslaviña. 1989. *La Herencia de los Chicago Boys.* Santiago: Las Ediciones del Ornitorrinco.

Del Pino, Jaime. 1993. "Análisis de las organizaciones económicas populares (1989–1991)." In 1992–1993 *Economía y Trabajo en Chile. Informe Anual.* Santiago: PET.

Diamond, Larry, Jonathan Hartlyn, Juan J. Linz, and Seymour Martin Lipset, eds. 1999. *Democracy in Developing Countries: Latin America.* 2d ed. Boulder, Colo.: Lynne Rienner.

Díaz, Cecilia, Ligia Galván, and Taller de Historia La Alborada. 1991. *En ese entonces... La alborada: Experiencia de reconstrucción histórica de una población de La Florida.* Santiago: ECO.

Domínguez, Jorge I. 1997. *Technopols: Freeing Politics and Markets in Latin America in the 1990s.* University Park: Pennsylvania State University Press.

Dubois, Lindsay. 1993. "Popular Memory in Practice and Theory: Reflections on a History Workshop in Argentina." Paper presented at the conference "For What and for Whom? Theory, Method and the Politics of History." Center for Studies of Social Change, New School for Social Research, New York, April 30.

Eley, Geoff. 1994. "Nations, Publics, and Political Cultures: Placing Habermas in the Nineteenth Century." In *Culture / Power / History: A Reader in Contemporary Social Theory.* Edited by Nicholas B. Dirks, Geoff Eley, and Sherry B. Ortner. Princeton, N.J.: Princeton University Press.

Elgueta, Gloria. 1992. "Los intelectuales han muerto (¡Vivan los intelectuales!)." *Página Abierta,* no. 74, 18–21.

Epstein, Steven. 1996. *Impure Science: AIDS, Activism, and the Politics of Knowledge.* Berkeley and Los Angeles: University of California Press.

Escobar, Arturo, and Sonia E. Álvarez, eds. 1992. *The Making of Social Movements in Latin America: Identity, Strategy, and Democracy.* Boulder, Colo.: Westview Press.

Espinoza, Vicente. 1988. *Para una historia de los pobres de la ciudad.* Santiago: Ediciones SUR.

———. 1994. "Tiempos cortos y largos en el movimiento poblacional." *Proposiciones* 24:246–50.

Farias, Ana María, Mario Garcés, and Nancy Nicholls. 1993. "Historias locales y democratización local: Ponencias, debate y sistematización del seminario sobre historias locales organizado por ECO." Santiago: ECO (Educación y Comunicaciones).

Farías O., X., R. Gómez M., and R. Ruiz S. 1977. "Expediente urbano de La Granja." Santiago Departamento de Planificación Urbano Regional, Secretaria Ministerial Metropolitana, Facultad de Arquitectura y Urbanismo, Universidad de Chile.

Fazio, Hugo. 1996. *El programa abandonado: Balance económico social del gobierno de Aylwin.* Santiago: LOM Ediciones.

———. 1997. *Mapa actual de la extrema riqueza en Chile.* Santiago: Lom Ediciones.

Fedorowicz, H. M. 1990. "Civil Society in Poland: Laboratory for Democratization in Central Europe?" *Plural Societies* 21:155–76.

Ferguson, James. 1993. "De-moralizing Economies: African Socialism, Scientific Capitalism and the Moral Politics of 'Structural Adjustment.'" In *Moralizing States and the Eth-*

nography of the Present. Edited by Sally Falk Moore. Arlington, Va.: American Anthropological Association.

———. 1999. "Transnational Topographies of Power: Toward an Ethnography of Governmentality in Africa." Presentation at the Princeton University, Department of Anthropology lecture series, March 9.

Fine, Michelle. 1992. "Passions, Politics, and Power: Feminist Research Possibilities." In *Disruptive Voices: The Possibilities of Feminist Research.* Edited by Michelle Fine. Ann Arbor: University of Michigan Press.

Fleet, Michael. 1985. *The Rise and Fall of Chilean Christian Democracy.* Princeton, N.J.: Princeton University Press.

Flisfisch, Angel. 1991. "The Challenges Faced by Latin America: Democracy, Structural Adjustment, and Social Cohesion." In *From Dictatorship to Democracy: Rebuilding Political Consensus in Chile.* Edited by Joseph S. Tulchin and Augusto Varas. Boulder, Colo.: Lynne Rienner.

Fontaine Aldunate, Arturo. 1988. *Los economistas y el Presidente Pinochet.* Santiago: Empresa Editora Zig-Zag, SA.

Foucault, Michel. 1980. *Power/Knowledge: Selected Interviews and Other Writings, 1972–1977.* Edited by Colin Gordon. New York: Pantheon.

———. 1991. "Governmentality." In *The Foucault Effect: Studies in Governmentality.* Edited by Graham Burchell, Colin Gordon, and Peter Miller. Chicago: University of Chicago Press.

Foweraker, Joe. 1995. *Theorizing Social Movements.* Boulder, Colo.: Pluto Press.

Frohmann, Alicia, and Teresa Valdés. 1995. "Democracy in the Country and in the Home: The Women's Movement in Chile." In *The Challenge of Local Feminisms: Women's Movements in Global Perspective.* Edited by Amrita Basu. Boulder, Colo.: Westview Press.

Fuenzalida, Valerio. 1984. *Estudios sobre la televisión Chilena.* Santiago: Corporación de Promoción Universitaria.

Gallardo, Bernarda. 1987. "El redescubrimiento del carácter social del hambre: Las ollas comunes." In *Espacio y poder: Los pobladores.* Edited by Jorge Chateau. Santiago: FLACSO.

Gamarekian, Barbara. 1988. "How U.S. Political Pros Get Out the Vote in Chile." *New York Times,* November 18.

Go, Julian. 1997. "Democracy, Domestication, and Doubling in the U.S. Colonial Philippines." *Political and Legal Anthropology Review* 20(1):50–61.

Gordon, Colin. 1991. "Governmental Rationality: An Introduction." In *The Foucault Effect: Studies in Governmentality.* Edited by Graham Burchell, Colin Gordon, and Peter Miller. Chicago: University of Chicago Press.

Green, Duncan. 1995. *Silent Revolution: The Rise of Market Economics in Latin America.* London: Cassell.

Gregory, Steven. 1993. "Race, Rubbish, and Resistance: Empowering Difference in Community Politics." *Cultural Anthropology* 8:24–48.

Grupo de Salud Llareta. 1991a. "Carta abierta a los pobladores de San Ramón con motivo del cabildo comunal." San Ramón, Santiago.

———. 1991b. "El grupo de salud 'Llareta' y el cabildo popular de San Ramón." Santiago.

Grupo Salud Poblacional and Manuel Paiva. 1989. "Pasado: Victoria del presente." Santiago.

Guha, Ranajit, and Gayatri Chakravorty Spivak, eds. 1988. *Selected Subaltern Studies*. New York: Oxford University Press.

Gupta, Akhil. 1994. "The Reincarnation of Souls and the Rebirth of Commodities: Representations of Time in 'East' and 'West.'" In *Remapping Memory: The Politics of Time-Space*. Edited by Jonathan Boyarin. Minneapolis: University of Minnesota Press.

Hagopian, Frances. 1990. "'Democracy by Undemocratic Means'? Elites, Political Pacts, and Regime Transition in Brazil." *Comparative Political Studies* 23:147–70.

Hale, Charles. 1994. *Resistance and Contradiction: Miskitu Indians and the Nicaraguan State, 1894–1987*. Stanford, Calif.: Stanford University Press.

Hardy, Clarisa. 1989. *La ciudad escindida*. Santiago: PET.

Hearn, Jonathan S. 1997. "Scottish Nationalism and the Civil Society Concept: Should Auld Acquaintance be Forgot?" *Political and Legal Anthropology Review* 20(1):32–39.

Hite, Katherine. 2000. *When the Romance Ended: Leaders of the Chilean Left, 1968–1998*. New York: Columbia University Press.

Holston, James, and Arjun Appadurai. 1996. "Cities and Citizenship." *Public Culture* 19:187–204.

Holston, James, and Teresa P. R. Caldeira. 1998. "Democracy, Law, and Violence: Disjunctions of Brazilian Citizenship." In *Fault Lines of Democracy in Post-transition Latin America*. Edited by Felipe Agüero and Jeffrey Stark. Miami: North-South Center Press.

Hunt, Scott A., Robert D. Benford, and David A. Snow. 1994. "Identity Fields: Framing Processes and the Social Construction of Movement Identities." In *New Social Movements: From Ideology to Identity*. Edited by Enrique Laraña, Hank Johnston, and Joseph R. Gusfield. Philadelphia: Temple University Press.

Hyatt, Susan Brin. 1997. "Poverty in a 'Post-welfare' Landscape: Tenant Management Policies, Self-Governance and the Democratization of Knowledge in Great Britain." In *Anthropology of Policy: Critical Perspectives on Governance and Power*. Edited by C. Shore and S. Wright. New York: Routledge.

———. 2001. "From Citizen to Volunteer: Neoliberal Governance and the Erasure of Poverty." In *New Poverty Studies: The Ethnography of Politics, Policy, and Impoverished People in the United States*. Edited by Judith Goode and Jeffry Maskovsky. New York: New York University Press.

Illanes G., Mónica, and Raúl Gutiérrez A. 1980. "'La Granja': Informe de práctica profesional." Universidad de Chile, Facultad de Arquitectura y Urbanismo, Depto de Diseño.

Jobet, Julio César. 1987. *Historia del Partido Socialista de Chile*. Santiago: Ediciones Documentas.

Kamm, Thomas. 1993. "Free-Market Model." *Wall Street Journal*, January 25, 1.

Kandell, Jonathan. 1991. "Prosperity Born of Pain." *New York Times*, July 7.

Krauss, Clifford. 1998. "Chilean Foreign Minister Flies to General's Defense." *New York Times*, November 27, A14.

Leiva, Fernando Ignacio. 1990. "Nos dan alas pero nos cortan las puntas: Nuevos actores sociales y educación popular sobre temas económicos en Chile." Santiago: Taller PIRET.

———. 1995. "Los límites de la actual estrategia de lucha contra la pobreza y el dilema de las ONGs." Santiago: Taller de Reflexion. Serie de Documentos de Analisis. Mayo.

———. 1998. "The New Market Discipline." *Connection to the Americas* 5(4):1–6.

Lemunir Epuyao, Juan. 1990. *Crónicas de la victoria: Testimonios de un poblador.* Santiago: CENPROS.

Loveman, Brian. 1988. *Chile: The Legacy of Hispanic Capitalism.* 2d ed. New York: Oxford University Press.

Maarek, Philippe J. 1995. *Political Marketing and Communication.* London: John Libbey.

Marcus, George. 1998. "The Uses of Complicity in the Changing Mise-en-Scène of Anthropological Fieldwork." In *Ethnography through Thick and Thin.* Princeton, N.J.: Princeton University Press.

Marcus, George E., and Michael M.J. Fischer. 1986. *Anthropology as Cultural Critique: An Experimental Moment in the Human Sciences.* Chicago: University of Chicago Press.

Martínez, Javier. 1989. "Los famosos 'indecisos'." In *La campaña del NO vista por sus creadores.* CIS (CED-ILET-SUR). Santiago: Ediciones Melquiades.

Martínez, Javier, and Alvaro Díaz. 1996. *Chile: The Great Transformation.* Washington, D.C., and Geneva: Brookings Institution and United Nations Research Institute for Social Development.

McAnany, E.G. 1987. "Cultural Policy and Television: Chile as a Case." *Studies in Latin American Popular Culture* 6:55–67.

Meiselas, Susan, ed. 1990. *Chile from Within.* New York: Norton.

Melucci, Alberto. 1989. *Nomads of the Present: Social Movements and Individual Needs in Contemporary Society.* Philadelphia: Temple University Press.

Mires, Fernando. 1993. Paper presented at the Nineteenth Congress of the Latin American Sociological Association. Caracas, May 30–June 4.

Mitchell, Timothy. 1991. "The Limits of the State: Beyond Statist Approaches and Their Critics." *American Political Science Review* 85:77–96.

Montecinos, Verónica, and John Markoff. 1993. "Democrats and Technocrats: Professional Economists and Regime Transitions in Latin America." *Canadian Journal of Development Studies* 14:7–22.

Moore, Sally Falk. 1987a. "Explaining the Present: Theoretical Dilemmas in Processual Ethnography." *American Ethnologist* 14:727–51.

———. 1987b. *Law as Process: An Anthropological Approach.* Boston: Routledge and Kegan Paul.

Morales, Eduardo, and Sergio Rojas. 1987. "Relocalización socioespacial de la pobreza: Política estatal y presión popular, 1979–1985." In *Espacio y poder: Los pobladores.* Edited by Jorge Chateau et al. Santiago: FLACSO.

Morales Herrera, Luis. 1989. *Voces de Chuchunco.* Santiago: Centro Esperanza.

Moulian, Tomás. 1997. *Chile actual: Anatomía de un mito.* Santiago: LOM Ediciones.

National Democratic Institute (NDI). 1988. "NDI's Work in Chile." *NDI Reports,* fall.

Nelson, Diane M. 1999. *A Finger in the Wound: Body Politics in Quincentennial Guatemala.* Berkeley and Los Angeles: University of California Press.

O'Barr, William M. 1994. *Culture and the Ad.* Boulder, Colo.: Westview Press.

O'Brien, Philip. 1981. "The New Leviathan: The Chicago School and the Chilean Regime, 1973–80." *Bulletin of the Institute of Development Studies* 13(1):38–50.

O'Donnell, Guillermo, and Phillip Schmitter. 1986. *Transitions from Authoritarian Rule: Tentative Conclusions about Uncertain Democracies.* Baltimore: Johns Hopkins University Press.

Oppenheim, Lois Hecht. 1993. *Politics in Chile: Democracy, Authoritarianism, and the Search for Development.* Boulder, Colo.: Westview Press.

O'Shaughnessy, Nicholas J. 1990. *The Phenomenon of Political Marketing*. New York: St. Martin's Press.

Otano, Rafael. 1995. *Crónica de la transición*. Santiago: Grupo Editorial Planeta.

Owusu, Maxwell. 1995. "Culture, Colonialism, and African Democracy: Problems and Prospects." In *Africa in World History: Old, New, Then, and Now*. Edited by Michael W. Coy Jr. and Leonard Plotnicov. Ethnology Monographs no. 16. Pittsburgh: Department of Anthropology, University of Pittsburgh.

———. 1997. Domesticating Democracy: Culture, Civil Society, and Constitutionalism in Africa. *Comparative Studies in Society and History* 39:120–52.

Oxhorn, Philip D. 1995. *Organizing Civil Society: The Popular Sectors and the Struggle for Democracy in Chile*. University Park: Pennsylvania State University Press.

Paley, Julia, and Juan Carrera. 1996. "Chilean Ephemera and the Politics of Knowledge." *Princeton University Library Chronicle* 57:442–64.

Perlman, Janice E. 1976. *The Myth of Marginality: Urban Poverty and Politics in Rio de Janeiro*. Berkeley and Los Angeles: University of California Press.

Petras, James, and Fernando Ignacio Leiva. 1988. "Chile: The Authoritarian Transition to Electoral Politics: A Critique." *Latin American Perspectives* 15(3):97–114.

———. 1994. *Democracy and Poverty in Chile: The Limits to Electoral Politics*. Boulder, Colo.: Westview Press.

Pinto, Ana María. 1986. "Condiciones de Vida y Relaciones Familiares: Sector Sur de Santiago. San Gregorio y La Bandera." Tésis para optar al Título de Asistente Social. Escuela de Trabajo Social, Pontífica Universidad Católica de Chile.

Pinto, Julio. 1994. "Permanencia del modelo primario-exportador de Chile." *Proposiciones* 24:42–46.

Piñuel Raigada, J. L. 1990. "La cultura política del ciudadano y la comunicación política en TV, en la transición política del plebiscito Chileno (Octubre 1988)." *Revista Española de Investigaciones Sociológicas* 50:125–237.

Poster, Mark. 1988. "Introduction." In *Jean Baudrillard, Selected Writings*. Edited by Mark Poster. Stanford, Calif.: Stanford University Press.

———. 1990. *The Mode of Information: Poststructuralism and Social Context*. Chicago: University of Chicago Press.

Puryear, Jeffrey M. 1994. *Thinking Politics: Intellectuals and Democracy in Chile, 1973–1988*. Baltimore: Johns Hopkins University Press.

Putnam, Robert. 1993. "The Prosperous Community: Social Capital and Economic Growth." *Current*, no. 356, 4.

Quintanilla, Rosa. N.d. [ca. 1990]. *Yo soy pobladora*. Santiago: PIRET.

Rabinow, Paul. 1989. *French Modern: Norms and Forms of the Social Environment*. Cambridge: MIT Press.

Rabinow, Paul, and William M. Sullivan, eds. 1987. *Interpretive Social Science: A Second Look*. Berkeley and Los Angeles: University of California Press.

Raczynski, Dagmar, and Claudia Serrano. 1985. *Vivir la pobreza: Testimonios de mujeres*. Santiago: CIEPLAN.

Razeto, Luis, Arno Klenner, Apolonia Ramírez, and Roberto Urmeneta. 1990. *Las organizaciones económicas populares 1973–1990*. 3d ed. Santiago: PET.

Rebolledo, César. 1993. "Resumen de exposición." In Publicidad de Bien Público y Marketing Social, cuarto panel del Seminario "Examen a la política de comunicaciones de gobierno," November 18–19.

Roberts, Kenneth M. 1995. "From the Barricades to the Ballot Box: Redemocratization and Political Realignment in the Chilean Left." *Politics and Society* 23:495–517.

Rojas, Sergio. 1984. *Políticas de erradicación y radicación de campamentos 1982–1984: Discursos, logros y problemas.* Santiago: FLACSO.

Rosaldo, Renato. 1980. *Ilongot Headhunting, 1883–1974: A Study in Society and History.* Stanford, Calif.: Stanford University Press.

Rose, Nikolas. 1996. "Governing 'Advanced' Liberal Democracies." In *Foucault and Political Reason: Liberalism, Neo-liberalism and Rationalities of Government.* Edited by Andrew Barry, Thomas Osborne, and Nikolas Rose. Chicago: University of Chicago Press.

Rowe, William, and Vivian Schelling. 1991. *Memory and Modernity: Popular Culture in Latin America.* New York: Verso.

Ruiz-Tagle, Jaime. 1996. "Desarrollo social y políticas públicas en Chile: 1985–1995." In *Economía y trabajo en Chile: Informe anual (P.E.T.).* Edited by Margarita Fernández. Santiago: Programa de Economía del Trabajo.

Saball, Paulina, and Eduardo Valenzuela. 1985a. "Pobladores 3: El Grupo Comunitario." Documento de Trabajo No. 47. Santiago: Centro de Estudios Sociales y Educación SUR.

———. 1985b. "Pobladores 5: La Acción Comunitaria." Documento de Trabajo No. 49. Santiago: Centro de Estudios Sociales y Educación SUR.

Sassoon, Anne Showstack. 1991. "Civil Society." In *A Dictionary of Marxist Thought,* 2d ed. Edited by Tom Bottomore. Cambridge: Blackwell.

Schaffer, Frederic C. 1997. "Political Concepts and the Study of Democracy: The Case of *Demokaraasi* in Senegal." *Political and Legal Anthropology Review* 20(1):40–49.

Schild, Verónica. 1998. "New Subjects of Rights? Women's Movements and the Construction of Citizenship in the 'New Democracies.'" In *Cultures of Politics, Politics of Cultures: Re-visioning Latin American Social Movements.* Edited by Sonia E. Alvarez, Evelina Dagnino, and Arturo Escobar. Boulder, Colo.: Westview Press.

———. 2000. "Neo-Liberalism's New Gendered Market Citizens: The 'Civilizing' Dimensions of Social Programmes in Chile." *Citizenship Studies* 4.

Schneider, Cathy Lisa. 1995. *Shantytown Protest in Pinochet's Chile.* Philadelphia: Temple University Press.

Scott, James. 1985. *Weapons of the Weak: Everyday Forms of Peasant Resistance.* New Haven, Conn.: Yale University Press.

Seligman, Adam B. 1992. *The Idea of Civil Society.* New York: Free Press.

Shaffer, Deborah. 1989. *Dance of Hope (Cueca de la Esperanza).* Film produced by Lavonne Poteet and Deborah Shaffer.

Silva, Patricio. 1991. "Technocrats and Politics in Chile: From the Chicago Boys to the CIEPLAN Monks." *Journal of Latin American Studies* 23:385–410.

———. 1992. "Social Democracy, Neoliberalism and Ideological Change in the Chilean Socialist Movement, 1973–1992." Paper presented at the Seventeenth International Congress of the Latin American Studies Association, Los Angeles, September 24–27.

Skidmore, Thomas E., and Peter H. Smith. 1997. *Modern Latin America.* 4th ed. New York: Oxford University Press.

Slater, David. 1998. "Rethinking the Spatialities of Social Movements. Questions of (B)orders, Culture, and Politics in Global Times." In *Cultures of Politics, Politics of Cultures: Re-visioning Latin American Social Movements.* Edited by Sonia E. Alvarez, Evelina Dagnino, and Arturo Escobar. Boulder, Colo.: Westview Press.

Snow, David A., and Robert D. Benford. 1992. "Master Frames and Cycles of Protest." In *Frontiers in Social Movement Theory.* Edited by Aldon D. Morris and Carol McClurg Mueller. New Haven, Conn.: Yale University Press.

Stahl, Karin. 1996. "Anti-poverty Programs: Making Structural Adjustment More Palatable." *NACLA, Report on the Americas* 29(6):32–36.

Stryker, Sean D. 1998. "Communicative Action in New Social Movements: The Experience of Students for a Democratic Society." *Current Perspectives in Social Theory* 18:79–98.

Taussig, Michael. 1992. *The Nervous System.* New York: Routledge.

Tauxe, Robert V., Eric D. Mintz, and Robert Equick. 1995. "Epidemic Cholera in the New World: Translating Field Epidemiology into New Prevention Strategies." *Emerging Infectious Diseases* 1(4):141–46.

Taylor, Charles. 1990. "Modes of Civil Society." *Public Culture* 3(1):95–118.

Terry, Jennifer. 1991. "Theorizing Deviant Historiography." *Differences* 3(2):55–74.

Tironi, Eugenio. 1988. *Los silencios de la revolución Chile: La otra cara de la modernización.* Santiago: Editorial La Puerta Abierta.

———. 1989. "La modernización de la politica." In *La campaña del NO vista por sus creadores.* CIS (CED-ILET-SUR). Santiago: Ediciones Melquiades.

———. 1990. *Autoritarismo, modernización y marginalidad: El caso de Chile 1973–1989.* Santiago: Ediciones SUR.

Tironi, Eugenio, Vicente Espinoza, and Fernando Echeverría. 1985a. "Pobladores 2: El Grupo Reivindicativo." Documento de Trabajo No. 46. Santiago: Centro de Estudios Sociales y Educación SUR.

———. 1985b. "Pobladores 4: La Acción Reivindicativa." Documento de Trabajo No. 48. Santiago: Centro de Estudios Sociales y Educación SUR.

Tironi, Eugenio, Eduardo Valenzuela, Vicente Espinoza, Paulina Saball, and Fernando Echeverría. 1985. "Pobladores 1: La Intervención Sociológica." Documento de Trabajo No. 45. Santiago: Centro de Estudios Sociales y Educación SUR.

Toledo Jofré, María Isabel. 1991. "La historia la construimos nosotros, los pobladores: Historia oral de una población marginal de Santiago de Chile (La Bandera 1969–1986)." Santiago: Universidad de Chile, Departamento de Antropología, Memoria para Optar al Titulo de Antropóloga Social.

Trouillot, Michel-Rolph. 1995. *Silencing the Past: Power and the Production of History.* Boston: Beacon Press.

Universidad de Chile. 1977. "La pobreza urbana: Desafío para el arquitecto? El caso de la población La Bandera." Facultad de Arquitectura y Urbanismo, Seminario DEPIR.

Valdés, Juan Gabriel. 1989. "Comisarios, Jerarcas y Creativos." In *La campaña del NO vista por sus creadores.* CIS (CED-ILET-SUR). Santiago: Ediciones Melquiades.

———. 1995. *Pinochet's Economists: The Chicago School in Chile.* Cambridge: Cambridge University Press.

Valdés, Teresa. 1988. *Venid, benditas de mi padre: Las pobladoras, sus rutinas y sus sueños.* Santiago: FLACSO.

Valdés, Teresa, and Marisa Weinstein. 1993. *Mujeres que sueñan: Las organizaciones de pobladoras en Chile, 1973–1989.* Santiago: FLACSO.

Valenzuela, Arturo. 1978. *The Breakdown of Democratic Regimes: Chile.* Baltimore: Johns Hopkins University Press.

Vergara, Carlos. 1989. "Los duros, los blandos y los otros." In *La campaña del NO vista por sus creadores.* CIS (CED-ILET-SUR). Santiago: Ediciones Melquiades.

Vergara, Pilar. 1996. "In Pursuit of 'Growth with Equity': The Limits of Chile's Free-Market Social Reforms." *NACLA, Report on the Americas* 29(6):37–42.

Walker, Ignacio. 1991. "Democratic Socialism in Comparative Perspective." *Comparative Politics* 23:439–58.

Warren, Kay B. 1998. *Indigenous Movements and Their Critics: Pan-Maya Activism in Guatemala.* Princeton, N.J.: Princeton University Press.

Weinstein, Eugenia. 1989. "Los del patio de atras." In *La campaña del NO vista por sus creadores.* CIS (CED-ILET-SUR). Santiago: Ediciones Melquiades.

Werner, David. 1992. *Where There Is No Doctor: A Village Health Care Handbook.* Palo Alto, Calif.: Hesperian Foundation.

White, Hayden. 1987. *The Content of the Form: Narrative Discourse and Historical Representation.* Baltimore: Johns Hopkins University Press.

Winn, Peter. 1986. *Weavers of Revolution: The Yarur Workers and Chile's Road to Socialism.* New York: Oxford University Press.

———. 1992. *Americas: The Changing Face of Latin America and the Caribbean.* Berkeley and Los Angeles: University of California Press.

Yúdice, George. 1995. "Civil Society, Consumption, and Governmentality in an Age of Global Restructuring: An Introduction." *Social Text* 45, 14(4):1–26.

———. 1998. "The Globalization of Culture and the New Civil Society." In *Cultures of Politics, Politics of Cultures: Re-visioning Latin American Social Movements.* Edited by Sonia E. Alvarez, Evelina Dagnino, and Arturo Escobar. Boulder, Colo.: Westview Press.

INDEX

United States Agency for International Development (USAID), 8, 145–46, 180, 231n7
University of Chicago, 8, 63
Urban Analysis Workshop, 184
urban poor: agency of, 179–80; attitudes toward, 171–72, 174–75, 194–95, 209–10; cholera outbreak and, 155–60; Communist Party's influence on, 42; decrease in, 91; economic development and, 53–54; exclusion of, 204, 206; as focus of organizing, 79; free market's impact on, 63–65; health conditions unique to, 196–98; knowledge production and, 200, 205–7; marketing images of, 122–23; recognition of, 56; research approach to, 182–88; support for, 198–99; visibility of, 50–51
urban space: abandoned, 174–75; art and culture's place in, 56–57; control of, 80; crime and, 24; forced relocation and, 70; research on, 216; state's role in, 51–52. *See also* garbage
Uruguay, human rights reports in, 127
USAID (United States Agency for International Development), 8, 145–46, 180, 231n7
U.S.-Chilean relations: under Allende, 7; influences on, 8, 99–100; military government and, 62–63; nationalization and, 58
U.S. Department of Commerce, 111

Valdés, Juan Gabriel, 119, 122, 132
Vekemans, Roger, 53
Velasco, Andrés, 203
Venezuela, study of democracy in, 2
Vicaría de la Solidaridad, 60, 67
Vicaría Sur, 128

La Victoria, political activism in, 22
violence: in Allá Viene, Allá Viene, 73–74; fear of, 71–73; images of, 118, *120*, 123–24; in military coup, 59–62. *See also* crime *(delincuencia)*
volunteerism, 8
voter registration, 118–19

welfare state. *See* public services
Whitman, Gordon: health group and, 100–103, 194, 208; history workshop and, 17, 29, 30–33, 34, 83–85; video by, 141
Winn, Peter, 57
women: as actors/agents, 159; housing concerns of, 46; protests by, 58, 80; reaching out to, 104–5, 230n11; in social science research, 201–2; violence feared by, 72–73; as workers, 64–65. *See also* cooking cooperatives *(ollas comunes)*; education and training; health promoters
work of ants *(trabajo de hormigas)*, 104–5, 230n11
World Bank, 99, 144
World Summit for Social Development, 231n7
writing: as collective project, 30, 34–37, *35, 36*–37; on history of *poblaciones*, 17–18; by indigenous intellectuals, 15, 206; legitimation via, 202–3

YES campaign, 117, 118–119, *120*
youth: *cabildo* goals and, 163; cholera campaign and, 150; club for, 56–57; political marketing to, 137; protests and, 29–30, 34, 81, 87; summer camps for, 90. *See also* children; history workshops